THE SUSQUEHANNOCKS

RECENT RESEARCH IN **PENNSYLVANIA ARCHAEOLOGY**

Paul A. Raber, *Series Editor*

The Archaic Period in Pennsylvania:
Hunter Gatherers of the Early and Middle
Holocene Period, Vol. 1
Edited by Paul A. Raber, Patricia E. Miller,
and Sarah M. Neusius
Published by the Pennsylvania
Historical and Museum Commission
in cooperation with the Pennsylvania
Archaeological Council

Ice Age Peoples of Pennsylvania, Vol. 2
Edited by Kurt W. Carr and James M.
Adovasio
Published by the Pennsylvania
Historical and Museum Commission
in cooperation with the Pennsylvania
Archaeological Council

Foragers and Farmers of the Early and
Middle Woodland Periods in Pennsylvania,
Vol. 3
Edited by Paul A. Raber and Verna L.
Cowin
Published by the Pennsylvania
Historical and Museum Commission
in cooperation with the Pennsylvania
Archaeological Council

The Nature and Pace of Change in
American Indian Cultures: Pennsylvania,
4000 to 3000 BP, Vol. 4
Edited by Michael R. Stewart, Kurt W.
Carr, and Paul A. Raber

The
SUSQUEHANNOCKS

NEW PERSPECTIVES ON SETTLEMENT
AND CULTURAL IDENTITY

Edited by

PAUL A. RABER

THE PENNSYLVANIA STATE UNIVERSITY PRESS | UNIVERSITY PARK, PENNSYLVANIA

This book is dedicated to the memory of Dr. Barry C. Kent (1939–2019), Pennsylvania State Archaeologist (1966–86), scholar, colleague, friend, and mentor.

Library of Congress Cataloging-in-Publication Data

Names: Raber, Paul A., editor.
Title: The Susquehannocks : new perspectives on settlement and cultural identity / edited by Paul A. Raber.
Description: University Park, Pennsylvania : The Pennsylvania State University Press, [2019] | Series: Recent research in Pennsylvania archaeology | Includes bibliographical references and index.
Summary: "Examines the native group in Pennsylvania known as the Susquehannocks, who were encountered by Europeans when they first entered the Susquehanna Valley. The studies presented draw on recent archaeological excavation and analyses to provide new perspectives on the Susquehannocks"—Provided by publisher.
Identifiers: LCCN 2019025518 | ISBN 9780271084763 (paperback)
Subjects: LCSH: Susquehanna Indians—Antiquities. | Excavations (Archaeology)—Susquehanna River Valley. | Excavations (Archaeology)—Pennsylvania. | Susquehanna River Valley—Antiquities. | Pennsylvania—Antiquities.
Classification: LCC E99.S9 S87 2019 | DDC 974.801—dc23
LC record available at https://lccn.loc.gov/2019025518

Copyright © 2019 The Pennsylvania State University

Published by The Pennsylvania State University Press,
University Park, PA 16802-1003

The Pennsylvania State University Press is a member of the Association of University Presses.

It is the policy of The Pennsylvania State University Press to use acid-free paper. Publications on uncoated stock satisfy the minimum requirements of American National Standard for Information Sciences—Permanence of Paper for Printed Library Material, ANSI Z39.48-1992.

CONTENTS

VI

FIGURES

TABLES

PREFACE AND ACKNOWLEDGMENTS

Paul A. Raber

Since John Smith first laid eyes on the people he described in 1608, non-Susquehannocks have struggled to develop a suitable frame of reference to deal with the "gyant-like" people who occupied the Lower Susquehanna River Valley when Europeans arrived there in numbers and began to pay attention to the native inhabitants. The views of these first European observers reflected their colonial preoccupations and attitudes that ranged from romanticized to contemptuous: the savages were either noble or naked—often both. European explorers and conquerors lacked ready comparisons to use in understanding not only the physical attributes of the Susquehannocks but also the way they lived, their houses and communities, and their relations with neighboring groups. This confusion, alternating with hostility and aggression, characterized European relations with the Susquehannocks through the eighteenth century.

The perplexity of the first European travelers through the lands of the Susquehannocks and contemporary native peoples was matched by that of later nineteenth- and twentieth-century archaeologists and historians who tried to systematize and understand the available documentary and archaeological information. Lacking even a firm knowledge of what the Susquehannocks called themselves (Kent 2001:28–33), archaeologists in particular fell back on standard contemporary culture historical analytical categories when arranging and systematizing the archaeological record. This approach was lent a scientific veneer when, as Snow notes in his introductory chapter to this volume, the Susquehannock archaeological record was systematized in terms of the Willey and Phillips (1958) units of classification, including culture, tradition, type, variety, component, phase, state, and site. The tendency to view pottery types as equivalent to cultures and essentialist views of culture and biology plagued early attempts at explanation. In this regard, of course, Susquehannock archaeology reflected the contemporary state of the discipline. This approach, however, whatever its merits, has persisted in the face of more refined and broader theoretical perspectives. Archaeologists have tended to view Susquehannock culture in terms of a trajectory of origins, growth, climax, and decline that grants little or no agency to the Susquehannocks themselves. That has begun to change, and archaeologists can now view Susquehannock history with a broader grasp of colonial relations of power and inequality (see Custer 2018; Beisaw, chapter 3; Lauria, chapter 4 in this volume).

This is not to imply that earlier archaeologists were unaware of these issues, although contemporary technical and theoretical perspectives may have limited what they could do with the available data. The earliest professional archaeological attention to the Susquehannocks dates to the late nineteenth and early twentieth centuries, although occasional earlier amateur excavations had unearthed pottery of Susquehannock origin (Kent 2001:110–11, 298). Pottery remained the primary evidence for placing the Susquehannocks in a culture-historical framework through the early decades of the twentieth century, as reflected in the efforts of Griffin (in Cadzow 1936), Holmes (1903), Skinner (in Moorehead 1938:46–67), and Wren (1914) to recognize Susquehannock pottery as a distinct type, connect it with the historical Susquehannocks, and arrange a pottery typology.

As Gollup and others suggest in their chapters in this volume, much of our information on the Susquehannocks comes from extensive and generally poorly planned private excavations of Susquehannock sites. This approach and the related sale of important collections have seriously constrained our ability to understand Susquehannock site structure and what it implies about their culture. Nowhere is this more apparent than in the case of early Susquehannock sites in the Upper Susquehanna River drainage basin where, as Gollup and Herbstritt note, the haphazard approach to excavation and reporting has led to a significant loss of knowledge about the genesis of the archaeological culture we know as Susquehannock.

The first real effort at systematization of the Susquehannock evidence was that of Cadzow (1936), based on the investigations in 1931 and 1932 that were sponsored by the Pennsylvania Historical Commission. Although his fieldwork was constrained by the scheduled flooding of the river behind the Safe Harbor Dam, Cadzow's 1936 Safe Harbor Report No. 2 presented the largest body of archaeological evidence

on the Susquehannocks to that time. He provided clear descriptions of the investigations and ample documentation of the pottery, native artifacts, trade items, burials, and other cultural features unearthed.

Witthoft and Kinsey (1959) summarized the evidence that had accumulated in the decades since Cadzow's work and offered an updated view of Susquehannock studies based on a Susquehannock symposium held in 1958 at Franklin and Marshall College. Theirs was a notable attempt to synthesize the archaeological and historical data available by the late 1950s, the highlights of which are Witthoft's (1959) summary of the excavations and pottery studies that he and others had completed, Kinsey's (1959) typology of Susquehannock pottery, and Witthoft, Kinsey, and Holzinger's (1959) report on the 1955–57 excavation of the Ibaugh cemetery at Washington Boro.

Continued investigations by the Pennsylvania Historical and Museum Commission, the Pennsylvania State University, and Franklin and Marshall College in the 1960s and 1970s yielded a wealth of new information from extensive exposures of village plans and cemeteries at the Strickler, Schultz-Funk, Washington Boro village, Frey-Haverstick, Eschelman cemetery, Ibaugh cemetery, and other sites. Although the emphasis on rapid and large exposures may have come at the expense of detail, these investigations added substantially to the information on community plans, native artifacts and trade goods, chronology, and social structure.

Barry Kent drew on the results of all these studies in his definitive 1984 synthesis (revised in 2001) of the history and archaeology of the Susquehannocks and related groups. Kent's *Susquehanna's Indians* remains the standard reference on the Susquehannocks and other groups of the region, summarizing all that was known of their culture history and material culture at the end of the twentieth century.

The present book is by no means intended to replace Kent's synthesis. Like the other volumes in the series *Recent Research in Pennsylvania Archaeology*, it grew out of a symposium organized by the Pennsylvania

Archaeological Council (in this case, a session in April 2012 on recent Susquehannock archaeology). The present seven chapters include expanded versions of some of the papers presented at that session, with the addition of invited chapters on various topics. The chapters reflect the diverse perspectives and approaches that have marked Susquehannock archaeology since Kent's synthesis: new excavations (Wyatt and Wall), new analyses of pottery and skeletal materials and their meaning (Becker, Beisaw, and Lauria), and new views on the origins and geographic spread of Susquehannock culture (Gollup, Herbstritt, and Wall). Dean Snow offers a summary and discussion of the trends apparent in the individual contributions, drawing on his wide experience in the archaeology of Iroquoian and related groups in northeastern North America.

No particular direction was imposed on the authors, but it will be apparent in reading the chapters that a number of key issues or themes have consistently arisen in recent studies. The origins of Susquehannock culture remain poorly known, hampered by a reliance on many private and poorly conceived and documented "excavations" of related early Susquehannock sites. As Gollup notes in chapter 1, this is a problem exacerbated by confusion and inconsistency in terminology that make the use of terms like "Proto-Susquehannocks" and "Protohistoric Susquehannocks" problematic. Gollup and Herbstritt make an important effort in their chapters to sort out the disparate and confusing strands of knowledge about the birth of a Susquehannock culture in the Upper Susquehanna River drainage basin.

A related issue is whether "ethnogenesis" (Herbstritt, chapter 2) or "nation-genesis" (Beisaw, chapter 3) better explains the origins and history of native identity. Herbstritt draws on a vast body of often insufficiently reported excavation data to trace the development of a Susquehannock ethnic identity in the fifteenth through seventeenth centuries. Beisaw claims that ethnogenesis homogenizes and thereby distorts the native experience, while nation-genesis, focusing on goals and means as they relate

to nationality, respects native agency and allows for a more nuanced understanding of the decisions made by native peoples in negotiating a complex and rapidly changing reality.

Wall (chapter 5) and Wyatt (chapter 6) address the potential of new excavation data and new technology to change our conceptions of Susquehannock settlement—in particular, the idea that the Susquehannocks occupied single villages sequentially. The discovery and intensive study of new Susquehannock villages—and hamlets and small camps—challenges prevailing models of Susquehannock settlement and opens our eyes to the variability and flexible adaptations that we should expect to see during the turbulent history of the Contact period.

Becker's contribution (chapter 7) emphasizes how little we presently know about the physical characteristics of a people early Euroamerican observers described as "gyant-like." Again, the haphazard approach to excavation and to the study and reporting of the physical anthropology of the Susquehannocks that marked the late nineteenth- and early twentieth-century history of Susquehannock archaeology has hampered a deeper understanding. As Snow emphasizes, new technology could make a substantial contribution here beyond defining their stature by addressing the impacts of disease and stress on this native population.

Pottery and other forms of material culture have been critical to Susquehannock studies. In general, however, they have simply been used uncritically as markers of ethnic identity, according to an implicit model of biological growth and decline that all too often betrays colonialist assumptions about the fate of native groups. Lauria (chapter 4) and Beisaw suggest an approach to pottery and introduced metal vessels that goes beyond ethnic identity to trace the use of pottery and other vessels as it reflects decisions made by Susquehannock women in response to their encounters with Euroamerican populations, an approach that grants agency to native peoples, especially women, rather than treating them as helpless victims.

I am grateful to the authors for their patience in what has been a longer than normal—but I hope not unbearable—gestation for this book. This publication was made possible with financial support from the Society for Pennsylvania Archaeology (SPA), the Pennsylvania Archaeological Council (PAC), and the Eastern States Archaeological Federation (ESAF). In particular, I want to express my gratitude to ESAF for the Louis A. Brennan Award in aid of publication. The members and officers of all three organizations have been outstanding in their patronage of this series and the present book. Their continued sponsorship is gratefully acknowledged. I would also like to express my profound appreciation for the excellent work and essential assistance of the Pennsylvania State University Press staff, especially Kathryn B. Yahner, acquisitions editor. James T. Herbstritt and Elizabeth Wagner of the State Museum of Pennsylvania kindly provided some of the images used on the book cover. Finally, I want to express my appreciation to Barry Kent, Fred Kinsey, Ira Smith, John Witthoft, and others who laid the foundations that made this book and the work it embodies possible.

REFERENCES

Cadzow, Donald A.

1936 *Archaeological Studies of the Susquehannock Indians of Pennsylvania*. Safe Harbor Report No. 2. Pennsylvania Historical Commission, Harrisburg.

Custer, Jay F.

2018 A Postcolonial Perspective on Contact Period Archaeology. In *Middle Atlantic Prehistory: Foundations and Practice*, edited by Heather A. Wholey and Carole L. Nash, 325–70. Rowman and Littlefield, New York.

Holmes, William H.

1903 Aboriginal Pottery of the Eastern United States. In *Twentieth Annual Report of the United State Bureaus of American Ethnology, 1893–1894*, 1–237. Government Printing Office, Washington, D.C.

Kent, Barry C.

2001 *Susquehanna's Indians*. Revised edition. The Pennsylvania Historical and Museum Commission, Harrisburg.

Kinsey, W. Fred, III

1959 Historic Susquehannock Pottery. In *Susquehannock Miscellany*, edited by J. Witthoft and W. F. Kinsey III, 61–98. Pennsylvania Historical and Museum Commission, Harrisburg.

Moorehead, Warren K.

1938 *A Report of the Susquehanna River Expedition*. Andover Press, Andover, Massachusetts.

Willey, Gordon R., and Philip Phillips

1958 *Method and Theory in American Archaeology*. University of Chicago Press, Chicago.

Witthoft, John

1959 Ancestry of the Susquehannocks. In *Susquehannock Miscellany*, edited by J. Witthoft and W. F. Kinsey III, 19–60. Pennsylvania Historical and Museum Commission, Harrisburg.

Witthoft, John, and W. Fred Kinsey III (editors)

1959 *Susquehannock Miscellany*. Pennsylvania Historical and Museum Commission, Harrisburg.

Witthoft, John, W. Fred Kinsey III, and Charles H. Holzinger

1959 A Susquehannock Cemetery: The Ibaugh Site. In *Susquehannock Miscellany*, edited by J. Witthoft and W. F. Kinsey III, 99–119. Pennsylvania Historical and Museum Commission, Harrisburg.

Wren, Christopher

1914 *A Study of North Appalachian Indian Pottery*. Republished from Proceedings of the Wyoming Historical and Geological Society, vol. 13. The E. B. Yordy Company, Wilkes-Barre, Pennsylvania.

Introduction

SUSQUEHANNOCK ARCHAEOLOGY

Dean R. Snow

ABSTRACT

New technologies and advances in theory have produced new kinds of data and at much higher resolutions than before, thereby benefiting archaeological research by resolving old problems and facilitating the development and solution of new ones. The Susquehannock case is informed by Northern Iroquoian cultural patterns, but it generally lacks reliable, specific, and detailed ethnohistorical sources. As a result, researchers are more dependent on archaeology in this part of Northern Iroquoia. The interactions of regional conflict, trade, epidemic diseases, and Susquehannock demography conditioned their settlement patterns, requiring an understanding of all of these subjects. The interaction of these factors led to the aggregation of widely scattered hamlets to a small region centered on Bradford County, followed by their merger into a single larger community that lived on a series of large sites nearer the mouth of the Susquehanna River. Smaller ancillary hamlets also existed, and the possibility of one more still-undiscovered larger village persists. New ceramic analysis informs Susquehannock origins, the production and uses of pottery vessels by women, and the symbolic importance of decorative ceramic attributes. New information has filled out the bigger picture of the place of the Susquehannock nation in the Colonial era and the centuries leading up to it and has set the agenda for new archaeological initiatives.

The chapters of this book reveal a profound and invigorating shift from the analytical categories and procedures of American archaeology as it was a half century ago (Willey and Phillips 1958). The standard units of classification and exposition used in that era included culture, tradition, type, variety, component, phase, stage, site, and other terms that were broad, often subjective, parochial, impressionistic, and in practice often only vaguely defined. Today, as evidenced by this volume, new technologies and improved method and theory in archaeological science have facilitated the emergence of higher-resolution tools and conceptual frameworks. These have allowed researchers to acquire much more detailed data and use them to build better logical structures of analysis and reporting. Computers are now fast and portable. Relatively inexpensive accelerator mass spectrometry (AMS) radiocarbon dating can now be used on larger numbers of much smaller samples. Inexpensive digital camera technology vastly improves the quality and quantity of visual records. Total stations can gather and preserve excavation data at a small scale, which computer-assisted drawing (CAD) software converts to visual form. Geographic positioning systems (GPS), coupled with geographic information systems (GIS) software, facilitate the acquisition, management, and analysis of large quantities of high-resolution spatial data gathered at a large scale. Microscopic analysis allows the extraction of lithic, floral, and faunal data that have a host of scientific uses. Ancient DNA (aDNA) analysis reveals human descent lines like never before. Database management systems have allowed us to control huge quantities of data in many forms for purposes of analysis that were inconceivable in the days of 3 × 5 cards and typewriters. More rigorous analytical procedures have facilitated productive use of all these new tools.

The Susquehannocks

A new generation of archaeologists is bringing these tools to bear on the Susquehannock case, as evidenced by the chapters that follow. As is so often the case in North American ethnohistory, we know the subjects of this volume by names supplied by others. John Smith (1580–1631) called them "Sasquesahanoughs" in 1608, a term given to him by an Eastern Algonquian interpreter (Barbour 1969:374). Smith also claimed that they were a nation of men like "giants." Marshall Becker's chapter indicates that the men Smith met probably averaged 174.7 centimeters (5 ft 8¾ in) in height, which is not particularly tall by modern standards but was probably 10 centimeters (4 in) taller than the average Englishman of Smith's time. One individual might have been over 180 centimeters (5 ft 11 in). That alone would have been sufficient to impress Smith enough to prompt him to make his

contribution to the sketchy anecdotal historical record we have available today.

Later English sources called these people "Conestogas," a term they had borrowed from one of the Iroquois languages. The French usually referred to them as "Andastes," a name shortened from the Huron "Andastoerrhonon." Dutch and Swedish colonial sources typically refer to them as "Minquas," a term given to them by Eastern Algonquians. A confusion of other names, some of them probably cognates of those mentioned here, turn up in various colonial documents (Jennings 1978). As Heisey and Witmer (1964:1) note, "If a people has a right to choose its own name, there probably never were any Susquehannocks." At least for now, however, how these people referred to themselves remains unknown. Historians and anthropologists have settled on calling them "Susquehannocks," which is at least consistent with the modern term "Susquehanna" for the river along which they lived in the seventeenth century.

By AD 950, Northern Iroquoians were living in dozens of hamlets broadly scattered across what are now central Pennsylvania, New York, and southern Ontario. By AD 1350, Northern Iroquoians had abandoned Pennsylvania, and a few were expanding down the St. Lawrence into modern Quebec. By the fifteenth century, the periodic relocations of hamlets every decade or two were producing clusters of archaeological sites, and by 1560, the sequences of recently abandoned hamlet sites were clustering where the historically known Northern Iroquoian nations emerged.

The gradual clustering of villages in areas that correspond to the homelands of historic Northern Iroquoian nations was a process that played out largely in the fifteenth century. Thus it is inappropriate to refer to any of the ancestors of the historic nations by names that probably did not arise until that process began. It is likely that the Susquehannocks had ancestors in common with the historic Cayugas and Onondagas, but it is not appropriate to derive any one of them from one of the others so named. Wallace Chafe has described the genesis of the Cayuga language, which is still spoken, as particularly complex (personal communication, 1995). This was probably occasioned by the movement of individuals and groups between communities over time in the formative era. The Susquehannock language was extinct by the end of the eighteenth century, and too little is known of it for its linguistic evolution to be characterized in any detail.

Susquehannock Demography

Hamlets previously scattered along the upper tributaries of the Susquehanna River in New York and Pennsylvania relocated to a cluster in and around Bradford County, Pennsylvania. These early sixteenth-century hamlets later began merging into much larger villages, often located within palisades on defensible hilltops. What had been clusters of small communities merged into a few much larger ones, even as the overall population was growing. This major demographic change was initially misinterpreted as evidence of overall decline by Ramenofsky because, while she was able to count the declining numbers of sites, she was unable to measure their growing aggregate populations (Ramenofsky 1988). This error was later corrected by better dating and new means to measure individual community sizes and aggregate population sizes (Snow 1995a).

Samuel de Champlain provides an insightful observation regarding Northern Iroquoian demography that applies throughout the centuries leading up to his early seventeenth-century travels in the region. Translated from French, he says, "They sometimes change their villages at intervals of ten, twenty, or thirty years, and transfer them to a distance of one, two, or three leagues from the preceding situation, except when compelled by their enemies to dislodge, in which case they retire to a greater distance, as the Antouhonorons, who went some forty to fifty leagues" (Champlain 1907:313–14). A league was about the distance encumbered people

can cover on foot in an hour, a variable measure of 3.25 to 4.68 kilometers (2.02 to 2.91 mi). The 40- to 50-league distances cited by Champlain thus amount to 130–234 kilometers, or 81–146 miles. Champlain was using a nation of what we now call the Neutral Confederacy (Antouhonorons) as his example, but the observation also applies to the ancestral Huron nations and other Northern Iroquoians, including the Susquehannocks.

The strong tendency for Northern Iroquoian communities to relocate every one to three decades is a great benefit to archaeologists. A single hamlet-sized community can produce a cluster of 3 to 10 spatially discrete sites in only a century, which are easier to study than are the components of longer occupations on single sites. Once hamlets congregated into large villages, the exhaustion of fields and firewood forced even more frequent relocation. This, in turn, produced larger and more easily discovered sites. Moreover, the internal structuring of Northern Iroquoian villages was consistent enough to allow archaeologists to derive reasonably accurate population estimates from site areas (Snow and Starna 1989). This has facilitated the development of credible demographic histories for the Mohawks and other Northern Iroquoian nations (Jones 2010; Snow 1995a).

Jasmine Gollup (chapter 1) and James Herbstritt (chapter 2) discuss ancestral Susquehannock communities that had been living scattered within the drainage basin of the Susquehanna River, which came together as a cluster of hamlets primarily along the main course of the river in northern Bradford County and the adjacent part of New York. Decades earlier, John Witthoft recognized the significance of the ceramics found on these sites, which he inferred were ancestral to later ceramics found on southern Pennsylvania village sites (Kent 1984:295–307; Witthoft 1959). The peripatetic Warren K. Moorehead had excavated two decades earlier in the same site cluster (Moorehead 1939). At least 18 sites were then located within the Bradford County site cluster. Gollup mentions more than twice that many and provides ceramic data for 31 of them. How many periodically relocating communities are represented by these sites has not been determined. This is not unusual in Northern Iroquoia. Small poorly sampled hamlets having few or no diagnostic artifacts cannot be dated with sufficient accuracy to allow them to be assigned to sufficiently short periods to solve the problem.

Herbstritt estimates that the Bradford cluster was established beginning in the middle of the sixteenth century and that the communities relocated to the southern Susquehanna Valley in the late part of the same century. Herbstritt summarizes what is known of the Bradford cluster's origins in remote upper tributary drainage basins. Unfortunately, sampling sites for diagnostic ceramic evidence has not provided information on community sizes or internal residential patterns. Many sites are now so damaged that such patterns cannot be recovered. At least for now, clarification of the Susquehannock case depends on inference by way of analogy with more completely known Northern Iroquoian cases in New York and Ontario.

The ancestral Susquehannocks were just one of a couple dozen sets of communities that moved first into clusters for mutual protection and then began merging into larger villages on defensible locations. As they made changes for the sake of defense and security, they also sought ways to take advantage of new opportunities. Neither threat nor opportunity lasts for long under such circumstances, and rapid culture change is not a surprising consequence. The sixteenth century was a chaotic time for everyone in Northern Iroquoia, full of metaphorical carrots and sticks. The climatic cooling of the Little Ice Age affected farming. Intervillage conflict was increasing, possibly stimulated by earlier conflicts among Mississippian polities in the Midwest (Milner 1999). Violence spiraled in Northern Iroquoia as random deaths provoked blame and revenge, which in turn prompted more of the same (Snow 1994:54–55). Europeans carrying exotic and desirable trade goods turned up along the Atlantic Coast while this was happening.

The Susquehannocks were mostly dispersed westward by colonial incursions and warfare in the first half of the eighteenth century. A remnant community of 20 people living near Conestoga was massacred by a mob referred to as the Paxton Boys in 1763, and with that, the Susquehannocks disappeared from Pennsylvania history. The atrocity was condemned by many, including Benjamin Franklin.

Likely, too little evidence remains for historians to do justice to the history of the Susquehannocks, documentary or otherwise, or for linguists to reconstruct their language in any detail. Exploration of the Susquehannocks has been left largely to archaeologists. Fortunately, what little we know from documentary sources indicates that Susquehannock culture was consistent with the general pattern of all Northern Iroquoians: "Many of the major patterns so well understood for the nineteenth-century Iroquois can be assumed to have been present among all the northern Iroquoians during earlier times" (Fenton 1978:296). We know that sixteenth-century Susquehannocks resided in Iroquoian longhouses and that Susquehannock women made Iroquoian-style collared pottery. Other details are similarly consistent with the larger pattern.

Jamestown, Virginia, was established by English colonists in 1607. From there, John Smith and others explored the Chesapeake Bay and beyond, seeking opportunities for their colony. Unfortunately, the arrival of European settlers, which included children, increased the likelihood that pathogens would join trade goods in moving along the well-established trails of the region; children were the primary carriers of infectious diseases, since adults typically had acquired immunity to the worst diseases in childhood (Snow and Lanphear 1988). Long voyages by adult crews kept childhood diseases from reaching America easily. Even after diseases arrived, epidemics were slower to spread than claimed by Dobyns and some other historians, mainly because of buffer zones between communities and the sporadic nature of trade (Dobyns 1983; Thornton 2000). Influenza, measles, and other less severe diseases may have dominated in early epidemics. Smallpox was particularly virulent, and mortality was high when it eventually appeared. The initial smallpox epidemic on the Mohawk River in New York produced 60% mortality in the winter of 1634–35 (Snow 1994:94–108; 1995a). The timing and severity were both contrary to Dobyns and those influenced by his exaggerated speculations (Henige 1998).

We know little about Susquehannock political organization apart from what can be inferred from their settlement pattern and by analogy from the nations in the League of the Iroquois. A French Jesuit source tells us that there was a single Susquehannock village with 1,300 warriors in 1647, a probable exaggeration. This mention dates over a decade after the horrible epidemic that struck the Mohawks during 1634–35. Moreover, a count of 1,300 warriors would imply a total population of at least 5,200. We know that the populations of Northern Iroquoian villages rarely reached 2,000 and that above that size, they became unstable for a variety of political and logistical reasons (Snow and Starna 1989). The Mohawk Failing site briefly had a population of 3,300 just before the epidemic struck, but within a year, the total Mohawk population had fallen to about 2,830 people housed in four much smaller villages (Snow 1995b:296–97). Consequently, we are better off depending on archaeological evidence rather than putting much stock in rare documentary sources of dubious veracity.

Trade and Exchange

Basque and French fishermen had started visiting the Gulf of St. Lawrence early in the sixteenth century. Their visits became so frequent that a trading jargon developed between Algonquian and Basque trading partners there. Fierce far-ranging travelers from the interior to the southwest of the Gulf sometimes appeared there in the warm months. These people were referred to by the Basques as *Hilokoa* or *Hirokoa*. One possibility is that the name derives from a Basque word meaning "killer people," but Basque grammar makes it more likely that it derives from a term meaning "walled-town people" (Bakker 1990; Loewen 2016). Later French explorers encountered the same people and adopted the same word from the Algonquians, silencing the *H* and giving it a spelling to fit the French language, *Iroquois*. It is still pronounced "Irokwa" in Canada. These were the same people who were in constant conflict with various neighbors around their homeland, in what is now New York State. It is not surprising that in the context of Iroquois predation and European trade, the ancestral Susquehannocks shifted generally southward down the Susquehanna River over time.

Historical documents from the sixteenth century, particularly those associated with the de Soto entrada, show that despite chronic warfare, trade in luxury goods thrived along the well-established trail network of the Eastern Woodlands, particularly that part of it that lay eastward beyond the Mississippian heartland. Marine shell from the Gulf Coast was particularly valued in the interior Northeast, and the overland trails that ran along the Piedmont and thence along both sides of the Susquehanna were important routes in the wider network (Bradley 2011; Sempowski 1989; Wallace 1952). As Spanish, English, and other ships touched the shores of Chesapeake Bay, European trade items began to flow into the existing trading system. The failed English colony on Roanoke Island, established in 1585, lasted long enough to have an impact on the trading system as well. None of this would have escaped the notice of the Susquehannocks living up the Susquehanna. Their response to the mix of threats and opportunities of the time led them to move downriver. They came together to form a single large community with at least five longhouses at the Schultz site (36LA7) on the east side of the Susquehanna in Lancaster County around 1590 (White 2001).

Settlement Changes

James Herbstritt discusses Susquehannock ethnogenesis empirically and in considerable detail. April Beisaw, however, argues that framing analysis of the process in terms of national genesis is preferable to framing it in terms of ethnogenesis because ethnogenesis is or can be treated abstractly, whereas framing the discussion in terms of national genesis more easily allows for the examination of agency and clarification of how individuals negotiated their lives and identities. Her argument revives the distinctions of culture and society made by an earlier generation but provides greater clarity, for it takes us beyond identity to a more nuanced appreciation of agency, from inferences about who these people were collectively to inferences about what they did individually. Most importantly, it takes researchers deeper into the available data, a more detailed approach that is bound to produce higher-resolution results. There is clearly value in working through analyses at multiple levels and with alternative perspectives. Herbstritt and Beisaw offer complementary analyses that are not mutually exclusive.

The period covered by the large Susquehannock villages along the lower course of the river includes their apparent initial consolidation at the Schultz site, the influx of European trade goods, the onset of epidemics, the dwindling of the Susquehannock population, and the extermination of their remnant community in 1763 (table I.1). There are only vague and sometimes contradictory documentary references available, but the archaeological evidence has tended to support the working hypothesis that the Schultz site represents the first of a series of large villages occupied by a single community that moved periodically in a typically Northern Iroquoian manner. The older Shenks Ferry culture sites of the area were abandoned and their populations apparently either displaced, extirpated, or absorbed by the Susquehannocks. April Beisaw argues that the dominant process was absorption and that it probably played out in more mutual than asymmetrical terms—that is, more merger than subjugation. When she examined the evidence in detail, she found evidence of the persistence of Shenks Ferry identities in later seventeenth-century sites.

There might have also been scattered hamlets associated with each main village. Such was the case for the Mohawks and several other Northern Iroquoian nations. The Mohawks had three main villages in 1580. These expanded to four villages after 1614, then reduced to three following the smallpox epidemic of 1634–35. The number reduced again to only two after 1679, then fragmented to six smaller communities before reconsolidation produced the two "castles" that persisted until the American Revolution (Snow 1995b). The point is that we should expect the Susquehannock picture to become more complicated as new archaeological evidence is uncovered.

Andrew Wyatt's discussion of new evidence from the Lemoyne site (36Cu194) provides just such an

TABLE I.1   Archaeological sites of the Washington Boro area, with occupation dates estimated by Kent (1984), White (2001), and Wyatt (chapter 6)

Site name	Site number	Type	Kent	White	Wyatt
Schultz	*36LA7*	*village*	*1575–1600*	*1590–1615*	*1595–1615*
Lemoyne	36CU194	hamlet	1625–45	1640–50	1610–20
Washington Boro	36LA8	village	1600–1625	1615–40	1615–35
UNKNOWN		village	1625–45	1640–50	
Strickler	36LA3	village	1645–65	1650–65	
Oscar Leibhart	36YO9	village	1665–74	1665–74	
Byrd Leibhart	36YO170	village	1676–80	1676–80	
UNKNOWN			1680–90		
Conestoga	36LA52	village	1690–1763		

occasion for reassessment. The community that built and occupied the Lemoyne site appears to have derived from Schultz near the end of its two-decade life. After a one-decade existence, the population of Lemoyne probably moved to the Washington Boro site, which had by then already been occupied for a few years (table I.1). It is not possible to accurately measure the size of the Lemoyne site, but a critical reading of the historical documents tends to support the hypothesis that there was only one large village community at the time and Lemoyne was likely a smaller community. Thus it is not necessary to force Lemoyne into the chronology between Schultz and Washington Boro by proposing an earlier abandonment of the former and/or a later founding of the latter.

There is a time gap of at least 10 years, perhaps more, between Washington Boro and Strickler: AD 1640–50. Kent could not account for where the Susquehannocks were living in this "transitional stage." He cites some evidence from two small sites and suggests that a main village might have been under the site of modern Columbia, Pennsylvania, and consequently is now destroyed. Marshall Becker introduces the possibility that the Susquehannocks broke up into a handful of much smaller communities due to smallpox and conflict in their increasingly complex colonial world. This would be analogous to what the Mohawks went through between 1693 and 1712 (Snow 1995b:4). Another gap appears after the abandonment of the Byrd Leibhart village site and before the return of dispersed Susquehannocks to live in Conestoga, but in this case, temporary dispersal is less speculative because it is generally explained by documents (Kent 1984:22–24).

A Lost City?

Lost cities are a popular topic outside professional archaeology. *The Lost City of Z* was published in 2005, and a movie version of it came out in 2016. But such stories are more about archaeologists than

archaeology and are largely if not entirely fictional at that. Nevertheless, Susquehannock archaeology might have its own lost city, which may or may not lie under modern Columbia. If Marshall Becker's hypothesis that the Susquehannocks resided in five much smaller communities for a decade or two is true, there may be no lost city to search for.

Much depends on the dating of the Washington Boro and the Strickler sites. Even high-resolution radiocarbon dating is too inaccurate to resolve these dates. The presence or absence of well-dated European trade goods is still a more accurate indicator. But here the logic of dating either site introduces uncertainties. The *terminus post quem*, the date after which a site must have been initially occupied, can be inferred only from the **presence** of diagnostic artifacts that establish the initial date. We can be certain that artifacts cannot have been deposited before they were available, and in this case, the evidence is positive and certainty is relatively strong. The *terminus ante quem*, the date by or before which a site must have been abandoned, can only be inferred by the **absence** of diagnostic artifacts that can reasonably be expected to have been in use and circulation after that date. Like it or not, this is a form of negative evidence. Artifact types like white ball clay (kaolin) smoking pipes were typically acquired, used, broken, and discarded quickly, and that is good for archaeology. Pipe styles changed frequently enough and their dates of manufacture are well-enough known for our purposes. However, other artifacts that are more durable and more likely to be curated as heirlooms might take a very long time to fall into the archaeological record. Thus overall there is less certainty in setting the *terminus ante quem* than is the case for a relatively more certain *terminus post quem* date.

The logic of using these concepts with trade goods to date sites can be illustrated by many examples. If, for instance, elderly Northern Iroquoian people are buried in clothing bearing curated beads and other ornamentation, key artifacts recovered from cemeteries will tend to predate those found discarded in the associated residential sites. Newly available objects tend to appear suddenly and enjoy popularity, often making their initial appearance a useful horizon marker. But if the same objects are treasured and curated, their disappearance might be gradual. Thus the *terminus ante quem* has to be based not simply on what is present but on the failure of some key artifact to appear when and where it can reasonably be expected to do so.

So far, the AD 1640–50 temporal gap between the Washington Boro and Strickler sites has been maintained by the presence and the absence of key artifacts at both sites. Perhaps new or reexamined evidence from one or both sites, or new evidence from elsewhere regarding the dating of trade goods, will close the gap. For now, however, the lost settlement of the Susquehannocks remains a possible hypothesis (White 2001:238).

The Uses of Ceramic Types

One can get a sense of the history of Susquehannock archaeological research through a careful reading of the chapters in this volume. Lisa Lauria's contribution is helpful in that regard. Cultures always evolve over time, and Lauria points out that characterizing change over time as either progress or degeneration typically tells us more about the scholars making those characterizations than it does about the case being described.

Lauria's argument builds on Strauss's observations regarding the relationship between vessel volume, decorative style, and social contexts of vessel use. Strauss noticed that the average vessel volume decreased over time, a change that was coincident with the increasing importance of brass trade vessels in cooking. Strauss also noted that ceramic vessels used earlier to cook food for nuclear families and the occasional visitor ranged in volume from 3.01 to 10 liters (Strauss 2000).

Lauria observes that cooking pots had to have occupied prominent places on the central aisleway fires of Susquehannock longhouses, just as they did in all Northern Iroquoian longhouses. Simmering pots were constantly and conspicuously visible. It should not surprise anyone that such prominence made the pots an excellent medium for the display of important iconic symbols. Whatever the intentions behind a Susquehannock woman's choice of decorative elements, we can be certain that they did not include a desire to facilitate the work of future archaeologists. Nevertheless, the potters' choices signaled, sometimes intentionally and sometimes unintentionally, information about community, matrilineage, family, sexuality, fashion, food preparation, diet, and so forth. We do not need to perceive specific meanings to appreciate the significance of the phenomenon. All of these symbols probably evolved over time, but some might have persisted because of intentional replication by the potters. Archaeologists working in the first half of the twentieth century were mainly concerned with building chronologies of culture history. What they needed were ceramic types that were time sensitive, types that could be used for cross dating, like geologists used key fossils. As a consequence, they tended to use projectile point types and pottery attributes as temporal keys without much questioning of the assumptions involved. While it might have been better to key on particular time-sensitive attributes, it appears that archaeologists typically felt compelled to use the fullest possible range of attributes in the definition of types and wares, so as to avoid criticism for being selective. This tendency could have easily introduced enough noise into the process to defeat their good intentions.

Archaeologists have traditionally used the broadly defined Richmond Mills Incised, Proto-Susquehannock, and Schultz Incised wares as temporally arranged in that order. That use assumes that the differences between the three are chronologically significant (largely, if not entirely so). If that were true, the 31 components shown in Jasmine Gollup's figure 1.5 Venn diagram should seriate cleanly. But the Venn diagram indicates that they will not, and any attempt to seriate the components does indeed produce unsatisfactory results. That means that some of the sites have two or more components, a significant portion of the attributes used are not time sensitive, or typological mistakes have been made. This is a common problem in ceramic seriation studies, and serious efforts to solve it usually show that the reuse of sampled sites by later populations is the principal difficulty (Snow 1969).

An examination of James Herbstritt's table 2.2 reveals that the Parker (36LU14) and Blackman (36BR83) sites were probably in continuous or discontinuous use for long periods. Parker in particular has 10 radiocarbon dates spanning 376 years. According to Jasmine Gollup's figure 1.5, only Schultz Incised wares are found at Parker. If we cannot count on sites having been occupied for sufficiently short durations, and if we cannot count on traditional pottery types to be sufficiently time sensitive, then researchers must reexamine ceramic assemblages to find truly time-sensitive attributes.

Reanalysis of the Bradford cluster of sites might produce better results. Gollup points out that some older type definitions are so vague or subjective that they cannot be reproduced. However, it is also the case that a clean seriation of the 31 components in her figure 1.5 can be achieved by selectively ignoring or redefining the objects in the assemblages of only four sites: Engelbert, BR1, BR5, and BR43. That means that any of us might be tempted to simply look at those four assemblages and find a way to modify the evidence to better fit our expectations. Subconscious cherry picking can be fatal to any scientific undertaking. Thus any reanalysis should be comprehensive, well-designed, focused on time-sensitive attributes, and accompanied to the extent possible by the precise application of high-definition AMS radiocarbon dating. To do otherwise can perpetuate the use of concepts too blunt to produce reliable results.

This leads to another point. The epistemology of archaeologists of the culture-history tradition of scholarship has long since been inverted by radiocarbon dating. The assumptions underlying typology, cross dating, and chronology in the procedures outlined by Willey and Phillips six decades ago have been upended. We can and should now be dating everything independently and in detail, using what we find out to understand the complex processes we once assumed in simple forms for other purposes (Snow 1978; Willey and Phillips 1958). Yet it is still the case that even high-precision AMS dating cannot yet replace the use of time-sensitive trade goods for the construction of Colonial-era chronologies.

This Is Us

Another key question is this: What archaeologically recoverable object(s) can be identified as exclusively emblematic of the Susquehannocks? How did they project their identity? Archaeological descriptions of physical remains often summarize archaeological cultures in terms of house styles, food resources used, projectile point types, and so forth. But these components of material culture are often shared with other cultures and thus fail tests of exclusivity. Every nation has something that says "This is us" both to its own members and to the outside world, and many examples can be found in the ethnohistorical literature.

A Susquehannock potter was not just applying pretty decorations to the vessels she made; she was consciously saying to her family, to her clan segment, to her community, and to visitors that "this is who we are." It does not matter that we cannot now know the precise symbolic meanings of most or all of the symbolism found on the collars of the vessels; it is sufficient for our purposes to be able to conclude that women in Northern Iroquoian societies were making explicit symbolic statements about their identities. Lauria observes that the standardization of this messaging increased over time through the course of the seventeenth century, even as large communal feasting appears to have waned. This kind of change certainly relates to other evolutionary changes in Susquehannock society; as Lauria reminds us, it is a mistake to characterize it simply as loss or deterioration.

Symbols of identity are often not obvious to us. There are many examples to illustrate the problem. For the Cheyenne nation, the key emblem was and is a crescentic artifact made from the thick portion of a freshwater mussel shell (Moore 1996:27–29). National identities in the former Yugoslavia were conveyed mostly by distinctive hats (Wobst 1977). Southwestern pottery provides what is probably a better analogy for understanding Susquehannock emblems of identity. Pueblo communities there were and remain matrilineal. In the Southwest, modern ceramics are typically easy for both insiders and outsiders to identify as Pueblo. It is an ironic twist that archaeologists have sometimes been scoffed at for calling artifacts that defy utilitarian explanation "ceremonial objects." Once thus labeled, such artifacts are often set aside and forgotten, the attribution acknowledged as a desperate default category invoked to cover for uncertainty. But ethnographers know that many culturally significant objects, or the decorations they bear, lack obvious utilitarian purposes. These often are indeed ceremonial or, more precisely, emblematic objects. This observation can be extended to the apparent nonutilitarian decoration of otherwise utilitarian artifacts. In both cases, special objects and decorative attributes may indeed have symbolic utility for their makers.

Thus it turns out that archaeologists can sometimes learn from marginalized objects in artifact assemblages. Their analysis in this case has the potential to lead to the definition of archaeological cultures that come much closer to mapping evolving nations as described by ethnographers. That said, it must be recognized that the defining emblems that are unique to nations are not necessarily parts of their material culture that we can expect to be preserved in the archaeological record. If key emblematic displays are to be found in, say, feather headdresses or perishable textiles, the archaeologist might be simply out of luck.

The evidence presented by Lisa Lauria makes it clear that Northern Iroquoian women were signaling at least group identity, and perhaps other unknown things, with the decorated collars of their pottery vessels. Evidence has been presented by April Beisaw that suggests that female makers of Shenks Ferry ceramics were absorbed into Susquehannock communities where they continued to produce pots bearing the symbolic elements they learned from their mothers rather than switching to Susquehannock styles. This might not have been the case had the circumstances been different, a possibility that prompts a digression.

Northern Iroquoian communities practiced planned parenthood. At first contact with Europeans, observers found that it was rare for a woman to have more than three children, and those she had were spaced over time. The reason was that women were responsible for most of the agricultural production; they could not afford to care for large numbers of children at the same time. Thus they lacked the hedge against childhood deaths by having large families like the Europeans did. European families had long since compensated for the effects of epidemics by having many children, only some of whom lived to adulthood. Thus when those epidemics began to appear in the Northeast, Iroquoian communities could not respond in the same way as Europeans had by increasing the birth rate.

The Northern Iroquoians had long taken prisoners in raids against other communities, particularly young women, and adopted them as a means to replace younger people who had died unexpectedly. Young men, typically war captives, were less often adopted and more frequently subjected to torture and death. But captives of both sexes who seemed adaptive to their captors could be adopted. All adoptions were regarded as complete and permanent by both captives and captors. An adopted man or woman was expected to replace a recently deceased person, in effect becoming that person in every way possible. Such an adoptee was expected to learn the language quickly and to assume the name, roles, tasks, and identity of the person (s)he was replacing. This set of assumptions was consistent with the Iroquoian political succession. The death of a chief was typically followed by the "raising up" of a new younger chief who took on the name and the identity of the deceased (Snow 1994:127–30).

For example, Pierre Radisson was captured and adopted by the Mohawks in 1651. For a long time, he went along with his captors and thereby avoided premature death. He bided his time, escaping three years after being captured and adopted and making his way back to Europe by way of Fort Orange, now Albany. While he hid out at Fort Orange, waiting for a ship to make good his escape, his adoptive parents and sisters tearfully roamed the settlement, pleading for their son/brother to come out and return with them to the Mohawk Valley. They eventually gave up and went home, no doubt thinking that Radisson (or whatever they called him) had acted in very bad faith (Snow, Gehring, and Starna 1996:62–92).

The nature of Northern Iroquoian adoption is relevant here because adoptees were expected to take on and exhibit the standard adopted emblems of ethnicity. A captured Susquehannock woman adopted into a Mohawk household would have been expected to learn how to decorate collared pots properly (i.e., the proper Mohawk way) and to immediately abandon the motifs and techniques of her birth mother. Radisson was shown how to paint his face like a proper Mohawk and was given strings of wampum to wear, this too no doubt in a precise Mohawk fashion (Snow, Gehring, and Starna 1996:70). It is very likely that the Susquehannocks had similar practices, which differed only in the codified details.

The contrast of this scenario with what April Beisaw infers for the absorption of Shenks Ferry people into Susquehannock society suggests that she is observing the playing out of a very different process. The absorption was more a merger than a conquest, with individuals retaining traditional identities in the new emergent community in the big villages of the Lower Susquehanna River (insofar as the signaling of ceramic vessel collars is concerned). As it happens, this practice also has analogues in the Mohawk Valley, where at different times both Oneida and Huron communities were taken in wholesale, their potters not expected to abandon their traditional styles for Mohawk ones (Snow 1995b:294, 403).

There remains the frequent reference to copper and brass bracelets and spirals as supposed Susquehannock emblems. Beisaw, Gollup, Herbstritt, and Wall all discuss these artifacts, which are common in sixteenth- and seventeenth-century Susquehannock assemblages. Although it is possible that they had pre-Contact prototypes made from native copper, most or all were probably made from repurposed trade kettles. Thus while the raw material was derived from European trade, the spirals and bracelets were native innovations. The question is whether or not they should be regarded as symbolic emblems of the Susquehannocks. We can probably set aside shell tempering as a possible signal of ethnicity. It appears to have been borrowed for technical reasons from the Upper Ohio by way of the West Branch Valley during the earliest years of the Upper West Branch phase (James Herbstritt, personal communication, 2018). We can also set aside things that from archaeological evidence were clearly pan-Iroquoian.

The spirals and bracelets deserve closer examination. The evidence indicates that neither object was exclusive to the Susquehannocks. In some parts of the Northeast, the spiral ornaments are sometimes referred to as "Basque earrings," a two-part name that is probably inappropriate on both counts. It is sufficient to point out that both spirals and bracelets were in widespread use in these two centuries, making their use important but not exclusive to the Susquehannocks. That said, it is also possible that the Susquehannocks wore either or both more frequently or in special exclusive ways that said "this is us." Trace element analysis and continued AMS dating could give researchers a means to become more certain of raw material sources, the high-resolution dates of the first appearance of the artifacts on regional sites, and by inference whether manufacture was localized or widespread. None of these problems has been solved yet, and interesting secondary questions regarding trade and exchange have not yet even been framed.

Vessel Volumes

Susquehannock ceramic vessels often display human effigies. Lauria observes that these usually occur on smaller vessels made for individual use. This is an accurate conclusion, but a review of older literature reveals that it differs sharply from some earlier erroneous archaeological inferences. William Ritchie used the Deowongo Island site as one of those defining what he saw as the Mohawk Iroquois Chance phase (AD 1400–1525). The island is on Canadarago Lake in north central Otsego County—technically not in Mohawk territory but in the part of Eastern New York in which at least two later Northern Iroquoian nations, Oneida and Mohawk, emerged. This was a hunting camp, and like the Susquehannock hamlet sites of the Upper Potomac discussed by Wall, it lacked longhouse patterns and some other features characteristic of main Mohawk or Oneida villages.

Ritchie was aware that Chance-phase ceramic cooking vessels typically came in one of two sizes. Analysis of many more complete vessels from Mohawk village sites confirmed this observation for Chance and later ceramics. Vessels plotted by volume produced a bimodal curve, excluding smaller numbers of very small (toy or paint) pots and very large special-use pots. Smaller vessels tend to cluster around 1.5 liter capacities, while larger vessels are five times larger, clustering around 7.5 liters. Ritchie found none of the smaller vessels at Deowongo Island, and he hypothesized that this was related to the food cooked in them. He reasoned that inasmuch as this was a hunting and fishing camp, the large vessels were intended for cooking meat and fish and, further, that small vessels were by default probably made for cooking corn mush. Ritchie offered no alternative hypotheses to this favored one (Ritchie 1952).

Ritchie did not often make use of ethnohistorical sources, and that was the source of his error. He was apparently unaware of the work of Gabriel Sagard, a Recollect friar who lived among the Hurons in the 1620s. Sagard was clear in describing pottery production as a women's activity. Moreover, he observed that women made cooking pots in two sizes, a large size for the cooking of food shared within nuclear families and smaller pots for the individual use of women while they were menstruating. This alone suffices to disprove Ritchie's corn mush hypothesis (Sagard 1968:102, 109; Snow 1994:107).

The menstrual pot hypothesis received further support when the New York State Museum undertook the inventory and preparation of burials and associated materials from the Mohawk Rice's Woods site for repatriation under the terms of the Native American Graves Protection and Repatriation Act (NAGPRA). Small (1.5 liter) pots found in burial contexts at the site were associated exclusively with the skeletal remains of women. There can be little doubt now regarding the function of smaller cooking pots in Northern Iroquoian communities. The cluster of Mohawk vessels averaging 1.5 liters falls comfortably into this range. Vessels having much larger than ±7.5-liter volumes appear not to have been used for daily cooking but rather for storage and perhaps occasional feasting by large groups. These very large vessels all but disappeared in the seventeenth century, a change apparently related to shifts in storage and communal eating.

While the evidence she has available for Susquehannock cases is not by itself sufficient to allow Lauria to be certain that these were used exclusively by women, she presents that conclusion as probable. The Mohawk cases, in which small vessels have been shown to associate exclusively with female burials, provide additional support for her conclusion. The manufacture and use of small vessels by women continued even as they chose to replace larger communal cooking vessels with brass trade kettles. Archaeology has come a long way since ceramic analysis was used primarily for the very limited purpose of working out chronologies.

Potomac Sites

As described by Robert Wall, seven short-term Susquehannock sites have been found along the Upper Potomac, in adjacent parts of the Maryland and West Virginia panhandles (table I.2). The North Branch Potomac River defines the state line west of Oldtown, Maryland, and three sites lie along the left bank there. The Barton and Flanigan sites are a straight-line distance of only about 16 kilometers (10 mi) apart, with the Llewellyn site lying between them. The South Branch flows down the middle of the West Virginia panhandle. Herriott Farm and Pancake Island are found close to each other nearer the junction of the two branches at Oldtown. The Crites site is farthest upstream to the southwest, a straight-line distance of about 46 kilometers (28.5 mi) from Herriott Farm. The Moorefield site lies only about 7 kilometers (4 mi) northeast of Crites.

Altogether, the sites can be perceived as a single cluster of hamlets or three clusters of two or three hamlets each. A straight line of about 64 kilometers (40 mi) links the two sites that have the greatest mutual separation. All of these sites fall into the short temporal range of a single decade, AD 1610–20, and none of them had the longhouses of larger Susquehannock towns in Pennsylvania.

TABLE I.2 Upper Potomac Susquehannock sites, AD 1610–20

Site name	Site number	Location
Barton	18AG3	Potomac North Branch, MD
Llewellyn	18AG26	Potomac North Branch, MD
Flanigan	18AG96	Potomac North Branch, MD
Herriott Farm	46HM1	Potomac South Branch, WV
Pancake Island	46HM73	Potomac South Branch, WV
Moorefield	46HY89	Potomac South Branch, WV
Crites	46HY25	Potomac South Branch, WV

Janet Brashler found pottery vessels of both large and small sizes on the Pancake Island site. Here, as on other Susquehannock sites, rim diameters projected from rim sherds can be used as a size proxy for unreconstructed fragmentary vessels. Although ovoid vessel mouths make assessment challenging in some cases, distinguishing the two sizes using rim sherds is possible. The importance of the distinction in this case is that the presence of vessels of both sizes indicates that both males and females were present at Pancake Island and presumably related sites in the Upper Potomac drainage basin. Thus, despite the absence of longhouses, these sites were not all-male hunting or trading camps. Nor do they represent residential mobility, as when whole Susquehannock towns relocated in the periodic way common among Northern Iroquoians. They were logistical hamlets that housed complete nuclear families (Brashler 1987). Wall mentions the possible reasons for their AD 1610–20 use, all of them related to opportunities for trade and exchange.

Conclusion

The chapters of this volume document the continuing growth of Susquehannock archaeology, in terms of both quantity and sophistication. They are in step with the emergence of archaeological science that has allowed hypothesis testing to replace interpretations dependent on impressionistic argumentation from archaeological evidence and what we think we already know about both prehistory and ethnohistory. At the same time, cultural resource management has become such a productive part of government agency and private business archaeology that it has replaced academic and avocational projects as the main source of new evidence. A major challenge now is the comprehensive and detailed preservation and archiving of burgeoning evidence in ways that will ensure access and productive continued use of large quantities of data into the future. The evolution of television from 1950 to today is an apt metaphor for the changes in resolution, clarity, precision, speed, volume, and diversity that archaeology currently enjoys. We can perceive the past more clearly now because of those changes. Those of us near the ends of our productive careers envy those near the beginning of theirs for the amazing new tools that are opening avenues of research that no one could imagine, let alone predict, a half century ago. Here too we need to recognize the importance of agency. Archaeology is in good hands, and the future of the study of the past is full of promise.

REFERENCES

Bakker, P.
1990 A Basque Etymology for the Word "Iroquois." *Man in the Northeast* 40:89–93.

Barbour, Philip L.
1969 *The Jamestown Voyages.* Vol. 2. 2 vols. Cambridge University Press, London.

Bradley, James W.
2011 Re-visiting Wampum and Other Seventeenth-Century Shell Games. *Archaeology of Eastern North America* 39:25–51.

Brashler, Janet G.
1987 A Middle 16th Century Susquehannock Village in Hampshire County. *West Virginia Archeologist* 39 (2): 1–30.

Champlain, Samuel de
1907 *Voyages of Samuel de Champlain: 1604–1618.* Original Narratives of Early American History. Charles Scribner's Sons, New York.

Dobyns, Henry F.
1983 *Their Number Become Thinned: Native American Population Dynamics in Eastern North America.* University of Tennessee Press, Knoxville.

Fenton, William N.
1978 Northern Iroquoian Culture Patterns. In *Handbook of North American Indians*, edited by B. G. Trigger, 296–321. Handbook of North American Indians 15. Smithsonian Institution, Washington, D.C.

Heisey, Henry W., and J. Paul Witmer
1964 The Shenk's Ferry People. *Pennsylvania Archaeologist* 34 (1): 1–34.

Henige, David P.
1998 *Numbers from Nowhere: The American Indian Contact Population Debate.* University of Oklahoma Press, Norman.

Jennings, Francis
1978 Susquehannock. In *Northeast*, edited by B. G. Trigger, 362–67. Handbook of North American Indians 15. Smithsonian Institution, Washington, D.C.

Jones, Eric E.
2010 Sixteenth and Seventeenth Century Haudenosaunee (Iroquois) Population Trends in Northeastern North America. *Journal of Field Archaeology* 35 (1): 5–18.

Kent, Barry C.
1984 *Susquehanna's Indians.* Pennsylvania Historical and Museum Commission, Harrisburg.

Loewen, Brad
2016 Intertwined Enigmas: Basques and Saint Lawrence Iroquoians in the Sixteenth Century. In *Contact in the 16th Century: Networks Among Fishers, Foragers, and Farmers*, edited by B. Loewen and C. Chapdelaine, 57–76. Mercury Series. University of Ottawa Press, Ottawa.

Milner, George R.
1999 Warfare in Prehistoric and Early Historic Eastern North America. *Journal of Archaeological Research* 7:105–51.

Moore, John H.
1996 *The Cheyenne.* Blackwell, Cambridge, Massachusetts.

Moorehead, Warren K.
1939 *A Report of the Susquehanna River Expedition.* Andover Press, Andover, Massachusetts.

Ramenofsky, Ann F.
1988 *Vectors of Death: The Archaeology of European Contact.* University of New Mexico Press, Albuquerque.

Ritchie, William A.
1952 *The Chance Horizon: An Early Stage of Mohawk Iroquois Cultural Development.* New York State Museum Circular 29. New York State Museum, Albany.

Sagard, Gabriel
1968 *Sagard's Long Journey to the Country of the Hurons.* Greenwood Press, New York.

Sempowski, Martha L.
1989 Fluctuations Through Time in the Use of Marine Shell at Seneca Iroquois Sites. In *Proceedings of the 1986 Shell Bead Conference*, edited by C. F. Hayes III, 81–96. Rochester Museum and Science Center, Rochester.

Snow, Dean R.

1969 Ceramic Sequence and Settlement Location in Pre-Hispanic Tlaxcala. *American Antiquity* 34 (2): 131–45.

1978 Shaking Down the New Paradigm. *Archaeology of Eastern North America* 6:87–91.

1994 *The Iroquois*. The Peoples of America Series. Blackwell, Cambridge, Massachusetts.

1995a Microchronology and Demographic Evidence Relating to the Size of Pre-Columbian North American Indian Populations. *Science* 268:1601–4.

1995b *Mohawk Valley Archaeology: The Sites*. Occasional Papers in Anthropology 23. Matson Museum of Anthropology, University Park.

Snow, Dean R., Charles T. Gehring, and William A. Starna (editors)

1996 *In Mohawk Country: Early Narratives About a Native People*. Syracuse University Press, Syracuse, New York.

Snow, Dean R., and Kim M. Lanphear

1988 European Contact and Indian Depopulation in the Northeast: The Timing of the First Epidemics. *Ethnohistory* 35 (1): 15–33.

Snow, Dean R., and William A. Starna

1989 Sixteenth Century Depopulation: A View from the Mohawk Valley. *American Anthropologist* 91:142–49.

Strauss, Alisa N.

2000 *Iroquoian Food Techniques and Technologies: An Examination of Susquehannock Vessel Form and Function*. Ph.D. dissertation, Department of Anthropology, The Pennsylvania State University, University Park. University Microfilms, Ann Arbor, Michigan.

Thornton, Russell G.

2000 Population History of Native North Americans. In *A Population History of North America*, edited by M. R. Haines and R. H. Steckel, 9–50. Cambridge University Press, New York.

Wallace, Paul A. W.

1952 Historic Indian Paths of Pennsylvania. *Pennsylvania Magazine of History and Biography* 76:4.

White, Sharon

2001 *To Secure a Lasting Peace: A Diachronic Analysis of Seventeenth-Century Susquehannock Political and Economic Strategies*. Ph.D. dissertation, Department of Anthropology, The Pennsylvania State University, University Park. University Microfilms, Ann Arbor, Michigan.

Willey, Gordon R., and Philip Phillips

1958 *Method and Theory in American Archaeology*. University of Chicago Press, Chicago.

Witthoft, John

1959 Ancestry of the Susquehannocks. In *Susquehannock Miscellany*, edited by J. Witthoft and W. F. Kinsey III, 19–60. Pennsylvania Historical and Museum Commission, Harrisburg.

Wobst, H. Martin

1977 Stylistic Behavior and Information Exchange. In *For the Director: Research Essays in Honor of James B. Griffin*, edited by C. C. Cleland, 317–42. University of Michigan Press, Ann Arbor.

PART I

Susquehannock Origins

1.

Tracking the Susquehannocks

"PROTO-SUSQUEHANNOCK" SITES

IN THE UPPER SUSQUEHANNA

RIVER VALLEY   Jasmine Gollup

ABSTRACT

The Susquehannock sites in the Upper Susquehanna Valley, called "Proto-Susquehannock" by many, are understudied and provide ambiguous answers to questions of Susquehannock origins. This chapter provides a compilation of Proto-Susquehannock research including information on excavation history, site location, artifact assemblages, and previous research on 45 sites identified as Proto-Susquehannock.

The chapter also delves into definitional problems hindering research in this area, focusing on terms such as "Protohistoric" and "Proto-Susquehannock" and the pottery variants often associated with the Susquehannocks (Richmond Mills Incised, Proto-Susquehannock, and Schultz Incised) and emphasizing the lack of consistent and operational definitions associated with each term.

Introduction

The Susquehannock Indians are historically known as the dominant indigenous tribe in seventeenth-century central Pennsylvania, controlling vast portions of the Chesapeake and Delaware Bay regions at the time of European exploration and settlement. Occupying a strategic position on the Susquehanna River in Lancaster County, the politically and economically influential Susquehannocks were prominent traders with the Dutch, English, French, and Swedish colonies throughout the seventeenth century, providing a crucial economic link between the early European coastal settlements and the fur-trapping tribes of the interior. By the time Europeans arrived, the Susquehannocks already held firm control over much of the Mid-Atlantic region, a hegemony achieved through raiding or subjugating local tribes. The apex of Susquehannock influence came in the mid-seventeenth century, after which a combination of infectious disease, broken alliances, and hostile actions by neighboring groups caused them to suffer a precipitous decline (Hunter 1959).

While relatively well-known historically, the origins of the Susquehannock people remain mired in antiquated theoretical models reliant on evidence obtained through outdated archaeological methods. The seventeenth-century Susquehannocks shared many traits with the member groups of the Five Nations Iroquois, including a similar language, culture, and religion. As a result of this similarity, the Susquehannocks are believed to be close relatives of the Five Nations Iroquois, and it is commonly believed that the Susquehannocks migrated south from present-day New York in the years immediately prior to European exploration. The Upper Susquehanna River Valley, an area straddling New York and Pennsylvania, has traditionally served as an alleged and convenient homeland for the Susquehannock people, termed the "Proto-Susquehannocks" by early researchers (see Herbstritt, chapter 2 in this volume). Unfortunately, the studies supporting this claim are undermined by deep terminological and theoretical problems that affect the foundation on which current Proto-Susquehannock research is built. Through the analysis of previous scholarship in the Upper Susquehanna River Valley, this chapter will illuminate the problems inherent in past Proto-Susquehannock research.

Susquehannock Scholarship

The Upper Susquehanna River Valley, including the North Branch in New York and the Tioga Point region along the New York–Pennsylvania border, contains dozens of small, multicomponent sites that have been attributed to the Proto-Susquehannock Indians. The Susquehannock presence on the North Branch begins south of the city of Binghamton and continues south through the Tioga Point region (Rippeteau 1981:128, 135).

It is believed that the Proto-Susquehannocks settled in the Upper Susquehanna River Valley region for an indeterminate amount of time (probably less than a century) and then began a swift migration south. Kent (2001) claims that the founding of the Schultz site in Lancaster County, Pennsylvania, can be dated to 1575. Some researchers believe that the Susquehannock presence in the Upper Susquehanna River Valley continued through the late sixteenth

century (Crannell 1970:158; Sempowski 1989:81; Witthoft 1959:22), claiming the possibility of several waves of migrations (Kent 2001:117). The majority of the Upper Susquehanna Valley Susquehannock sites contains few European trade items and, as a result, has been thought to date to the sixteenth century. Researchers are unsure why the Susquehannocks moved almost 200 miles down the Susquehanna River in such a short time period (the typical community move of Iroquoian groups at the time being 2 to 3.4 miles per move [Engelbrecht 2003:101]), hypothesizing that they were either pulled by economic opportunities or pushed by Iroquoian aggression (Bradley 2005:98).

With an assumed ancestry from at least one of the Five Nations Iroquois groups, Susquehannock research in the twentieth century has focused on trying to pinpoint the moment the Susquehannocks split from the mother group. Researchers have been particularly interested in determining if the tribe left New York as culturally recognized Susquehannocks or if they formed their group identity during their journey south. Some propose an in situ approach to the Susquehannocks, claiming that a Susquehannock identity arose among people already living in the area between the Wyoming Valley in Pennsylvania and the New York Finger Lakes (Crannell 1970:58; Witthoft 1959:21). Others claim they are an example of relocation, creating their cultural identity while moving either as refugees from Iroquois aggression or as economic opportunists (Engelbrecht 2003:143; Kent 2001).

Kent (2001) provides another view on the issue, challenging the notion that the Susquehannocks were an example of pure divergence or convergence with the Iroquois. A divergence implies a common ancestry and separate development, while convergence refers to parallel development and circulation of ideas (Kent 2001:15). Kent concludes that the Susquehannocks are an example of both processes, stating their potential common roots with the New York Iroquois are evidenced through ceramic seriation (Kent 2001:15–16).

Although presently established as relatives of the New York Iroquois, it is unknown when, where, or from whom the Susquehannocks actually split. The majority of observations on this topic point toward a western Iroquoian, particularly Cayuga or Seneca, ancestry for the Susquehannock tribe. Some researchers believe that the Susquehannock split occurred before the Seneca and Cayuga split (Lenig 1960:12–13; Witthoft 1959:20), citing linguistic and material culture similarities, while others believe that the post-split Cayuga were the predecessors of the Susquehannocks, a belief based primarily on ceramic seriation and geographic proximity (Crannell 1970:154; Kent 2001:117; Rippeteau 1981:135). In one of the more recent studies, Niemczycki (1984) questions the proposed evolutionary relationship between the Cayuga and Seneca, consequently casting doubt on Susquehannock origin theories that reference such relationships.

While the details are disputed, researchers do agree on several main ideas. The first is that the people in the Upper Susquehanna Valley reflect the "Proto-Susquehannocks," a term used to denote them as almost, but not quite, culturally identical to the historically known Susquehannocks of the Lower Susquehanna River Valley. They are undeniably Iroquoian both linguistically and culturally, most likely descended from the Seneca and/or Cayuga as the result of a recent (between AD 1400 and 1500) split. Researchers also agree that they completely relocated to the Lower Susquehanna River Valley by the end of the sixteenth century, a move of almost 200 miles in less than 100 years.

The problem with these conclusions is that researchers have arrived at similar assumptions while utilizing conflicting ideas and evidence. Of primary importance is a problem of definition: the terminology and the material culture markers used to describe early Susquehannocks are not well defined or uniformly adhered to and are often contradictory. This problem is exemplified by the ceramic analysis of Proto-Susquehannock sites and the seriation of three similar and—in many cases—contemporaneous types.

Another issue lies with the quality of the data, with the vast majority of information coming from local collectors or from excavations predating 1950. There has been very little artifact analysis beyond basic identification and no discussion of stratigraphy or context. Instead of reanalyzing these past conclusions with new, systematically obtained evidence, recent studies simply use the Proto-Susquehannock foundation created by these past excavations, building on past research rather than questioning obvious flaws.

The final problem is perhaps the most troubling, in that our current understanding of Susquehannock culture is based on outdated and discredited theoretical paradigms. The culture-history approach to archaeological analysis has been discredited since the mid-twentieth century, a time that conveniently coincides with the apex of excavations in the Upper Susquehanna River Valley. Rather than reassessing the evidence using updated interpretive frameworks, researchers have stubbornly adhered to the idea of a monolithic Susquehannock culture reflected by a unique, identifiable, and culturally delineated set of materials. By repeatedly building on this shaky foundation, researchers are ignoring and perpetuating problems inherent in Proto-Susquehannock studies.

Material Culture Markers

Within the field of archaeology, certain artifacts are often seen as indicative of a specific culture, identified here as material culture markers. Seen within the culture-history framework, the mere presence of these artifact types, usually regardless of amount, on a site has led to the automatic identification of the site as belonging to one particular group. Though viewed with increasing skepticism today, the continued reliance on conclusions previously reached through this mode of thinking only perpetuates the problem. Two types of artifacts are used as material culture markers to denote Proto-Susquehannock presence: copper spirals and hoops and shell-tempered pottery.

Spirals and hoops manufactured from copper appear to cluster in northeastern North America during the sixteenth century (Bradley and Childs 2007:290). Found primarily along the Susquehanna River and its associated drainage basins, archaeologists have connected these artifacts with the Five Nations Iroquois (particularly the Seneca) and the Susquehannocks during the sixteenth century. Assumed by early researchers to be of European manufacture, the presence of copper spirals on American Indian sites was seen as the earliest example of indigenous adoption of European material culture (Witthoft 1959).

As few of the purported Proto-Susquehannock sites contain other European-manufactured items, copper spirals appear to be the object that places the Proto-Susquehannocks in the Protohistoric period. Unfortunately, the lack of stratigraphic control and temporal analysis common in most excavations, combined with the multicomponent nature of the majority of Proto-Susquehannock sites, complicates this association. The correlation of copper spirals and hoops with the Five Nations Iroquois as well as the Susquehannocks shows that sites cannot be labeled Proto-Susquehannock based simply on the presence of the artifacts. Furthermore, concluding a Proto-Susquehannock presence based simply on the presence of copper spirals completely ignores the vibrant trade networks functioning throughout North America.

Shell-tempered pottery is seen as the single most distinctive Susquehannock trait and has been utilized by the majority of researchers as a diagnostic indicator of Susquehannock culture (Beisaw 2007:3; chapter 3 in this volume). In his seminal work, Kent states, "Pottery is the key, in fact the only identifiable archaeological remain by which we can confidently recognize the occupation sites and trace the movements of our Susquehannocks" (Kent 2001:295; see also Kinsey 1959). The role of ceramic seriation to Susquehannock studies, particularly in Susquehannock origin research, is paramount.

Theoretically, the direct historical approach is the method most often used for ceramic analysis, as it allows researchers to trace and connect historically known cultures to their undocumented ancestors. Typically conducted through ceramic seriation, this method rests on the belief that the evolution of pottery involves the addition and subtraction of attributes within the manufacturing process and that the possibilities for new types depend largely on contingencies inherent in older types (Garrahan 1990:17). Utilizing this approach, researchers have connected the historically known Lower Susquehanna Valley ware called Schultz Incised to two earlier types thought to represent ties to the Upper Susquehanna Valley: Richmond Mills Incised and Proto-Susquehannock ware.

Schultz Incised pottery is generally accepted by most scholars as the first distinctive Susquehannock ware, as it is the first to include the distinguishing shell temper present in all later Susquehannock ceramics. Closely related to other wares produced by Iroquoian-speaking peoples in New York and Pennsylvania, Schultz Incised wares seem to carry over decorative elements from earlier forms and are most distinguishable by their use of shell temper (Bradley 2005:58; Kent 2001:113).

Witthoft differentiates between two varieties of Schultz Incised pottery, which he terms Early and Late, claiming that the early varieties are represented in the Upper Susquehanna Valley and the late type in the Lower. Claiming that the Early Schultz Incised pottery often exhibits "a crisper, more expert design and execution, and slightly better form and proportion, as compared to the Lancaster County examples," Witthoft distinguishes between the types based on ethereal concepts that are, in his words, more important than technical attributes such as lip treatment or rim form (Witthoft 1959:28).

Others have had difficulty applying his two types to actual artifacts, as his distinctions are subjective and require access to visual examples (Crannell 1970:146). As the differences stated by Witthoft are not operationally feasible, few researchers utilize the Early/Late Schultz Incised concept. However, some alleged Proto-Susquehannock sites have been noted as containing Early Schultz Incised pottery. The Engelbert site's shell-tempered sherds were described by Crannell (1970) as Early Schultz, although Crannell noted that her conclusions were tentative due to confusion regarding what traits actually constitute Early Schultz Incised pottery (see also Caister 2007). Kent labels all shell-tempered pottery found in Bradford (Pennsylvania) and Tioga (New York) counties as Early Schultz Incised (Kent 2001:306), though it is unknown if the sherds actually exhibit the traits mentioned or if the division is simply temporally and geographically convenient.

Schultz Incised shares many similarities with wares present in the Upper Susquehanna Valley from the early sixteenth century and, more generally, with the Five Nations Iroquois in New York. Because of this, scholars have posited an evolutionary relationship between Schultz Incised and the earlier Richmond Mills and so-called Proto-Susquehannock wares. Richmond Mills Incised vessels are often associated with the late prehistoric Cayuga in the southern New York and northern Pennsylvania region, although some researchers have equated the tradition with the Susquehannocks (Lucy 1991:8; MacNeish 1952:51; see also Pratt 1960 and Wren 1914). Grumet (1995:332–33) succinctly illustrates this relationship, claiming that Richmond Mills Incised represents the first evidence, or the derivation, of the Susquehannock pottery tradition. Richmond Mills Incised vessels are grit-tempered, globular vessels with a constricted neck and high collar (2.5–3.5 in). The collars are decorated with incised designs and typically display four castellations (MacNeish 1952:51).

Proto-Susquehannock ware is generally believed to be the closest ancestor to the Lower Susquehanna Valley Schultz Incised type (Stewart 1973:1). Assumed to have developed out of the Richmond Mills Incised tradition, Proto-Susquehannock ware is seen as the enviable "missing link" connecting known Cayuga (Richmond Mills) and Susquehannock (Schultz Incised) wares. Proto-Susquehannock ware shares many traits with its predecessor, Richmond Mills

Incised, with a globular body, a high collar (typically comprising one-half the overall height of the vessel), and a fine grit tempering. Although rare, sculpted human faces are seen as highly characteristic of these vessels, a trait that later became conventionalized in the Schultz (1575–1600) and Washington Boro (1600–1625) phases (Kent 1980a:99; Lucy and McCracken 1985:24; Lucy and Vanderpoel 1979:9, 391) and that was observed at the Murray Garden (36BR2) site. Contrary to Grumet, others declare this pottery type to be the earliest distinguishable form of Susquehannock culture (Kent 2001; Witthoft 1959).

Ceramic seriation appears to support linguistic evidence and suggests a Cayuga/Seneca ancestor for the Susquehannocks. Witthoft (1959) notes overlapping ceramic styles between the Cayuga and Susquehannocks, shown through the pottery types of Richmond Mills Incised and Proto-Susquehannock ware respectively. With identical shape, finish, and decoration, the two types of pottery exhibit only superficial differences (Witthoft 1959:35). Witthoft suggests that the Susquehannocks split from the Cayuga around 1400, but their pottery only became distinct as they began their southward migration around 1550 (1959:39, 59; see also Crannell 1970 and Rippeteau 1981:12–13). Kent (2001:117) likewise states that the Susquehannocks split from the Cayuga based on ceramic seriation, noting the emergence of Proto-Susquehannock pottery from Richmond Mills Incised as the precise point of the cultural split. The exact relationship between Richmond Mills Incised, Proto-Susquehannock ware, and Schultz Incised pottery is unresolved, but the general consensus agrees with Kent's (2001:115) idea of a direct progression (see also Lucy and McCracken 1985:11). Found in roughly the same geographical region, these three types are differentiated primarily on the basis of temper type and minor design elements.

The primary issue facing ceramic seriation is the similarity of the pottery in the region; the broad and often inoperative descriptions of each type, particularly when applied to smaller sherds; and the difficulty that researchers face when attempting to recognize distinction. Kent (2001:131–32) defines five general attributes of Susquehannock pottery as the following:

1. The top of the collar is bounded by one or two lines of horizontal incising or punctation.
2. Broad shallow incising is present.
3. Triangular, diamond, or rectangular plats are combined to form numerous geometric patterns.
4. Enclosed right triangular plats are filled with elliptical punch marks, short lines of incising, or parallel horizontal incisings.
5. Smoothed collars into which incising is applied are present.

These traits are similar to those presented by Bailey (1938) in his description of a generic, pan-Iroquoian ceramic tradition. Bailey notes that Iroquoian pottery expresses several pan-regional characteristics including a globular body, round bottom, and an emphasized collar with geometric decorative motifs (1938:333). Early Schultz Incised typically exhibits all of the traits listed by Kent, while Proto-Susquehannock pottery demonstrates all but number four. However, Ithaca Linear, a definite Cayuga type with no known ties to the Susquehannocks, also exhibits all five traits (Kent 2001:132).

Furthermore, the three types mentioned are very similar, with only minor design elements separating Richmond Mills Incised and Proto-Susquehannock ware, elements that would be impossible to identify on smaller sherds. The addition of crushed shell temper appears to be the only distinctive indicator of Schultz Incised. It is quite difficult, particularly for the untrained researcher, to correctly identify and distinguish between these different pottery styles.

While the difficulties caused by questionable ceramic identification (in turn caused by nebulous descriptions) are a major concern, the main problem with Proto-Susquehannock ceramic seriation is one of definitions. Shell-tempered pottery is seen as the main cultural indicator of the Susquehannocks. Yet many scholars claim that the grit-tempered Richmond Mills Incised and Proto-Susquehannock ware are indicative of early Susquehannock culture, often within the same publication. This means that researchers are simultaneously claiming that the Susquehannocks are defined by shell-tempered pottery and, conversely, that the grit-tempered Proto-Susquehannock ware is identifiably Susquehannock. This creates an inconsistency that undermines the conclusions reached in previous studies and that is undeniably caused by irresponsible use of nebulous terminology.

Terminology

The main question that arises from the discrepancies of Susquehannock ceramic seriation concerns the definition of the prefix "proto" and what difference, if any, is implied by utilizing the term "Proto-Susquehannock" versus "Susquehannock." The term "Protohistoric" has been used by both professionals and amateurs to describe the Susquehannocks of the Upper Susquehanna River Valley. While most researchers of this region utilize the term, few provide an explicit definition, and the delineations given by those few rarely agree. As a result, different interpretations of the term have emerged, leading disparate sites to be labeled as Protohistoric and creating confusion for area scholars.

In simplest terms, the prefix "proto" means the first, foremost, or earliest form of (Dictionary.com Unabridged 2010). The term "Protohistoric" then quite literally means the earliest form of the historic period. Researchers utilize the term as an important descriptive link between the prehistoric and the historic eras (Noble 2004:179). Wilcox and Masse define the Protohistoric period in the American Southwest as the time "between prehistory and the ethnographic present . . . a time of transition during which the societies of the North American Southwest experienced radical systematic changes brought about by their articulation with the European world system" (1981:1).

While this definition may adequately reflect the time period, it is not archaeologically operational.

The only article on northeastern Indigenous archaeology to provide a definition of the term "Protohistoric" (Noble 2004) references an article written by Bernard Fontana (1965) that defined a fivefold classification system of historic sites. Fontana's system places sites into one of five temporal categories—Protohistoric, Contact, post-Contact, frontier, and nonaboriginal—based on the degree to which a site is "Indian" (Fontana 1965:61). Fontana defines the Protohistoric period sites as "aboriginal sites in which there is evidence of nonaboriginal culture but which were occupied before the arrival of nonaborigines on the immediate scene" (1965:62). European objects are present, but Europeans themselves are not. Fontana (1965:62) claims that Protohistoric sites can be distinguished by the presence of European goods and a lack of documentary evidence about the site itself.

There are several problems with this definition, the first being that it is necessarily fluid. Defining Protohistoric sites must be done on a site-by-site basis and must focus on the physical site itself, not the people occupying it. Indigenous groups that occupied multiple sites may fall into different categories. Individuals in the form of trading parties, travelers, or warriors may have had contact with Europeans, yet the physical presence of a European on the indigenous site is crucial. Fontana (1965:62) describes the Contact period sites as those actually visited by non-Indians and states that they are usually documented. The key problem with this definition is that it relies on documentation to distinguish between the phases, an unrealistic assumption.

Despite the differing definitions provided by Fontana, the term "Protohistoric" is sometimes used synonymously and interchangeably with Contact terminology. Grumet (1995:28) describes the Contact period as a time when the trade of European objects began and makes no distinction between the presence of items and the presence of people. Silliman notes that Fontana's five-part classification is often condensed, with the first three categories of Protohistoric, Contact, and post-Contact lumped together under the umbrella term "Contact," which is then used to describe all indigenous-European encounters (Silliman 2005:60). The confusion resulting from these insubstantial definitions has led to liberal use of the term "Protohistoric." Based on the aforementioned research (Fontana 1965:61; Noble 2004:180), along with the dictionary definition, for the purposes of this study, the term "Protohistoric" can be tentatively defined as referring to a period marked by the appearance of European trade goods without the documented presence of Europeans themselves.

This definition leads to yet another terminological issue. The terms "Proto-Susquehannock" and "Protohistoric Susquehannock" have been used interchangeably in the literature, often without explicit definition, to reference what seem to be two different concepts. No author has given a definition of the term "Proto-Susquehannock." Literally, the term "Proto-Susquehannock" should mean early Susquehannock, a definition that focuses on culture rather than temporality. This definition implies that those labeled Proto-Susquehannock are culturally identifiable as Susquehannocks.

The literature provides mixed answers. Kent (2001:15) labels Proto-Susquehannock pottery as the earliest distinguishable form of Susquehannock culture, and many others seem to agree that the Proto-Susquehannocks are Susquehannocks culturally. However, it is also stated that shell-tempered pottery is the principal cultural indicator of the Susquehannocks. These two ideas are unquestioningly deemed to be true even though the evidence they present offers differing, and irreconcilable, views. In this view, the grit-tempered Proto-Susquehannock ware would not be affiliated with the Proto-Susquehannock people. The pottery appears to imply that the Proto-Susquehannocks are different, a nascent form of the later Susquehannocks seen in the Lower Susquehanna River Valley.

The term "Protohistoric Susquehannock" is equally perplexing. Literally meaning early historic Susquehannock, the term focuses on temporality and implies that the group in reference is fully Susquehannock culturally. Thus "Protohistoric Susquehannock" does not carry the same inferences as the term "Proto-Susquehannock." However, these two terms are used almost interchangeably without reference to definition, although they seem to refer to two different concepts. The term "Proto-Susquehannock," within this area of research, is used to exclusively reference a particular culture or cultural attributes and is utilized by at least 15 area researchers (Crannell 1970; Grumet 1995; Kent 1980a, 1980b, 2001; Lenig 1960; Lipe 1976; Lucy 1959, 1991; Lucy and McCracken 1985; Lucy and Vanderpoel 1979; McCracken and Lucy 1989; Smith 1970, 1977; Witthoft n.d.). The term "Protohistoric Susquehannock" is less clear. Although by definition it should express temporality, it is used by four authors in reference to time only (Lipe 1976; Noble 2004; Reinhart 2000; Wilcox and Masse 1981), one in reference to culture only (Cobb and Nassaney 1995), and six with ambiguous meaning (Beisaw 2006; Brashler 1987; Jennings 1978; McCann 1962; Sempowski 2007; Stewart 1973). One author (Lipe 1976) uses both terms, but neither is solidly defined.

Without a clear definition of the term "Proto-Susquehannock," many researchers are using the term as a catchall, ignoring potential differences that may alter our current understanding of the Susquehannocks. By using ambiguous terminology and poorly defined ceramic types, researchers are reaching similar conclusions with conflicting data. Through vague ceramic typologies, sites are pushed into a temporal niche that they may not belong in by excavators, many of them amateurs, without a clear understanding of the subtle differences in ceramic types, if they do in fact exist. This is the foundation that Proto-Susquehannock archaeology was, and continues to be, built on: a foundation held together by disjointed ideas and unaddressed contradictions.

Excavation History

The Upper Susquehanna River Valley region, generally running from Binghamton, New York, to just south of Bradford County, Pennsylvania, has endured centuries of archaeological exploration, both professional and amateur. Witthoft (n.d.) succinctly illustrates the current state of archaeology in the Upper Susquehanna Valley: "The great difficulty with most excavations . . . conducted in the region [around Tioga Point] is that they have been hit and run operations, not part of any overall program, with rapid excavation and too little precise dissection of features and levels and too little careful observation of unspectacular evidence."

Few professional excavations have been conducted in the area, the majority of which predate 1980. Warren K. Moorehead performed the first professional exploration of the Upper Susquehanna River Valley sites in 1916. The term "professional" is loosely applied, as Moorehead's expedition was little more than a glorified (and well-funded) treasure hunt focused on the exhumation of burials and acquisition of museum-worthy curios (Moorehead 1938; see also Custer 1986). Predictably, the records left by Moorehead lack necessary and critical scientific information, particularly in comparison with modern reports. Nevertheless, the expedition, as the first major archaeological investigation in the region, does provide crucial information on area sites. James Griffin, funded by the Tioga Point Museum, later undertook excavations in 1931 at four area sites: Ahbe-Brennan (36BR42), Thurston Farm (36BR5/41), Murray Farm (36BR5), and Spanish Hill (36BR27; Kent 2001:301). Griffin's work was meant to determine which sites warranted more extensive excavation and to generate local interest in area archaeology (Griffin 1931:3, 2003a:37).

The Susquehanna River Archaeological Survey, led by Ira F. Smith III of the Pennsylvania State Museum, was meant to find and identify Clemson Island sites in eastern Pennsylvania. Spanning four years (1972–73 and 1975–76), the group surveyed

26

stream terraces, conducted surface collections, and interviewed landowners, amateur archaeologists, and collectors (Smith 1977:27). In 1975, the survey, attempting to determine the relationship of sites in Bradford and Elk counties to known Susquehannock sites, excavated the Blackman (36BR83) and Kennedy (36BR43) sites (Smith 1977:29). In 2003, AD Marble and Company completed a research program focused on the compilation of area site information in the municipalities of Athens, Litchfield, Ridgebury, Sayre, Sheshequin, Smithfield, South Waverly, and Ulster (AD Marble and Company 2003:1–22).

When analyzing Upper Susquehanna archaeology, particularly in the Tioga Point area, one cannot ignore the presence and influence of local collectors or avocational archaeologists. In this case, the term "collector" is defined as any person without professional archaeological training *and* employment. The Tioga Point area is unique in that collecting is not just a hobby practiced by a small portion of the population but a cultural phenomenon with its origins in the mid-nineteenth century with the beginnings of intensive plow agriculture (AD Marble and Company 2003:26). The rise of local prominent collectors such as Louise Welles Murray led to the creation of several local museums such as the Tioga Point Museum (AD Marble and Company 2003:30) and the Susquehanna River Archaeological Center. Some collectors have kept detailed records of their finds, noting general location. Many of the sites noted as Proto-Susquehannock were identified based solely on collector activity. Many locals have private collections, often the result of decades of activity, with some collections containing thousands of artifacts. The collection of Ted Keir of Athens, Pennsylvania, is acknowledged as one of the area's largest, while others, such as the Gillette, Rowe, and Vanderpoel collections, are also notable in Tioga Point archaeology. As this area has been largely ignored by professionals in recent decades, the activity of collectors in part fills the void of data created by their absence.

Forty-five sites are noted as Proto-Susquehannock in the Upper Susquehanna River Valley, identified as such by the archaeologist or collector, often based on the presence of shell-tempered pottery or copper spirals (figure 1.1; site locations approximate). Very little archaeological excavation has occurred in the area post-1980, with the height of archaeological interest in the early to mid-twentieth century. Few of the excavations can be called professional, as many of the sites were excavated with the goal of artifact acquisition rather than careful, scientific analysis of stratigraphy and context. A further complication to site analysis is the multicomponent nature of each site. With little attention paid to provenience, the presence or absence of an artifact itself must determine the cultural designation of a site.

Alleged Proto-Susquehannock sites include 7 sites in New York; 36 sites in Bradford County, Pennsylvania; and 2 in Luzerne County, Pennsylvania. The Tioga Point area, at the confluence of the Chemung and Susquehanna and straddling both New York and Pennsylvania, contains the greatest concentration of Proto-Susquehannock sites in the Susquehanna Valley. The sites identified in this chapter are listed in table 1.1. Information for sites without citations was acquired from unpublished documents located at the Tioga Point Museum and Susquehanna River Archaeological Center, from the Pennsylvania Historical and Museum Commission Cultural Resources Geographical Information System, and from informant interviews with local collectors.

For additional information on excavation and site analysis for these sites, see AD Marble and Company (2003); Beisaw (2006, 2007); Caister (2007); Casterline and Sokash (2003); Cowles (1932–33); Crannell (1970); Dunbar and Ruhl (1974); Frost (1935); Funk (1993); Funk, Rippeteau, and Houck (1973, 1974); Griffin (2003b); Lipe (1976); Lucy (2003); Lucy and McCracken (1985); Lucy and Vanderpoel (1979); McCann (1962); McCracken and Lucy (1989); Murray (1921, 1931); Semowich (1980–81); and Triple Cities Chapter (2005).

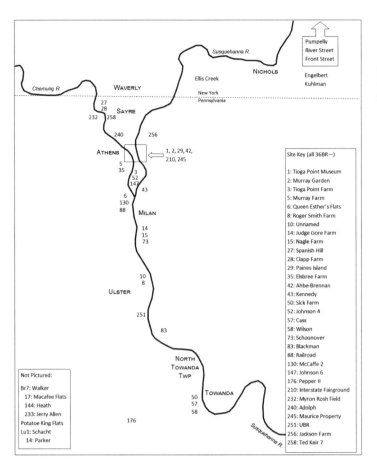

FIGURE 1.1

Proto-Susquehannock sites in the Upper
Susquehanna River Valley

Discussion

While the lack of contextual information makes analysis difficult, it is possible to identify several patterns among Upper Susquehanna River Valley sites. Although the exact location of the majority of sites is unknown, a general placement is possible for many. Topographically, most sites are found on the flats of Tioga Point. Typically occupying a position on the peninsula between the Chemung and Susquehanna Rivers or on either side of the rivers' banks, these sites exploit a strategic economic position. Six sites (36BR1, 2, 29, 42, 210, and 245) are found at the narrowest point on the peninsula, an area only 200 meters wide, which would have provided excellent control of both rivers.

Only two sites of known location were placed on defensible knolls—Engelbert and Spanish Hill—

neither of which has produced concrete evidence of Susquehannock occupation. Only one site, Blackman, provided evidence of a stockade. The placement of the sites indicates an emphasis on trade and little fear of hostilities, hinting that the Susquehannocks' migration south was more likely a result of economic opportunism than an escape from competitive aggression. This may also indicate that the Susquehannocks' homelands were thought to be generally secure because of their warlike reputation, as several groups in the Chesapeake and Delaware regions are known to have abandoned sections of their ancestral territory due in part to Susquehannock belligerence.

Temporal analysis of the sites is difficult. There has been little attempt to order the sites into a sequence, and they are thought by many to be contemporaneous. The narrow time frame given for this region, typically lasting less than 100 years—from 1450 to 1550—and

TABLE 1.1   Proto-Susquehannock archaeological sites in the Upper Susquehanna River Valley

Site number	Site name	Citation
New York		
NA	Pumpelly Creek	NA
NA	River Street	Crannell 1970
NA	Front Street	NA
SUBi-300	Engelbert	Beisaw 2006, 2007, 2008, and 2010; Caister 2007; Crannell 1970; Dunbar 1974; Elliot and Lipe 1970; Lipe 1976; Reinhart 2000; Semowich 1980–81; Stewart 1973; Versaggi et al. 1996
30TI24	Ellis Creek	Lucy 1959
NA	Potatoe King Flats	NA
NA	Kuhlman/Kahlman	Crannell 1970; Beisaw 2007
Tioga Point Region		
36BR1	Tioga Point Museum	Murray 1921
36BR2	Murray Garden	Murray 1921; Kent 2001; Twigg 2009a
36BR3	Tioga Point Farm	Murray 1921; Lucy 1991; Lucy and Vanderpoel 1979; Kent 2001
36BR5	Murray Farm	Murray 1921; Moorehead 1938; Kent 2001; Twigg 2010
36BR6	Queen Esther's Flats	Murray 1921; Moorehead 1938
36BR7	Walker	NA
36BR8	Roger Smith Farm	NA
36BR10	unnamed	NA
36BR14	Judge Gore Farm	Murray 1921; Moorehead 1938; Witthoft 1959, n.d.
36BR15	Nagle Farm	Murray 1921; Moorehead 1938; Witthoft 1959, n.d.
36BR17	Macafee Flats	Murray 1921
36BR27	Spanish Hill	Murray 1921, 1931; Griffin 1931, n.d.; Moorehead 1938; Hunter 1959; McCracken 1985; Funk 1993; Kent 2001; Twigg 2005, 2009b, 2010
36BR28	Clapp Farm	NA
36BR29	Paines Island	NA
36BR35	Elsbree Farm	NA
36BR5/41	Thurston Farm	Griffin n.d.; Kent 2001; Twigg 2010
36BR42	Ahbe-Brennan	Griffin n.d.; Kent 2001; Twigg 2010
36BR43	Kennedy	Lucy 2003; Casterline and Sokash 2003; Smith 1977; Kent 2001
36BR50	Sick Farm 3	Lucy and McCracken 1985; Witthoft n.d.
36BR52	Johnson 4	NA
36BR57	Cass	NA
36BR58	Wilson	McCann 1962; Witthoft n.d.
36BR73	Schoonover	NA
36BR83	Blackman	Smith 1977; Lucy 1985; Herbstritt 1988; McCracken and Lucy 1989
36BR88	Railroad	NA
36BR130	McCaffe 2	NA
36BR144	Heath	NA
36BR147	Johnson 6	NA
36BR176	Pepper II	McCracken 1989
36BR210	Interstate Fairgrounds	NA
36BR232	Myron Rosh Field	NA
36BR240	Adolph	NA
36BR245	Maurice Property	NA

(continued)

Site number	Site name	Citation
Tioga Point Region		
36BR251	UBR	NA
36BR256	Jackson Farm	NA
36BR258	Ted Keir 7	NA
Luzerne County		
36LU1	Schacht	Kent 1970, 2001
36LU14	Parker	Kent 1970, 2001

the lack of stratigraphic context for the vast majority of artifacts makes temporal interpretation nearly impossible. The small geographical range (the Tioga Point region is only eight miles north-south and six miles at its widest) further obfuscates the interpretation. The multicomponent nature of every site likewise complicates temporal analysis, particularly when combined with poor excavation documentation. At present, the sites are thought to be roughly contemporaneous, dating solidly within the sixteenth century, though it is not possible to know if the area saw widespread settlement or gradual migration.

The type of settlement also plays an important role in interpretation. Past researchers have stated that the Proto-Susquehannocks lived in small hamlets that were very different from the large, nucleated villages of the Lower Susquehanna. These smaller occupations, with consequent household moves every couple of decades, seem to provide the best interpretation of sites in the area, none of which have produced evidence of large-scale occupation. Assuming that the sites are contemporaneous, or at least within a 50- to 100-year time frame, the distribution of occupation sites in the region appears to support that claim, with small occupation sites spread over roughly 16 square miles. There is a possibility that the sites represent sequential moves; unfortunately, the short time frame and the general lack of stratigraphic evidence from most sites restrict any such interpretation.

The relatively large number of sites that date to roughly the same time period of both occupation and burial context appears to corroborate this settlement pattern. The geographic location of different site types, burial or occupation, is noted in figure 1.2. The identification of sites as burials or occupations, based on the conclusions reached by past researchers about the Susquehannock component only, is not available for many of the sites and is often questionable. Burial sites are identified by the presence of human remains and occupation sites by a large number of artifacts and/or the lack of human remains. It must be noted that many of the earlier professional excavations (the Moorehead expedition, in particular) were focused almost exclusively on the exhumation of burials.

The New York sites are all described as burial sites only and, aside from Engelbert, represent what appear to be isolated graves. There is a definite cluster of sites, both burial and occupation, situated on and around Tioga Point. Of the identified Proto-Susquehannock sites in this area, five are occupation only, two are burial only, and six contain both occupation and burial components (further information is not provided for the majority of sites). Farther downriver, less than four miles away, are the Sheshequin sites, one of which is burial only (36BR73), while the other (36BR15) contains elements of both uses. Sites in Ulster (36BR83) and Towanda (36BR58) are described as occupation only. Tentatively, there appear to be more burial sites in the northern part of the study area, while occupation sites are generally found farther south.

Proto-Susquehannock burial practices are often assumed to be similar to those of the historic Susquehannocks, who lived in palisaded villages and

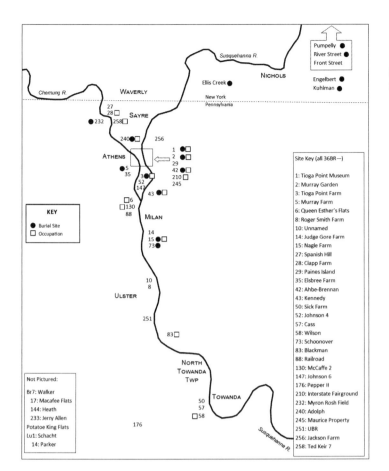

FIGURE 1.2
Proto-Susquehannock sites by type

Site Key (all 36BR—)

1: Tioga Point Museum
2: Murray Garden
3: Tioga Point Farm
5: Murray Farm
6: Queen Esther's Flats
8: Roger Smith Farm
10: Unnamed
14: Judge Gore Farm
15: Nagle Farm
27: Spanish Hill
28: Clapp Farm
29: Paines Island
35: Elsbree Farm
42: Ahbe-Brennan
43: Kennedy
50: Sick Farm
52: Johnson 4
57: Cass
58: Wilson
73: Schoonover
83: Blackman
88: Railroad
130: McCaffe 2
147: Johnson 6
176: Pepper II
210: Interstate Fairground
232: Myron Rosh Field
240: Adolph
245: Maurice Property
251: UBR
256: Jackson Farm
258: Ted Keir 7

KEY

● Burial Site
□ Occupation

Not Pictured:

Br7: Walker
  17: Macafee Flats
  144: Heath
  233: Jerry Allen
Potatoe King Flats
Lu1: Schacht
  14: Parker

buried their deceased in large cemeteries outside of their towns. This assumption ignores the evidence from earlier upriver sites. The Proto-Susquehannocks, presumably living in small hamlets instead of towns, may have utilized a different model, burying their dead within the occupation area. This seems to be the case with the six sites on Tioga Point that contain elements of both burial and occupation. Other sites, such as Queen Esther's Flats (BR6), were documented as occupation only but are also noted as containing one or two burials (which may or may not relate to the Susquehannock component). All occupation sites in the Athens region are within half a mile of a burial site.

Excavation methodology and intent may further compound the issue as the majority of early excavations, by professionals and collectors, focused almost entirely on burials in an effort to collect grave artifacts.

Furthermore, as there has been little archaeological research conducted in the area since the 1980s, it is quite possible that much information remains to be found or has been lost with recent residential and commercial expansion.

Nevertheless, there appears to be a difference between the New York and Pennsylvania sites. The Engelbert site's Susquehannock cemetery provides an interesting example. Noting that 10 of the 15 individuals found in the Engelbert Susquehannock "cemetery" were found in double graves, with the more recently deceased individual (thought to be Susquehannock) overlying the potentially earlier interment, Beisaw (2010) hypothesized that this unique burial practice was an attempt to reconnect with ancestors. Described by Beisaw (2010) as reburial (and defined as the purposeful internment of deceased individuals into existing graves), this practice may explain the presence of

Susquehannock burials without related occupation areas, particularly in New York State.

The distribution of copper objects may further illuminate this issue because five of the six (83%) New York sites—but only 8 of the 36 (22%) Bradford County sites—contained copper objects. The prevalence of copper in New York suggests a later time period than the Bradford County sites, corroborated by the higher frequencies of Schultz Incised pottery in the area (figure 1.3), and is at odds with the currently accepted migration model for the Susquehannocks. Furthermore, the nascent trade system evidenced by the flow of copper from the Mid-Atlantic also supports the belief that the Susquehannocks moved south in search of economic opportunities rather than in response to Iroquois aggression (see Beisaw, chapter 3 in this volume).

As all of the New York sites correspond to burials only (no occupation sites have yet been found) and contain objects assumed to represent a later time period than the Tioga Point sites, it is possible that they signify a later people, consistent with Beisaw's reburial hypothesis. However, as the prevalence of European trade objects is still relatively low at these sites, it is possible that if they do represent reburial or extralocal burial, the individuals found represent inhabitants of the lower Bradford County sites, particularly those past Sheshequin that do not have an associated burial site. With only 30 miles separating Towanda from Nichols and a convenient water transportation route available, this hypothesis does not seem impossible.

The relationship between Richmond Mills Incised, Proto-Susquehannock, and Schultz Incised pottery is unclear. All three types are found at roughly contemporaneous sites, contradicting the direct temporal progression proposed by Kent (2001). In the area studied, at least four sites, and possibly three others, contained both Proto-Susquehannock and Schultz Incised pottery in direct relation to each other, while three sites contain all three pottery varieties.

Furthermore, four sites contained both Richmond Mills Incised and Schultz Incised but not Proto-Susquehannock ware, further suggesting that the evolutionary model accepted by current scholars should be rethought (figure 1.4).

Geographically, both Richmond Mills Incised and Schultz Incised, the polar ends of the supposed temporal and locational continuum, are found throughout the region from Nichols, New York, to Towanda, Pennsylvania; Proto-Susquehannock wares are found only in Pennsylvania. All three varieties are concentrated primarily in the Athens region, which could be a result of the large number of sites in the area or their position along a major trade route. Interestingly, many sites contain more than one pottery variety, and Richmond Mills Incised is found in association with Proto-Susquehannock wares roughly as often as with Schultz Incised.

The three types are prevalent in roughly an equal number of sites in the region. Richmond Mills Incised ware was found at a total of 12 sites (figure 1.2). Proto-Susquehannock ware was found at 17 and Schultz Incised (early or nondifferentiated) was found at 16 sites. Seven sites contained pottery simply denoted as Susquehannock or as shell-tempered but not Schultz Incised: Kuhlman, 36BR3, 6, 10, 29, 50, and 88. Three sites (36BR2, 3, and 176) demonstrate contemporaneous usage of all three types (figure 1.5).

The problem of definitions is again raised when attempting to culturally and temporally define sites by pottery type. The issue is particularly evident with Proto-Susquehannock and Schultz Incised wares. Although described as grit-tempered in the majority of literature, some sherds labeled Proto-Susquehannock are noted as being sand (36BR50) or shell (36BR245) tempered. Sites with pottery noted simply as Susquehannock could represent an inability to distinguish between the different types or other shell-tempered sherds from unrelated groups described as Susquehannock simply because they are shell tempered.

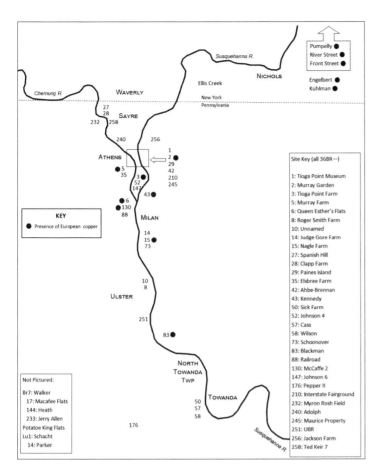

FIGURE 1.3. Presence of copper objects by site

Site Key (all 36BR—)

1: Tioga Point Museum
2: Murray Garden
3: Tioga Point Farm
5: Murray Farm
6: Queen Esther's Flats
8: Roger Smith Farm
10: Unnamed
14: Judge Gore Farm
15: Nagle Farm
27: Spanish Hill
28: Clapp Farm
29: Paines Island
35: Elsbree Farm
42: Ahbe-Brennan
43: Kennedy
50: Sick Farm
52: Johnson 4
57: Cass
58: Wilson
73: Schoonover
83: Blackman
88: Railroad
130: McCaffe 2
147: Johnson 6
176: Pepper II
210: Interstate Fairground
232: Myron Rosh Field
240: Adolph
245: Maurice Property
251: UBR
256: Jackson Farm
258: Ted Keir 7

KEY
● Presence of European copper

Not Pictured:

Br7: Walker
17: Macafee Flats
144: Heath
233: Jerry Allen
Potatoe King Flats
Lu1: Schacht
14: Parker

Pumpelly ●
River Street ●
Front Street ●

Engelbert ●
Kuhlman ●

Furthermore, every site examined contained a wide variety of pottery sherds, and perhaps most importantly, few sites described as Proto-Susquehannock actually contained a sizeable amount or percentage of Susquehannock pottery. The fact that all of these sites are multicomponent may be the reason for this low proportion, although without detailed contextual information it is impossible to determine percentages for a particular area of a site. Significant trade with regional groups may likewise be a factor in the prevalence of foreign pottery. Another possibility is that the Susquehannocks did not occupy the site and that the Susquehannock pottery found represents some form of intergroup contact.

Unfortunately, few excavators give actual counts, weights, or percentages of pottery types from their sites, and numbers for only five sites were available for analysis. The Murray Garden site (36BR2) contained 7 Schultz Incised sherds, representing 24.1% of the total ceramic assemblage, and 6 Proto-Susquehannock sherds, equaling 20.7%. The Tioga Point Farm site (36BR3) contained 7 sherds of Schultz Incised (0.55%), 16 sherds of Proto-Susquehannock ware (1.27%), 56 sherds of Richmond Mills Incised (4.45%), and 7 sherds of Susquehannock pottery (shell tempered but not Schultz Incised: 0.55%).

The Wilson site (36BR58) contained the largest percentage of identifiable Susquehannock pottery, with Schultz Incised representing 44.4% of the total (eight sherds) and Proto-Susquehannock representing 5.5% (one sherd). Unlike the majority of identified sites, the sherds found at the Wilson site do not represent a burial context. The Maurice Property site (36BR245) represents the largest percentage of

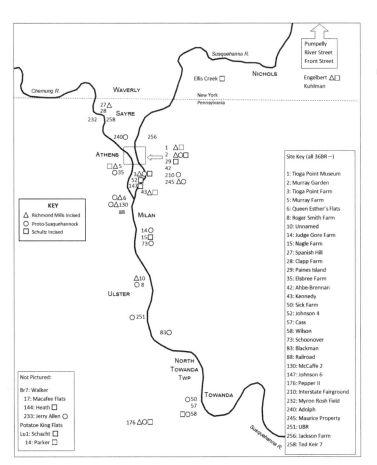

FIGURE 1.4. Pottery type by sites

shell-tempered pottery (80.2%, no quantity given), although it is unclear whether the sherds are stylistically Susquehannock. As the site is located in the center of Athens, an area with a relative abundance of Schultz Incised sherds, it is probable that the sherds are Susquehannock. At no site, with the possible exceptions of the Maurice Property and Wilson sites, is there an overwhelming majority of Susquehannock pottery that may indicate Susquehannock occupation.

The sample size at every site is small, while the percentage of pottery attributable to the Proto-Susquehannocks ranges drastically. The great variety shown through these percentages, from less than 1% to more than 80%, and the similar conclusions reached through them reflect an important interpretational issue in the use of material culture markers.

Sites in the Upper Susquehanna River Valley are typically denoted as Susquehannock if shell-tempered pottery—or in the cases of Richmond Mills Incised and Proto-Susquehannock ware, grit-tempered pottery—is found, regardless of the amount recovered. These widely varied percentages likely represent a variety of social and economic processes by which these assemblages were accumulated. It is an intellectual fallacy to assume that the simple presence of one type of pottery automatically indicates occupation by a particular group.

Conclusion

Rather than further building on it, the collapsing foundation of Proto-Susquehannock archaeology

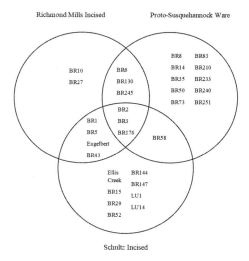

Richmond Mills Incised   Proto-Susquehannock Ware

BR10
BR27

BR6
BR130
BR245

BR8 BR83
BR14 BR210
BR35 BR233
BR50 BR240
BR73 BR251

BR2
BR1 BR3
BR5 BR176
Engelbert BR58
BR43

Ellis BR144
Creek BR147
BR15 LU1
BR29 LU14
BR52

Schultz Incised

FIGURE 1.5
Relationships between pottery types by site

must be addressed. The Upper Susquehanna River Valley region is undeniably an important piece of the Susquehannock puzzle, but it is relatively unknown archaeologically. The 45 sites discussed here represent those that past researchers have deemed the most likely to contain evidence of Proto-Susquehannock peoples, based primarily on ceramic seriation. Determining whether or not the sites are Proto-Susquehannock will require substantial changes in the terminology and theory used to support these assertions.

The definitions used to frame the groundwork of Proto-Susquehannock studies are nebulous and misused. The term "Protohistoric" is used in a variety of ways by both regional and national scholars. Without an accepted definition, the use of the term merely hampers interpretation rather than enhancing temporal clarity. The terms "Protohistoric Susquehannock" and "Proto-Susquehannock" suffer from similar issues. The etymology of the terms implies separate meanings, yet they are often used interchangeably or synonymously.

The loose definitions of the three main pottery types associated with the Proto-Susquehannocks—Richmond Mills Incised, Proto-Susquehannock ware,

and Schultz Incised—compounded by the structural and decorative similarities of the types, leads to a different interpretation of each by individual researchers. Although unsound, the differentiation between these types has become the primary method of determining the presence of Susquehannock people. It is difficult to describe the sites analyzed as Proto-Susquehannock when the term itself and the main artifact type used to define it are vague and interpretively nonoperational.

Of utmost importance is a reanalysis and complete overhaul of the theoretical framework common in indigenous origin research. The culture-history approach has been discredited for decades, yet its tenets still dominate our understanding of the Proto-Susquehannocks and other native peoples in the Middle-Atlantic region. In this view, shell-tempered pottery and copper spirals are equated with the Proto-Susquehannocks to such a degree that the mere presence of one of these objects on a site is enough to indicate Proto-Susquehannock habitation. To state that any site that includes one or more of these traits is Susquehannock based only on the presence of what may be a single object is to completely disregard the interconnectedness of American Indian societies and to infer that economic and social interactions were nonexistent or insignificant.

The Upper Susquehanna River Valley region has the potential to reveal a great deal about the history of the Susquehannock people. While the current evidence appears to support claims of the area as a homeland or birthplace of the Proto-Susquehannocks, close analysis of the available evidence reveals a shaky foundation built on antiquated theoretical paradigms and poorly defined cultural definitions. A complete reanalysis of the excavation and artifact evidence is needed within a new foundation built on solid definitions and relevant theory. Only after these problems have been addressed can we truly begin to understand the archaeological history of the Susquehannocks.

AD Marble and Company

2003   *Alternative Mitigation to the Interstate Fairgrounds Site (36Br210): Athens Bridge Replacement Project, S.R. 1056, Section 001. Athens Township, Bradford County, Pennsylvania.* Two volumes. Report prepared for the Pennsylvania Department of Transportation, District 3-0. AD Marble and Company, Conshohocken, Pennsylvania.

Bailey, John H.

1938   An Analysis of Iroquoian Ceramic Types. *American Antiquity* 3 (4): 333–38.

Beisaw, April M.

2006   Deer, Toads, Dogs, and Frogs: A New Interpretation of the Faunal Remains from the Engelbert Site, Tioga County, New York. *Northeast Anthropology* 72:1–23.

2008   *Untangling Susquehannock Multiple Burials.* Scholar in Residence Final Report: FC#4100045134, ME#20801. Report Submitted to the Pennsylvania Historical and Museum Commission, Harrisburg.

2007   *Osteoarchaeology of the Engelbert Site: Evaluating Occupational Continuity Through the Taphonomy of Human and Animal Remains.* Ph.D. dissertation, Department of Anthropology, State University of New York, Binghamton.

2010   Memory, Identity, and N.A.G.P.R.A. in the Northeastern United States. *American Anthropologist* 112 (2): 244–56.

Bradley, James W.

2005   *Evolution of the Onondaga Iroquois: Accommodating Change, 1500–1655.* University of Nebraska Press, Lincoln.

Bradley, James W., and S. Terry Childs

2007   Basque Earrings and Panthers Tails. In *Archaeology of the Iroquois*, edited by Jordan E. Kerber, 290–305. Syracuse University Press, Syracuse, New York.

Brashler, Janet G.

1987   A Middle Sixteenth Century Susquehannock Village in Hampshire County, West Virginia. *West Virginia Archaeologist* 39 (2): 1–31.

Caister, Dan

2007   Recalling the Engelbert Site. *Susquehanna River Archaeological Center of Native Studies Newsletter* 3 (1): 1–6.

Casterline, Richard, and John A. Sokash

2003   A Report on the Susquehannock Burials at the Kennedy Site. Report from the Kings College Excavations, 1974. In *Alternative Mitigation to the Interstate Fairgrounds Site (36Br210): Athens Bridge Replacement Project.* Vol. 2. Report prepared for the Pennsylvania Department of Transportation,

District 3-0. AD Marble and Company, Conshohocken, Pennsylvania.

Cobb, Charles R., and Michael S. Nassaney

1995   Integration and Interaction in the Late Woodland Southeast. In *Native American Interactions: Multiscalar Analyses and Interpretations in the Eastern Woodlands*, edited by Michael S. Nassaney and Kenneth S. Sassaman, 205–26. University of Tennessee Press, Knoxville.

Cowles, Ellsworth C.

1932–33   Excavating an Indian Site Near Sayre, Pennsylvania. *Pennsylvania Archaeologist* 3 (2): 14–15; 3 (3): 12–15; 3 (4): 16–21.

Crannell, Marilyn A.

1970   *Shell-Tempered Pottery Vessels from the Engelbert Site, Nichols, New York.* M.A. thesis, Department of Anthropology, State University of New York, Binghamton.

Custer, Jay F.

1986   Pennsylvania Profiles: The Susquehanna River Expedition of 1916. *Pennsylvania Archaeologist* 56 (3–4): 52–58.

Dictionary.com Unabridged

2010   s.v. "proto," accessed June 27, 2010, http://dictionary .reference.com/browse/proto.

Dunbar, Helene R., and Katherine C. Ruhl

1974   Copper Artifacts from the Engelbert Site. *New York State Archaeological Association Bulletin* 61:1–10.

Elliott, Dolores N., and William D. Lipe

1970   *The Engelbert Site Project.* Tioga County Historical Society, Owego, New York.

Engelbrecht, William

2003   *Iroquoia.* Syracuse University Press, Syracuse, New York.

Fitzgerald, William R., and Peter S. Ramsden

1988   Copper-Based Metal Testing as an Aid to Understanding Early European-Amerindian Interaction: Scratching the Surface. *Canadian Journal of Archaeology* 12:153–61.

Fontana, Bernard L.

1965   On the Meaning of Historic Sites Archaeology. *American Antiquity* 31 (1): 61–65.

Frost, Stuart W.

1935   Historic Sequence of Indian Occupation in Bradford County. *Pennsylvania Archaeologist* 4 (4): 20–21.

Funk, Robert E.

1993   *Archaeological Investigations in the Upper Susquehanna Valley, New York State.* Vol. 1. Persimmon Press, Buffalo, New York.

Funk, Robert E., Bruce E. Rippeteau, and Ralph M. Houck

1973 A Preliminary Cultural Framework for the Upper Susquehanna Valley. *New York State Archaeological Association Bulletin* 57:11–27.

1974 Recent Research in the Upper Susquehanna Valley, New York. *Pennsylvania Archaeologist* 44 (3): 1–31.

Garrahan, Francis D.

1990 Airport II Site: A Clemson Island / Owasco Settlement on the North Branch of the Susquehanna River. *Pennsylvania Archaeologist* 60 (1): 1–31.

Griffin, James B.

1931 The Athens Excavations. *Society for Pennsylvania Archaeology Bulletin* 2 (2): 3.

2003a The Tioga Point Museum Expedition for 1913. In *Alternative Mitigation to the Interstate Fairgrounds Site (36Br210): Athens Bridge Replacement Project.* Vol. 2. Report prepared for the Pennsylvania Department of Transportation, District 3-0. AD Marble and Company, Conshohocken, Pennsylvania.

2003b Griffin Excavation and Spanish Hill. In *Alternative Mitigation to the Interstate Fairgrounds Site (36Br210): Athens Bridge Replacement Project.* Vol. 2. Report prepared for the Pennsylvania Department of Transportation, District 3-0. AD Marble and Company, Conshohocken, Pennsylvania.

Griffith, Daniel R., and Jay F. Custer

1985 Late Woodland Ceramics of Delaware: Implications for the Late Prehistoric Archaeology of Northeast North America. *Pennsylvania Archaeologist* 55 (3): 5–20.

Grumet, Robert S.

1995 *Historic Contact.* University of Oklahoma Press, Norman.

Hart, John P., and Hetty Jo Brumbach

2003 The Death of Owasco. *American Antiquity* 68 (4): 737–52.

Herbstritt, James T.

1988 A Reference for Pennsylvania Radiocarbon Dates. *Pennsylvania Archaeologist* 58 (2): 1–29.

Hunter, William A.

1959 The Historic Role of the Susquehannocks. In *Susquehannock Miscellany*, edited by John Witthoft and W. Fred Kinsey III, 8–18. The Pennsylvania Historical and Museum Commission, Harrisburg.

Jennings, Francis

1978 Susquehannock. In *Northeast*, edited by B. G. Trigger, 362–67. Handbook of North American Indians 15. Smithsonian Institution, Washington, D.C.

Kent, Barry C.

1970 An Unusual Cache from the Wyoming Valley, Pennsylvania. *American Antiquity* 35 (2): 185–93.

1980a An Update on Susquehannock Iroquoian Pottery. In *Proceedings of the 1979 Iroquois Pottery Conference,* edited by Charles F. Hayes III, 99–103. Research Records 13. Rochester Museum and Science Center, Rochester, New York.

1980b *Discovering Pennsylvania's Archaeological Heritage.* Pennsylvania Historical and Museum Commission, Harrisburg.

2001 *Susquehanna's Indians.* Revised edition. Pennsylvania Historical and Museum Commission, Harrisburg.

Kinsey, W. Fred, III

1959 Historic Susquehannock Pottery. In *Susquehannock Miscellany*, edited by John Witthoft and W. Fred Kinsey III, 61–98. Pennsylvania Historical and Museum Commission, Harrisburg.

Lenig, Don

1960 The Oak Hill Horizon I. *New York State Archaeological Association Bulletin* 19:12–14.

Lipe, William D.

1976 The Engelbert Site Archaeological Project, Tioga County, New York. *National Geographic Society Research Reports* 17: 205–11.

Lucy, Charles L.

1959 Pottery Types of the Upper Susquehanna. *Pennsylvania Archaeologist* 20 (3–4): 28–37.

1991 The Tioga Point Farm Sites 36Br3 and 36Br52: 1983 Excavations. *Pennsylvania Archaeologist* 61 (1): 1–18.

2003 The Kennedy Site (36Br43) Athens Township, Bradford County, Pennsylvania. Excavations by Pennsylvania Historical and Museum Commission 1975. In *Alternative Mitigation to the Interstate Fairgrounds Site (36Br210): Athens Bridge Replacement Project.* Vol. 2. Report prepared for the Pennsylvania Department of Transportation, District 3-0. AD Marble and Company, Conshohocken, Pennsylvania.

Lucy, Charles L., and Richard J. McCracken

1985 The Blackman Site (36Br83): A Proto-Susquehannock Village. *Pennsylvania Archaeologist* 55 (1–2): 5–29.

Lucy, Charles L., and Leroy Vanderpoel

1979 The Tioga Point Farm Site. *Pennsylvania Archaeologist* 49 (1–2): 1–12.

MacNeish, Richard S.

1952 *Iroquois Pottery Types: A Technique for the Study of Iroquois Prehistory.* National Museum of Canada Bulletin 124. The Department of Resources and Development, Ottawa.

McCann, Catherine

1962 The Wilson Site, Bradford County, Pennsylvania. *Pennsylvania Archaeologist* 32 (2): 43–55.

McCracken, Richard J.

1985 Susquehannocks, Brûlé, and Carantouannais: A Continuing Research Problem. *New York State Archaeological Association Bulletin* 91:39–51.

McCracken, Richard J., and Charles L. Lucy

1989 Analysis of a Radiocarbon Date from the Blackman Site, an Early Susquehannock Village in Bradford County, Pennsylvania. *Pennsylvania Archaeologist* 59 (1): 14–18.

Moorehead, Warren King.

1938 *A Report of the Susquehanna River Expedition.* Andover Press, Andover, Massachusetts.

Murray, Louise Welles

1921 Aboriginal Sites in and near "Teaoga," Now Athens, Pennsylvania. *Pennsylvania Archaeologist* 23 (2): 183–214; 23 (3): 268–97.

1931 Selected Manuscripts of General John S. Clark Relating to the Aboriginal History of the Susquehanna. *Publications of the Society for Pennsylvania Archaeology.* Vol. 1. Athens, Pennsylvania.

Niemczycki, Mary Ann Palmer

1984 *The Origin and Development of the Seneca and Cayuga Tribes of New York State.* Research Division, Rochester Museum and Science Center, Rochester, New York.

Noble, William C.

2004 The Protohistoric Period Revisited. In *A Passion for the Past: Papers in Honor of James F. Pendergast,* edited by James V. Wright and Jean-Luc Pilon, 179–91. Canadian Museum of Civilization, Quebec.

Pratt, Peter P.

1960 A Criticism of MacNeish's Iroquoian Pottery Types. *Pennsylvania Archaeologist* 30 (3–4): 106–10.

Ramsden, Peter G.

1977 *A Refinement of Some Aspects of Huron Ceramic Analysis.* Archaeological Survey of Canada 63. The Department of Resources and Development, Ottawa.

Reinhart, Niels

2000 The Faunal Assemblage from the Engelbert Site, Nichols, New York: An Analysis of Subsistence and Paleoecology. *Northeast Anthropology* 59:1–22.

Rippeteau, Bruce E.

1981 The Upper Susquehanna Valley Iroquois: An Iroquoian Enigma. Occasional Publications in Northeastern Anthropology 5, 123–57. Essays in Northeastern Anthropology, University of Michigan, Ann Arbor.

Semowich, Charles

1980–81 Historic Ceramics from the Engelbert Site: An Evaluation of Artifacts from a Salvage Operation. *New York State Archaeological Association Bulletin* 80/81:19–25.

Sempowski, Martha L.

1989 Fluctuations Through Time in the Use of Marine Shell at Seneca Iroquois Sites. In *Proceedings of the 1986 Shell Bead Conference,* edited by C. F. Hayes III, 81–96. Rochester Museum and Science Center, Rochester.

2007 Early Historic Exchange Between the Seneca and the Susquehannock. In *Archaeology of the Iroquois,* edited by Jordan E. Kerber, 194–218. Syracuse University Press, Syracuse, New York.

Silliman, Stephen W.

2005 Culture Contact or Colonialism? Challenges in the Archaeology of Native North America. *American Antiquity* 70 (1): 55–74.

Smith, Ira F., III

1970 Schultz Site Settlement Patterns and External Relations: A Preliminary Discussion and Possible Interpretation. *New York State Archaeological Association Bulletin* 50:27–34.

1977 The Susquehanna River Valley Archaeological Survey. *Pennsylvania Archaeologist* 47 (4): 27–29.

Snow, Dean R.

2007 Migration in Prehistory: The Northern Iroquoian Case. In *Archaeology of the Iroquois,* edited by Jordan E. Kerber, 6–29. Syracuse University Press, Syracuse, New York.

Stewart, Marilyn C.

1973 A Proto-Historic Susquehannock Cemetery near Nichols, Tioga County, New York. *New York State Archaeological Association Bulletin* 58:1–21.

Triple Cities Chapter

2005 *The Richard Engelbert Collection of Prehistoric Artifacts.* New York State Archaeological Association. Cady Memorial Library Nichols, New York.

Twigg, Deb

2005 Revisiting the Mystery of "Carantouan" and Spanish Hill. *Pennsylvania Archaeologist* 75 (2): 24–33.

2009a Louise Welles Murray and Her Garden. *Susquehanna River Archaeological Center of Native Studies Newsletter* 5 (1): 1–5.

2009b The 1916 Susquehanna River Expedition. *Susquehanna River Archaeological Center of Native Studies Newsletter* 5 (2): 1–5.

2010 The James Griffin Report: 1931. *Susquehanna River Archaeological Center of Native Studies Newsletter* 6 (1): 1–7.

Versaggi, Nina, Peter Stahl, Timothy Knapp, and Diana Loren

1996 *Binghamton University Draft NAGPRA Inventory Addendum Engelbert Site (SUBi-300).* Report Submitted to the National Park Service. Binghamton University Public Archaeology Facility, Vestal, New York.

Wilcox, David R., and W. Bruce Masse

1981 A History of Protohistoric Studies in the North American Southwest. In *The Protohistoric Period in the North American Southwest, AD 1450–1700,* edited by

David R. Wilcox and W. Bruce Masse, 213–56. Arizona State University Anthropological Research Papers 24, Tempe.

Witthoft, John

1959   Ancestry of the Susquehannocks. In *Susquehannock Miscellany*, edited by John Witthoft and W. Fred Kinsey III, 19–60. Pennsylvania Historical and Museum Commission, Harrisburg.

n.d.   Archaeological Resources of the Susquehanna Drainage. Undated notes in the collections of the Tioga Point Museum, Athens, Pennsylvania.

Wren, Christopher

1914   *A Study of North Appalachian Indian Pottery.* Republished from Proceedings of the Wyoming Historical and Geological Society, vol. 13. The E. B. Yordy Company, Wilkes-Barre, Pennsylvania.

2.

Becoming Susquehannock

THE WEST BRANCH AND

NORTH BRANCH TRADITIONS   James T. Herbstritt

ABSTRACT

Native people of two contemporary Late Woodland cultural traditions occupied the Susquehanna Valley from AD 1200–1550. The territory of the West Branch tradition included the headwaters of the Upper West Branch in the Deep Valleys section of the Appalachian Plateaus to the "Forks of the Susquehanna" at Sunbury, Pennsylvania. The territory of the North Branch tradition extended from the Susquehanna Lowland and Anthracite Valley sections along the Susquehanna's North Branch from Nanticoke, Pennsylvania, to the southern end of Tioga County, New York. After ca. AD 1475–1500, the archaeological evidence suggests that these traditions underwent an ethnogenic transformation. A changing settlement pattern of terminal West Branch and North Branch tradition groups is thus indicated by the disappearance of large palisaded settlements and the emergence of small-sized hamlets around the first quarter of the sixteenth century. The coalescence of West Branch tradition (terminal Quiggle phase) makers of shell-tempered incised pottery and North Branch tradition (Wyoming Valley Complex) makers of Chance/Garoga-phase incised pottery resulted in the emergence of makers of Schultz Incised pottery near the Upper Susquehanna headwaters of the Susquehannock. The principal land route linking these cotraditions was the Sheshequin Indian path (Wallace 1965) that connected the Lycoming Creek and Towanda Creek headwaters in Sullivan and Bradford counties in Pennsylvania—the gateway to the Endless Mountains. By the mid-sixteenth century, the Susquehannocks shifted their settlements from the Towanda and Sugar Creeks to the Susquehanna's main river valley around the Chemung / North Branch confluence before migrating south to the Lower Susquehanna and the Potomac's South Branch Valleys sometime in the latter half of the sixteenth century.

Introduction

In his seminal work, *Susquehanna's Indians*, Barry Kent summarized an enormous body of information on the Susquehannocks, who, by the early eighteenth century, were collectively known as the Susquehanna or Conestoga Indians (B. Kent 1984). From an archaeological and historical perspective, their lifeways and material culture are trackable over more than 200 years. History reveals that at their end, 20 of the 22 known Conestoga Indians were murdered on December 27, 1763, by a roving band of vigilantes. The only documented surviving residents—Michael and his spouse, Mary, who themselves were not Susquehannocks—were not at the Conestoga town when the massacre happened. Eight months later, Governor John Penn granted them asylum (Eshleman 1908:386–87) at the manor of Christian Hershey in Lancaster County, Pennsylvania, where they lived out the remaining years of their lives. Michael and Mary were laid to rest "in a lonely spot in one of the back pastures of this homestead [Hershey Manor]." (B. Kent 1984:68). Having no documented descendants, the passing of Michael and Mary literally marked the end of an era for the Conestoga Indians.

Three decades after Kent's synthesis appeared in print, a large body of additional information from sites in the Susquehanna Valley has shed new light on Susquehannock culture (Herbstritt 2020; see Beisaw, chapter 3; Lauria, chapter 4; and Wyatt, chapter 6 in this volume). Reanalysis of ceramics and other material remains suggests that the Susquehannocks developed through an emergent evolutionary process of ethnogenesis that early on embraced regional populations of different people from the hinterlands of northern Pennsylvania.

The formative period began ca. AD 1200 and ended by AD 1550, a time span when interaction between contemporary native groups grew increasingly widespread in northern Pennsylvania. This "ethnogenic process" was neither instantaneous nor short lived but developed at a rate suitable for group reorganization and assimilation to take place, eventually leading to a Susquehannock identity.

After "becoming" Susquehannock, these people shifted their habitation sites from the Lycoming and Towanda / Sugar Creek headwaters to the Chemung-Susquehanna confluence in northeastern Bradford County, Pennsylvania, and southern Tioga County,

New York (Bradley 1987; B. Kent 1984; Witthoft 1959; see Gollup, chapter 1 in this volume).

The Susquehannocks were allies of the Huron (or Wendat) nation, which knew them as the "Andastoerrhonons." By the latter decades of the seventeenth century, a name for them (used with different spellings) was "Gandastogue," which by the eighteenth century became corrupted to "Canastogues," or Conestoga. Whichever name these Indians were called by their native or European counterparts, they were the Susquehannocks, who resided in the Susquehanna River Valley for more than two centuries. This we know from history, but what of their true ancestry?

After ca. AD 1500, the internal flow of native trade and exchange in many ways contributed to the ethnogenic process, as the native's worldview was, in part, replaced by non-Indian aspects centered on ideological, technological, and social differences. The internal complexity brought about by such changes in the Susquehannocks' worldview contributed to the ushering in of the Contact period, a time when many Susquehannocks began to move to the Lower Susquehanna. This settlement relocation is believed to have resulted, in part, from competition driven by outside influences for control of the beaver skin trade. By the mid- to late sixteenth century, droughts and foreign diseases spreading up the Susquehanna took their toll on the local Shenks Ferry populations, significantly reducing their numbers and their villages to farmsteads. The decline of the Shenks Ferry groups and the Luray groups located on the Potomac opened their territories to Susquehannock migrations, which by the late sixteenth century were complete.

Northern Pennsylvania was once covered by an old growth forest of conifers and deciduous trees. Early explorers and cartographers gave various names to this landscape: "Dismal Vale" (Bartram 1751), the "Dismal Wilderness" (Wallace 1945, cited in Turnbaugh 1977), "Great Swamp," "Endless Mountains," "Magnolia Hills" (Evans 1755), and the "Shades of Death" (Pownall 1776; see also figure 2.1).

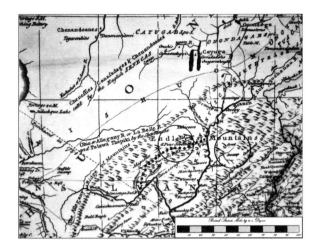

FIGURE 2.1
Inset of Lewis Evans's 1755 map of Pennsylvania showing the West Branch and North Branch of the Susquehanna and prominent landmarks mentioned in chapter 2. Dotted line is the Sheshequin Indian Path that connected the West Branch and North Branch Valleys. Library of Congress, Washington, D.C.

As the region became more populated, the forest-cloaked river valleys were reduced to meadows and grasslands (Meginness 1889). Fire was a valuable land-clearing tool used often by Indians, and its effects in forest clearing are evident in the dendrochronological record (Brose et al. 2015). By the middle to late nineteenth century, much of the old growth forest was commercially timbered off for the shipbuilding, lumber, and tanning industries (Taber 1972).

At the onset of the Little Ice Age, ca. AD 1350, northern Pennsylvania was a vast region where native peoples shared a common semisedentary economy based on hunting, fishing, trapping, wild plant foraging, and agriculture, which had been brought to the region from the lower eastern Great Lakes (Crawford and Smith 1996; Ellis and Ferris 1990) and the Finger Lakes region of central New York (Hart 1999). These later agriculturally driven events set into motion an ethnogenic flow of technological, sociological, and ideological concepts culminating in the emergence of the West Branch (Quiggle phase) and North Branch (Wyoming Valley phase) cultural traditions.

The Late Woodland groups of north-central Pennsylvania have antecedents in the proto-Iroquoians

defined by Ritchie (1980) as Owasco. Later, Ritchie and Funk (1973) viewed the essential core region of Owasco as eastern and south-central New York. As Hart and Brumbach (2003:743) so cogently note, Ritchie (1980:272–300) described the principal elements of Owasco culture as maize-bean-squash agriculture, nucleated villages, longhouses with inferred matrilocal residence, and a series of discrete pottery types. Hart and Brumbach (2003) questioned the definition of Owasco on the very basis of Ritchie's original criteria and viewed Owasco as a subjectively defined unit, though agreeing with Ritchie that the Willey and Phillips (1958) approach had merit in controlling spatial and temporal variation within assigned analytical units.

While some inherent limitations of the culture-historical "component-phase-tradition" approach formulated by Willey and Phillips (1958) exist, the scheme is used herein to define a three-stage cultural development for the West Branch tradition—Initial stage / Kalgren-Bell phase, ca. AD 1200–1300; Intermediate stage / Stewart phase, ca. AD 1300–1400/1425; and Terminal stage / Quiggle phase, ca. AD 1425–1525/1580. The North Branch tradition is similarly broken up into Transitional Iroquois / Castle Creek and Oak Hill; Early Iroquois (Chance), ca. AD 1250–1475; and Protohistoric Iroquois (Garoga), ca. AD 1500/1520–1600 (figure 2.2). The West Branch tradition endured for three centuries before undergoing a significant ethnogenic change involving the North Branch tradition, ca. AD 1525, in the Upper Susquehanna. The social transformation ended with the emergence of the historically documented Susquehannocks of the seventeenth century.

West Branch: Deep Valleys and Unglaciated Plateau

The West Branch and North Branch traditions were regionally defined cultural equivalents in the Susquehanna Valley from ca. AD 1200 to 1525/1550. Both traditions can be traced through the different

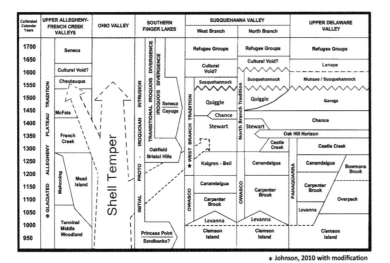

FIGURE 2.2

Late Woodland to Contact period chronology for northern Pennsylvania

※ Johnson, 2010 with modification
★ Graybill, 1987 with modification

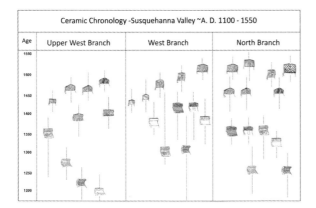

FIGURE 2.3

Ceramic motif chronology for the Susquehanna Valley, AD 1200–1550

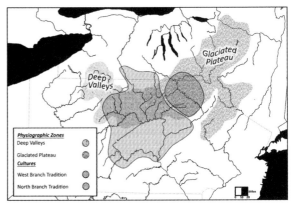

FIGURE 2.4

West Branch and North Branch traditions, showing their locations within the Deep Valley and Glaciated Plateau physiographic sections

decorative traits of northern proto-Iroquoian potters and their descendants (figure 2.3). The Deep Valleys section was, in a sense, a cultural nexus of the Upper Allegheny and Niagara Escarpment and the Susquehanna's West Branch Valley (figure 2.4). Over an approximate span of 350 years, key pottery forms were used contemporaneously in these areas—for example, Carpenter Brook Cord-on-Cord, Canandaigua (a.k.a. Sackett Corded), Stewart Incised, and Castle Creek Incised—despite subtle differences in regional settlement patterns (Bressler and Rainey 2003; Bressler and Rockey 1997; Funk 1993; Lucy 1959, 1991a; Ritchie and Funk 1973).

West Branch Tradition Synopsis

Upper West Branch Kalgren-Bell Phase (ca. AD 1200–1300/25)

The Upper West Branch Kalgren-Bell phase is a compound name derived from the first and second Late Woodland village sites to be systematically studied in the Upper West Branch Valley of Clearfield County, Pennsylvania. Excavations were conducted at the Kalgren (a.k.a. Dodd) site from 1978 to 1994 (Herbstritt 2014a) and the Bell (a.k.a. Hegarty) site from 1979 to

1985 (Matlack 1986). The distribution of the Upper West Branch Kalgren-Bell-phase sites extends from the Upper Ohio Valley / West Branch Susquehanna divide around Sabula, Pennsylvania, eastward to the Deep Valleys section / Allegheny Front boundary at Lock Haven, Pennsylvania (figure 2.5; table 2.1). Similarities in settlement/community organization, mortuary patterns, and artifact assemblages are the principal material hallmarks of the dozen or so known Kalgren-Bell-phase sites. This cultural manifestation is ancestral to the Stewart-Quiggle phase (figure 2.6).

TABLE 2.1 Susquehanna Valley archaeological sites: key ceramics

Phase	Number	Percentage
Late Owasco	15	12.1
Kalgren-Bell	7	5.6
Stewart-Owasco	9	7.3
Stewart	29	23.4
Stewart-Montgomery	6	4.9
Transitional Iroquois	3	2.4
Chance/Garoga	9	7.3
Quiggle	14	11.3
Lancaster / Funk / Grubb Creek	7	5.6
Early Schultz Susquehannock	25	20.2
Total	124	100

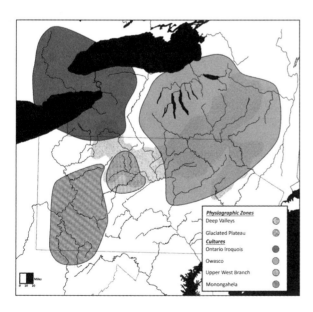

FIGURE 2.5
Late Woodland–phase interaction, ca. AD 1200–1300/1350

The earliest upland sites of the Upper West Branch Kalgren-Bell phase were palisaded settlements less than 0.3 hectare in size enclosing wigwam-shaped houses 5–10 meters in diameter (figure 2.7a). Later, slightly larger settlements featured short oblong longhouses with rounded ends, 15–20 meters in length,

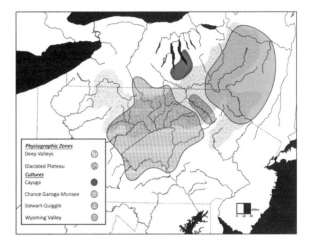

FIGURE 2.6
Late Woodland and Proto-Contact phases, ca. AD 1250/1275–1500

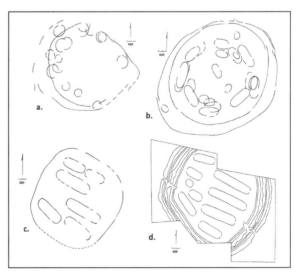

FIGURE 2.7
West Branch tradition village plans. a. Bell site: Kalgren-Bell phase (initial period occupation); b. Kalgren site: Kalgren-Bell phase (middle and late period occupations); c. Simmons-Nash site: Stewart-phase occupation; d. Simmons-Nash site: Quiggle-phase occupation. Courtesy of the State Museum of Pennsylvania, Pennsylvania Historical and Museum Commission.

surrounded by a compound of well-built, walled fortifications and ditch trenches. One or more freestanding semisubterranean keyhole structures (Herbstritt 2014a) attended most houses and served multiple purposes, which included use as storage facilities, smokehouses, and on occasion, as sweat lodges.

The Kalgren site occupies a height of land on the Upper Ohio / Susquehanna divide between Narrows Creek and the Sinnemahoning Creek headwaters in northern Clearfield County. The Bell site is in a similar upland setting in central Clearfield County within the Susquehanna's West Branch Little Clearfield Creek drainage basin. Although the Clearfield County sites are three-dimensional circular earthworks or earthrings, most surface traces of the earthring and ditch trench features have been obliterated by nearly two centuries of continuous farming.

Two rebuildings were confirmed by overlapping palisades, overlapping houses, and overlapping pits at the Kalgren and Bell sites. Later houses were superimposed on earlier ones (figure 2.7b), indicating a need for repair and replacement over time. Generally, these fortified villages were reoccupied with some architectural changes (Herbstritt 2014a). Some of the upland settlements of the Kalgren-Bell phase show evidence of Initial (Upper West Branch), Intermediate (Stewart), and Terminal (Quiggle) stage West Branch tradition reoccupations from ca. AD 1200 to AD 1550 based on architectural differences, suggesting that these settlements were better suited for reuse owing to their ecological surroundings—principally the wetlands, meadows, and dense mast-bearing forests of mixed deciduous trees.

The principal pottery types of the Kalgren-Bell phase are Upper West Branch Cord-Marked—a shell or, rarely, grit-tempered collarless pottery marked by lip incising—and Upper West Branch Incised—a low incipient collared shell-tempered pottery with cord-marked or plain necks displaying simple line incising (table 2.1; see also Wren 1914: plate 9, figure 4). Both types, embellished with final

Z-twist cordmarkings, are early utilitarian wares that share lower Upper Ohio Valley (Monongahela) and proto-Iroquoian (Owasco) affinities (figure 2.8a). Upper West Branch Cord-Marked and Upper West Branch Incised are the assumed cognates to Stewart Incised, the dominant pottery type of the West Branch tradition's Intermediate (Stewart) phase and not something entirely derived from the mixing of pottery forms from elsewhere. Smoking pipes are simple, obtuse-angled, and barrel-shaped forms, many with delicate rouletting that extends onto the stem, and some of these could be characterized as Owasco forms akin to those at the Upper Susquehanna Willow Point site in New York (Ritchie and Funk 1973: plates 152, 161, and 162).

Stewart Phase (ca. AD 1300–1400/1425)

The Charles Stewart site near McElhattan, Pennsylvania, is the type site for the Stewart phase. Sites are common in the lower reaches of the Deep Valleys section to the southeastern edge of the Pittsburgh Low

FIGURE 2.8
Pottery types of the West Branch and North Branch traditions. a. Upper West Branch Incised; b. Stewart Incised; c. Quiggle Incised; d. Chance Incised; e. Garoga / Munsee Incised; f. local rendition of Niagara Frontier Iroquois; g. local rendition of Indian Hill Stamped; h. early Quiggle-Schultz Incised. Courtesy of the State Museum of Pennsylvania, Pennsylvania Historical and Museum Commission.

Plateau and Allegheny Front, then southward into the Juniata River's Raystown Branch where the Sheep Rock and Workman sites are located (figure 2.6; table 2.1). Stewart-phase sites, however, are most common on the main stem of the Susquehanna's West Branch. Other sites occur from the upper Clearfield Creek and upper Chest Creek drainage basins to locations as far south as Cambria County.

The North Branch Stewart-phase sites are sporadic from the Pennsylvania / New York state line south into the Wyoming Valley and consist mostly of isolated pits containing a mix of Stewart Incised and Owasco Sackett Corded and Castle Creek Incised pottery. Longhouses may be associated with some of these sites in the Cowanesque/Tioga River Valley (East et al. 2006). From the Wyoming Valley south to the Conococheague Creek headwaters in Franklin County, these pottery types co-occur with Mason Island (Page) and Montgomery Complex (Shepard) wares. Pottery pipes of Owasco forms are common types of the Stewart phase but not of the slightly later Shenks Ferry Blue Rock phase south of Blue Mountain, where pipes are much more like the small barrel-shaped styles of the Montgomery Complex.

Dwellings associated with Stewart-phase site components on the West Branch Susquehanna River proper were of the longhouse type, 15 to 28 meters long, with well-defined interior cubicles, centrally aligned hearths, and a doorway at each end of the structures. These architectural elements presumably characterize the social structure of Stewart-phase groups as matrilineal. Their longhouses were usually arranged in parallel rows aligned east-west and surrounded by a single or double wall of palisades encompassing areas of approximating half a hectare (figure 2.7c). Many of the settlements had encircling ditch trenches, a defining carry-over from the earlier Kalgren-Bell-phase era. Freestanding keyhole structures of a slightly squared or oblong form (figure 2.9c), in contrast to the oval-shaped bodies of Kalgren-Bell-phase keyholes (figure 2.9a–b), are architecturally more like the

FIGURE 2.9
Semisubterranean keyhole structures from sites of the West Branch and North Branch traditions. a. compound form (Quiggle phase), Kalgren site; b. freestanding form (Kalgren-Bell phase), Kalgren site; c. freestanding form (Stewart phase), Nash-Simmons site; d. freestanding form (Chance/Garoga phase), Parker site. Courtesy of the State Museum of Pennsylvania, Pennsylvania Historical and Museum Commission.

semisubterranean sweat lodges of Southern Ontario Middleport Stage sites (Dodd et al. 1990).

Stewart-phase pottery is a form of low-collared incised pottery (figure 2.8b) that in some respects is like the slightly later grit-tempered Shenks Ferry Incised pottery of the Lower Susquehanna (Witthoft 1954). Both pottery types were embellished with final Z-twist cordmarkings beneath an applied motif of a multibanded, horizontally decorated collar; incising was always over a plain neck—all traits that also appear on miniature toy pots of the Stewart phase. Its descendent, Shenks Ferry Incised, was the earliest pottery type of the Shenks Ferry culture in the Lower Susquehanna Valley several decades later. Some Stewart-phase pots were castellated, a rim trait common to Middle Ontario Iroquois and late-stage Owasco (Transitional Iroquois) collared pottery from the Upper Susquehanna, which may reflect a codevelopment in collar design for these contemporary pot forms. These traits, however, are rarely seen on Shenks Ferry Incised pots of the Lower Susquehanna Valley.

Quiggle Phase (ca. AD 1425–1525/50)

The type site for the Quiggle phase is the Quiggle (a.k.a. Quiggle-Lapp) site located at Pine Station in Clinton County, Pennsylvania (Ritchie 1929; Smith 1984). The distribution of Quiggle-phase settlements and their hallmark pottery and pipe forms encompasses much of the former territory of the Kalgren-Bell and Stewart phases and includes a fringe region extending into the Upper Genesee River drainage basin to Belmont, New York, as well as northeast to the Upper Delaware and the mountain tributaries of south-central Pennsylvania (figure 2.6; table 2.1). Early stage Quiggle-phase settlements were built on hilltops and bench promontories overlooking drainage basin divides, while most late-stage settlements occupied floodplain settings near major stream confluences.

Strongly fortified like the Kalgren-Bell- and Stewart-phase settlements, Quiggle-phase settlements were slightly larger than Stewart-phase settlements, averaging 0.6 hectare in size, and had multiple longhouses of 12 to 42 meters in length either arranged along the inside wall of a palisade or set in rows (figure 2.7, d) in an orientation like that of the Stewart-phase houses. Semisubterranean keyhole structures take on two forms during the Quiggle phase: an oval-bodied form (figure 2.9a–b) placed at different locations around the house ring on upland settlements is typical, while the oblong/square-bodied forms (figure 2.9, c) are most common at farmstead/hamlet sites where each house had direct access to one or more keyholes.

Certain pottery motifs of the preceding Stewart phase are transitional carryovers onto Quiggle-phase pots, which implies that a strong level of social cohesion existed between the Intermediate and Terminal stage groups of the West Branch tradition. Collared pottery increased in height through time and carried common motifs composed of line-filled trapezoids, triangles, and parallelograms. The lips and bases of pot collars incorporated dowel- or wedge-shaped punctates, and castellations appear as important temporal markers that increase through time, a parallel also seen in the Cayuga pottery series of the Finger Lakes region of central New York (figure 2.8c). Collars of terminal Quiggle-phase pots (post AD 1500–1550) display castellations with raised ladder appliqués that sometimes have triangular panels filled with jab punctates placed over a treatment of final Z-twist cordmarking like the later motifs of Schultz Incised (figure 2.8h). During the first half of the sixteenth century, these ladder appliques begin to show up in the Wyoming Valley complex (figure 2.8d–e) and the later proto-Contact Seneca Adams (Wray et al 1987, figure 3–40e–f, h–i and figure 3–41f–h), Mohawk (Snow 1995), Oneida (Pratt 1976), and the Susquehannock Schultz sites (B. Kent 1984, figure 15). Figure 2.10 depicts the hypothesized evolution of collar motif designs and decorative ladder appliques in a sequence from the Initial Quiggle and Wyoming Valley stages through early Schultz Susquehannock.

Niagara Frontier and Finger Lakes region pottery attributes—that is, collar spouts and exotic double-necked pot shapes—begin to show up on terminal Quiggle-phase borderland settlements of

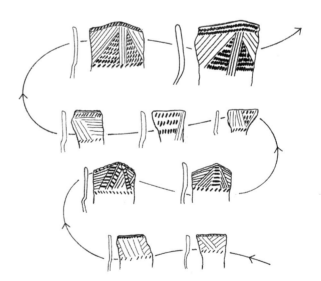

FIGURE 2.10
Pot collar motif evolution of Quiggle Incised / Chance / Cayuga / Garoga to Schultz Incised based on the in situ development model; Late Woodland through Protohistoric Susquehanna Valley, AD 1200–1550/1575

the late sixteenth century (figure 2.8f). A few of these unusual pots appear (figure 2.8g) to mimic the "cord impressed" decorative technique observed on Conemaugh Corded (Johnson 1998) and the proto-Contact to Contact period Indian Hills Stamped pots from northeastern Ohio. As such, these styles demonstrate a strong ethnogenic pathway of ideas, trade, and social interaction among these different tribal groups.

The clay pipes of the Quiggle phase developed from the evolutionary "follow-throughs" of Stewart- and Castle Creek Owasco–phase times, when the principal bowl and neck decorations on pipes were embellished with rouletting in the Willow Point style (figure 2.11b; see Ritchie and Funk 1973: plates 152 and 161–66), rarely with human face appliques (Matlack 1986: figure 10). Beginning in the early fifteenth century, these pipe forms transitioned into the trumpet styles not unlike the proto-Iroquois or Iroquois pipes of the Northern Iroquoians. These bowl forms became more strongly exaggerated through time (figure 2.11e). Tapered stone tube pipes, not to be confused with the Early Woodland stone tube pipes of the Ohio Valley, were carved from local fireclay found

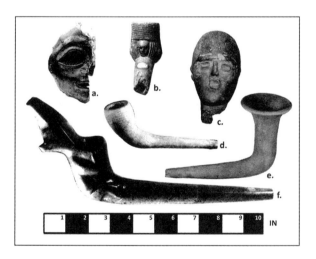

FIGURE 2.11
West Branch and North Branch tradition pipe styles. a., c. Chance-phase face pipes; b. Willow Point rouletted bowl face pipe; d. Kalgren-Bell-phase rouletted barrel bowl pipe; e. Quiggle-phase trumpet bowl pipe; f. animal effigy (full form) fireclay pipe. Courtesy of the State Museum of Pennsylvania, Pennsylvania Historical and Museum Commission.

with the soft coal beds of the Upper West Branch Valley. Occasionally, pipes of this stone and others of modeled clay portraying anthropomorphic and zoomorphic figures (figure 2.11f) were incorporated into the pipe maker's world, and these appeared by the late fifteenth century.

North Branch: Deep Valleys and Glaciated Plateau

The Upper Susquehanna River drainage basin extends from Wyalusing, Pennsylvania, to Cooperstown, New York. At Towanda, Pennsylvania, the valley reopens onto a broad floodplain where Native American occupations of Owasco through Chance/Garoga, Susquehannock, and possibly Munsee are present (figures 2.5 and 2.6; Lucy 1959; Lucy and Vanderpoel 1979; Murray 1921; Witthoft 1959).

Unlike the broad fertile floodplains of the Wyoming Valley, this segment of the river from West Pittston to Wyalusing is entrenched in the rugged mountains of the Glaciated Plateau, where few sizable floodplains were wide enough for large-scale agricultural settlements. South of the Wyoming Valley, large nucleated villages are also conspicuously absent from the valley from Nanticoke, Pennsylvania, to the forks of the Susquehanna at Northumberland, Pennsylvania. After AD 1450, this stretch of the river seems to have been vacant territory separating West Branch and North Branch tradition groups.

North Branch Tradition Synopsis

Transitional Iroquois: Castle Creek Owasco and Oak Hill Phases (ca. AD 1200–1375/1400)

These native occupations occur from the Wyoming Valley north into Tioga, Chemung, and Steuben counties in New York. Although post molds have been reported from sites in the Wyoming and North Branch Valleys (Sweeney 1966; Witthoft 1959), the community pattern data for the Transitional Iroquois period are scant save for the 24-foot subcircular-shaped house pattern (figure 2.12a) excavated at the Tioga Point Farm site (36Br3). Mixed assemblages of Sackett Corded, Owasco Corded Collar (a.k.a. Kelso Corded), and Transitional Iroquois sherds link this architectural feature to a middle or late Owasco occupation (table 2.1; Lucy 1991b). The North Branch Valley smoking pipe styles are also dominated by Sackett Corded, Castle Creek Owasco, and Transitional Iroquois forms (see Ritchie 1980: plate 100).

Stewart Incised, Sick Incised, and related pottery hybrids sharing mixed northern Transitional Iroquois traits are associated with traces of carbonized corn and bean cultigens, and Castle Creek / Kelso-Oak Hill pottery contexts indicate contemporaneity with other proto-Iroquoians in the southern New York / Upper Delaware areas, ca. AD 1250–1350 (see, for examples, Knapp 2009; Prezzano 1992). A subsistence economy centered on maize, beans, and squash agriculture was being broadly practiced by these and other Transitional Iroquois groups linked to the North Branch tradition in much of the Wyoming Valley (see, for example, Kohler and Orlandini 1985) as well as

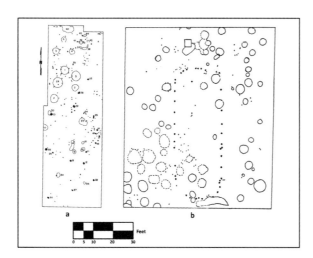

FIGURE 2.12
Upper Susquehanna Valley house patterns. a. Tioga Point Farm site (Late Owasco); b. Kennedy site (early Schultz-Susquehannock). Courtesy of the State Museum of Pennsylvania, Pennsylvania Historical and Museum Commission.

other regions of the Upper Susquehanna (see East et al. 2006) where these cultigens have been found in sealed archaeological contexts.

Early Iroquois (ca. AD 1400–1475/1500) and Protohistoric Iroquois (ca. AD 1500–1575)

Chance (Early Iroquois; figure 2.8d), Cayadutta (an intermediate Iroquoian pottery type), and Garoga (Protohistoric) pottery (figure 2.8e) is reported from five archaeological sites in the Wyoming Valley: Rusbar, Wermuth, Parker, Schacht-Dundee, and Shawnee Flats (table 2.1). The assemblages are most like those of the Onondaga, Oneida, and Mohawk, where settlement sequences are generally well defined (Pratt 1976; Snow 1995; Tuck 1971). Upriver from Wyoming Valley, these Iroquoian pottery types are known only as sporadic discoveries at multicomponent rock shelters and small, short-term, open-air habitation sites.

That not a single "pure" Chance/Garoga-phase–component has been identified for the Upper Susquehanna complicates the problem of following the archaeological record of these native occupations. Chance- and Cayuga-like pottery from plow zone and pit contexts at Tioga Point Farm and a few other sites around the Chemung/Susquehanna confluence at Athens, Pennsylvania, however, has been variously described by different scholars as Cayuga Horizontal, Richmond Incised, and Proto-Susquehannock Incised (see Lucy and Vanderpoel 1979), leading one to question which types are actually valid. In fact, it is virtually impossible to distinguish these types from a handful of mixed grit-tempered incised sherds (see MacNeish 1952; Niemczycki 1984; Pratt 1960). This typology problem is not entirely unique to Upper Susquehanna pottery, as researchers working elsewhere in the Northeast have discovered when attempting to link Iroquoian-like ceramics to other ethnic groups (Brumbach 1975; Pratt 1960; Smith 1973).

We know practically nothing of the architecture of North Branch tradition Chance-phase households, although their houses must have been comparable to those at Iroquoian sites in New York (Funk and Kuhn 2003; Ritchie and Funk 1973; Tuck 1971) and the tribal groups living in the Upper Delaware Valley (Kinsey 1972; Kraft 1975, 2001; Puniello 1980). Avocational archaeologists report uncovering lines of post molds on some of the Wyoming Valley sites where Chance-phase pottery and trumpet and face pipes have been found. The latter human face forms (figure 2.11a, c) are diagnostic of the Chance phase (see Snow 1995: figure 3.27). Smith (1973) suggests some level of socio-religious continuity with the False Face Society of the northern Iroquoians, beginning as early as the Chance phase.

Ending the local North Branch tradition sequence are the sites ascribed to the Wyoming Valley Garoga phase (figure 2.6). In Onondaga / Oneida / Mohawk and Munsee territories, the Garoga phase is dated ca. AD 1525–80, when European metals arrive at native villages (Snow 1995). As with the Chance pottery/ pipe sequence, there appears to be a corresponding relationship with the Upper Susquehanna's Garoga/ Munsee lobed pottery (Brumbach 1975; Funk and Kuhn 2003; see also Kraft 2001: figure 7.61; Smith 1973: figures 29 and 32a) and some pipe styles of other contemporary northeastern groups (Kraft 2001). The similarity between Mohawk / Upper Delaware Valley Munsee and terminal stage material culture of North Branch tradition Iroquoians (part of Sweeney's [1966] *Wyoming Valley Complex*) is dramatic. In fact, the pottery types and their narrowly defined motifs, the trumpet and effigy face pipes, and the radiocarbon chronologies are closest to these groups than to any others.

Fortified settlements of the Wyoming Valley's Chance/Garoga phases were surrounded by multiple palisades (see Smith 1973: figures 5 and 30) like the Mohawk settlements of New York (Funk and Kuhn 2003; Snow 1995). The best evidence we have for this are the fortified settlements of Schacht and Parker that had a complex system of multiple palisades and ditch trenches (figure 2.13a–b), which poses an interesting question: Who were their enemies?

The pattern appears to have been quite different for the Munsee settlements on the Upper Delaware, where palisades were evidently unimportant considerations for the safety of the inhabitants (Kraft 2001). With few exceptions, the sites of the Transitional Iroquois through the Mohawk/Munsee continuum were confined to the east bank of the Delaware River, where the occupations were identified archaeologically by food pits containing pottery; traces of corn, beans, and squash; and butchered animals but few post mold patterns (Moeller 1992).

Judging from the archaeological excavations at the Schacht-Dundee and Parker sites, Chance/Garoga North Branch tradition houses were 60 to 80 feet long. These figures are in line with the shorter class of West Branch tradition longhouses of the "Intermediate"

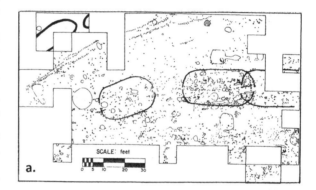

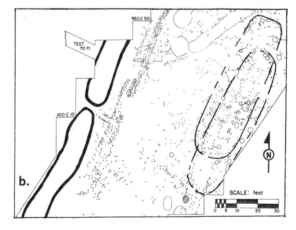

FIGURE 2.13

North Branch tradition (Wyoming Valley Complex) house patterns. a. Schacht site; b. Parker site. Courtesy of the State Museum of Pennsylvania, Pennsylvania Historical and Museum Commission.

through "Late" stages but smaller than their Iroquoian counterparts in New York. Several longhouses at the Schacht-Dundee and Parker sites had interior compartments with substantial side wall supports bordering hearths and a central corridor (figure 2.13a–b). Evidently, some dwellings were rebuilt during their span of use.

The community pattern of North Branch Valley settlements north of the Wyoming Valley is unknown, so village demographics cannot be addressed; nor has a refined chronology sequence of the settlements been adequately worked out. If, however, pottery styles can be judged as a temporally sensitive marker for the ethnogenic process, we might venture that a trend through time began with the earliest sites (Wermuth and Rusbar), followed by Schacht-Dundee and Parker, then ending with Shawnee Flats. (Note that Smith [1973], who was unaware of the Shawnee Flats village site, placed Schacht-Dundee as the latest site in the sequence, based on the preponderance of "lobed"

pottery and two small copper beads allegedly found on the site.) Hybridized Quiggle Incised rim sherds are reported from the Shawnee Flats site, suggesting a very late terminal Quiggle / Wyoming Valley occupation (Herbstritt 2014b). The Schacht-Dundee and Shawnee Flats villages are located at the lower end of the Wyoming Valley, their chronological lateness perhaps indicating a gradual downriver shift of Wyoming Valley settlements over time.

Radiocarbon dates from the Schacht-Dundee, Parker, and Shawnee Flats sites (table 2.2) place the Wyoming Valley Chance-Garoga pottery sequence occupations of the North Branch tradition in a period beginning in the early sixteenth century. The lateness of these sites is likely comparable to those of the Mohawk heartland and other tribal areas of Iroquoia, where sites encompassing the Protohistoric Garoga phase suggest that the first evidence of worked copper at native settlements was no earlier than the early sixteenth century (see, for example, Snow 1995:144).

TABLE 2.2   Radiocarbon dates from Susquehanna Valley Late Woodland / Protohistoric sites

Site name	Site number	C-14 date	Lab number	Calib 7.0 median probability	Component phase	Citation
Blackman	36Br83	545±55	A-12220	AD 1383	Chance/Garoga	Herbstritt (2020)
Blackman	36Br83	465±75	A-12221	AD 1448	Chance/Garoga	Herbstritt (2020)
Blackman	36Br83	410±60	Beta-20200	AD 1499	Chance/Garoga	McCracken and Lucy (1989)
Blackman	36Br83	350±65	A-12219	AD 1550	Chance/Garoga	Herbstritt (2020)
Dundee	36Lu11	680±60 BP	Beta-87328	AD 1313	Transitional Iroquois	Herbstritt (2020)
Dundee	36Lu11	620±70	Beta-48221	AD 1347	Transitional Iroquois	Herbstritt (2020)
Dundee	36Lu11	510±45	AA-35924	AD 1415	Quiggle	Herbstritt (2020)
Hegarty-Bell	36Cd34	632±83	AA-86832	AD 1343	Stewart	Herbstritt (2020)
Hegarty-Bell	36Cd34	615±70	Pitt—0000	AD 1348	Stewart	Herbstritt (2020)
Hegarty-Bell	36Cd34	591±37	AA-86829	AD 1348	Stewart	Herbstritt (2020)
Hegarty-Bell	36Cd34	562±69	AA-67348	AD 1363	Stewart	Herbstritt (2020)
Hegarty-Bell	36Cd34	550±90	A-10716	AD 1379	Stewart	Herbstritt (2020)
Hegarty-Bell	36Cd34	500±110	AA-86833	AD 1427	Stewart	Herbstritt (2020)
Hegarty-Bell	36Cd34	424±30	AA-86834	AD 1456	Quiggle	Herbstritt (2020)
Hegarty-Bell	36Cd34	405±29	AA-86828	AD 1470	Quiggle	Herbstritt (2020)
Hegarty-Bell	36Cd34	412±36	AA-67347	AD 1472	Quiggle	Herbstritt (2020)
Hegarty-Bell	36Cd34	430±110	DIC-1898	AD 1498	Quiggle	Herbstritt, 1988:9
Hegarty-Bell	36Cd34	367±29	AA-86831	AD 1517	Quiggle	Herbstritt (2020)
Hegarty-Bell	36Cd34	380±130	DIC-1897	AD 1550	Quiggle	Herbstritt, 1988:9
Kalgren	36Cd7	755±40	Pitt-0299	AD 1258	Kalgren-Bell	Herbstritt (2020)

Site name	Site number	C-14 date	Lab number	Calib 7.0 median probability	Component phase	Citation
Kalgren	36Cd7	740±60	DIC-1894	AD 1264	Kalgren-Bell	Herbstritt, 1988:9
Kalgren	36Cd7	740±60	Beta-53148	AD 1264	Kalgren-Bell	Herbstritt (2020)
Kalgren	36Cd7	530±50	DIC-1895	AD 1400	Chance/Quiggle	Herbstritt (1988:9)
Kalgren	36Cd7	500±50	Pitt-0298	AD 1419	Chance/Quiggle	Herbstritt (2020)
Kalgren	36Cd7	500±26	AA-75027	AD 1424	Chance/Quiggle	Herbstritt (2020)
Kalgren	36Cd7	487±69	AA-75029	AD 1428	Chance/Quiggle	Herbstritt (2020)
Kalgren	36Cd7	480±32	AA-75030	AD 1430	Chance/Quiggle	Herbstritt (2020)
Kalgren	36Cd7	465±47	AA-75025	AD 1438	Chance/Quiggle	Herbstritt (2020)
Kalgren	36Cd7	470±70	Beta-62853	AD 1442	Chance/Quiggle	Herbstritt (2020)
Kalgren	36Cd7	450±70	Beta-77496	AD 1462	Chance/Quiggle	Herbstritt (2020)
Kalgren	36Cd7	402±26	AA-75028	AD 1469	Chance/Quiggle	Herbstritt (2020)
Kalgren	36Cd7	420±60	Beta-20203	AD 1488	Chance/Quiggle	Herbstritt (1988:9)
Kalgren	36Cd7	410±60	Beta-67430	AD 1499	Chance/Quiggle	Herbstritt (2020)
Kalgren	36Cd7	280±50	Beta-20202	AD 1585	Quiggle	Herbstritt (1988:9)
Kalgren	36Cd7	265±40	Pitt-0550	AD 1631	Quiggle	Herbstritt (2020)
Kalgren	36Cd7	255±70	Pitt-1262	AD 1647	Quiggle	Herbstritt (2020)
Maurice	36Br245	480±40	Beta-172458	AD 1430	Chance	AD Marble and Company (2003)
Packers Island	36Nb27	618±37	AA-80400	AD 1348	Stewart	Herbstritt (2020)
Parker	36Lu14	710±50	A-12225	AD 1285	Transitional Iroquois	Herbstritt (2020)
Parker	36Lu14	700±45	A-12226	AD 1291	Transitional Iroquois	Herbstritt (2020)
Parker	36Lu14	690±55	A-12227	AD 1303	Transitional Iroquois	Herbstritt (2020)
Parker	36Lu14	575±35	A-12223	AD 1349	Chance/Garoga	Herbstritt (2020)
Parker	36Lu14	500±35	Pitt-0661	AD 1423	Chance/Garoga	Herbstritt (2020)
Parker	36Lu14	480±90	I-4880	AD 1439	Chance/Garoga	Buckley and Willis (1972)
Parker	36Lu14	450±45	A-12224	AD 1446	Chance/Garoga	Herbstritt (2020)
Parker	36Lu14	350±90	I-4881	AD 1557	Garoga	Buckley and Willis (1972)
Parker	36Lu14	345±95	Pitt-0662	AD 1562	Garoga	Herbstritt (2020)
Parker	36Lu14	250±90	I-4879	AD 1661	Garoga	Buckley and Willis (1972)
Pinnacle Rock Shelter	36EL49	663±34	AA-75024	AD 1324	Stewart	Herbstritt (2020)
Piper Airport 1	36Cn210	730±60	Beta-136222	AD 1272	Stewart/Owasco	Payne (2000)
Piper Airport 1	36Cn210	590±60	Beta-151167	AD 1352	Stewart	Payne (2000)
Piper Airport 1	36Cn210	560±60	Beta-136220	AD 1362	Stewart	Payne (2000)
Piper Airport 1	36Cn210	540±60	Beta-134673	AD 1387	Stewart	Payne (2000)
Piper Airport 1	36Cn210	420±60	Beta-136219	AD 1488	Quiggle	Payne (2000)
Piper Airport 1	36Cn210	420±70	Beta-136221	AD 1495	Quiggle	Payne (2000)
Piper Airport 1	36Cn210	420±80	Beta-134670	AD 1500	Quiggle	Payne (2000)
Piper Airport 1	36Cn210	380±50	Beta-134797	AD 1520	Quiggle	Payne (2000)
Piper Airport 1	36Cn210	370±60	Beta-13471	AD 1536	Quiggle	Payne (2000)
Piper Airport 1	36Cn210	590±70	Beta-134672	AD 1353	Stewart	Payne (2000)
Quiggle	36Cn6	690±30	Pitt-0667	AD 1291	Stewart/Owasco	Herbstritt (2020)
Quiggle	36Cn6	585±30	A-15280	AD 1346	Stewart	Herbstritt (2020)
Quiggle	36Cn6	500±40	A-10714	AD 1422	Quiggle	Herbstritt (2020)
Quiggle	36Cn6	455±40	A-15282	AD 1441	Quiggle	Herbstritt (2020)
Quiggle	36Cn6	430±50	A-10715	AD 1469	Quiggle	Herbstritt (2020)
Quiggle	36Cn6	390±40	Pitt-0666	AD 1502	Quiggle	Herbstritt (2020)
Quiggle	36Cn6	355±35	A-15278	AD 1547	Quiggle	Herbstritt (2020)

(continued)

TABLE 2.2 *(continued)*

Site name	Site number	C-14 date	Lab number	Calib 7.0 median probability	Component phase	Citation
Quiggle	36Cn6	335±45	A-15281	AD 1556	Quiggle	Herbstritt (2020)
Quiggle	36Cn6	295±35	A-15279	AD 1566	Quiggle	Herbstritt (2020)
Quiggle Flats	36Cn6	710±40	A-13724	AD 1283	Stewart/Owasco	Herbstritt (2020)
Shawnee Flats	36Lu9	800±40	AA-35926	AD 1232	Stewart/Owasco	Herbstritt (2020)
Shawnee Flats	36Lu9	680±60	Beta-87328	AD 1313	Stewart/Owasco	Herbstritt (2020)
Shawnee Flats II	36Lu175	535±50	A-14056	AD 1396	Chance/Garoga	Herbstritt (2020)
Shawnee Flats II	36Lu175	350±45	A-15276	AD 1559	Susquehannock	Herbstritt (2020)
Simmons-Nash	36Cn17	455±50	A-13695	AD 1445	Quiggle	Herbstritt (2020)
Simmons-Nash	36Cn17	860±90	Beta-98777	AD 1160	Kalgren-Bell/Owasco	Herbstritt (2020)
Simmons-Nash	36Cn17	860±85	A-12044	AD 1161	Kalgren-Bell/Owasco	Herbstritt (2020)
Simmons-Nash	36Cn17	835±90	A-13894	AD 1179	Stewart/Owasco	Herbstritt (2020)
Simmons-Nash	36Cn17	750±50	A-12047	AD 1259	Stewart	Herbstritt (2020)
Simmons-Nash	36Cn17	740±85	A-13891	AD 1261	Stewart	Herbstritt (2020)
Simmons-Nash	36Cn17	745±40	A-12418	AD 1264	Stewart	Herbstritt (2020)
Simmons-Nash	36Cn17	675±40	A-12417	AD 1311	Stewart	Herbstritt (2020)
Simmons-Nash	36Cn17	520±45	A-12045	AD 1410	Quiggle	Herbstritt (2020)
Simmons-Nash	36Cn17	495±45	A-13241	AD 1423	Quiggle	Herbstritt (2020)
Simmons-Nash	36Cn17	495±45	A-11295	AD 1423	Quiggle	Herbstritt (2020)
Simmons-Nash	36Cn17	470±45	A-11296	AD 1435	Quiggle	Herbstritt (2020)
Simmons-Nash	36Cn17	390±40	A-15092	AD 1502	Quiggle	Herbstritt (2020)
Simmons-Nash	36Cn17	375±35	A-13696	AD 1513	Quiggle	Herbstritt (2020)
Simmons-Nash	36Cn17	365±50	A-11297	AD 1538	Quiggle	Herbstritt (2020)
Simmons-Nash	36Cn17	410±40	A-15066	AD 1540	Quiggle	Herbstritt (2020)
Simmons-Nash	36Cn17	340±45	A-12046	AD 1554	Quiggle	Herbstritt (2020)
Tioga Point Farm	36Br3	493±38	AA-86835	AD 1425	Chance/Cayuga	Herbstritt (2020)
Wilson Fairgrounds	36Br58	340±40	Beta-172893	AD 1556	Susquehannock	A. D. Marble & Co. (2003)

Iroquoians and the Biodiversity of the Glaciated Plateau

The "Endless Mountains" is an eighteenth-century cartographic description of the Glaciated High Plateau / Glaciated Pocono Plateau (figures 2.1 and 2.4) bordering the Deep Valleys section and the southern edge of the valley and ridge of extreme northern Pennsylvania. The earliest cartographic reference to the region is found on the 1755 and 1759 Lewis Evans maps and the slightly later William Scull map (1770), which, with its greater detail, locates "a Pine Swamp" and "Great Swamp" here (figure 2.1). The Lackawaxen, Lehigh, and Lackawanna headwaters emanating from the Great Swamp linked key Indian paths between the

Upper Susquehanna and the Upper/Middle Delaware (Smith 1973; Wallace 1965). Today, as in prehistory, one might characterize the general region as a large wilderness rich in wetlands with an extremely high biotic density. Here, the plateau is pocked with small kettle lakes, swamps, and open meadowland modified by thousands of years of late glacial activity that created an exceptionally diverse habitat for creatures important to Native Americans in their quest for food and other life-sustaining resources. It is within these ecological settings that bears and other mammals were hunted for food and hides for clothing (Guilday and Parmalee 1965; Guilday, Parmalee, and Tanner 1962; Guilday and Tanner 1961; Webster 1983) The meadows and marshland of the Glaciated Plateau were also places where bear cubs were captured, taken back to the village, and penned for ritual use (Speck 1931). Elk, otter, fisher, marten, bobcat, wolf, fox, rabbit, muskrat, raccoon, and different species of birds, all significant members of the "creature community," were also used based on the butchered faunal evidence from North Branch tradition sites. Then as now, the region remains ecologically unique, as the carrying capacity of the Glaciated Plateau demonstrates. It should then come as no surprise that material objects of the Quiggle / Mohawk / Munsee people are associated with some rock shelter and campsites (Schrabisch 1926, 1930), as these specialized activity sites are located on or near old Indian paths (e.g., Smith 1973; Wallace 1965).

With a growing native population in the Susquehanna Valley in the period leading up to and including the opening years of the fur trade, the hunting and trapping of mammals for their hides and fur must have accelerated among groups, with deer (Gramly 1977), otter, and beaver (van den Bogaert 1988) as principal targets. After the extirpation of beaver from Europe, parts of eastern North America became the primary source of felt for much of the hatting industry. Key to the success of the beaver pelt trade was the unbroken chain formed between local native groups, the middlemen, and the Europeans.

Access to the beaver population in northeastern Pennsylvania was through the Quiggle and Wyoming Valley peoples and later the Susquehannocks. Given the complex problems linked to outside competition, access to these remote hunting territories would have been discouraged and jealously guarded, and the absence of nucleated settlements on the Delaware's west bank or any of its tributaries into the "Great Swamp" may have served as warnings to outsiders—no trespassing, no hunting, and no unsolicited contact!

It may follow, then, that access to the east side of the Delaware River Valley was viewed differently with respect to the hunting and trapping rights of people living there, since small planned settlements seem to have been established along the river north of the Delaware Water Gap adjacent to other equally favorable hunting territories that were also prime resource locations (Kraft 1972; Kraft 1975:75–86). Habitation sites at most of these places contain pit features with debris resulting from different methods of food gathering and food processing activities (Moeller 1992).

The rise in shellfish collecting and consumption—inferred from the shell-filled pits at terminal Upper Delaware Valley and North Branch tradition site occupations—may indicate a periodic partial shifting from the traditional subsistence pattern of taking great numbers of large mammals and practicing widespread "three sisters" agriculture to one based on the harvesting of shellfish of the genus *Elliptio* and small fin fish—river mussels, eels, and minnows—with a lesser reliance on traditional agriculture. Assuming that environmental risk was a major factor dictating the success or failure of maize crops during periods of drought and considering the widely variable weather conditions of the neo-Boreal climatic episode, a modified subsistence strategy focused on a greater variety of foods may have been the optimum strategy for a population's survival. Factoring climatic deterioration and the inherent problems of risky maize/beans/squash agriculture into the equation, local populations may have had to periodically expand their catchment zones into more isolated and more reliably productive areas where food resources were more abundant—in the present case, the Glaciated Plateau (Herbstritt 2014a).

The absence of large villages on the Delaware's west bank contrasts greatly with the presence of large palisaded villages in the Wyoming Valley, where identical kinds of pottery were being used and perhaps traded. The contrast in settlement patterns likely relates to variation in the different hunting/trapping strategies of Wyoming Valley and Munsee people, patterns that were dictated by climate, territory, and carrying capacity. Catchment zones closer to the Wyoming Valley may have at times embraced sections of the Glaciated Low Plateau west of the North Branch proper closer to the "Pine Swamp" (figure 2.1) for certain resources rather than the more remote Lackawanna, Lackawaxen, and Lehigh "Great Swamp" (figure 2.1) headwaters in the higher elevations of the Endless Mountains. These were likely the ecological forces that lured native groups to the hinterlands of the Upper Susquehanna drainage basin.

Ethnogenesis and the Emergence of a New Culture

I am proposing here an ethnogenic tribal model for the emergence of a new culture following the abandonment of central and northern Pennsylvania by the West Branch and North Branch tradition people sometime in the first half of the sixteenth century. The model is partly based on the ceramic data assembled by Witthoft (1959) and others (Crannell 1970; McCracken and Lucy 1989). Witthoft, specifically, suggested that Cayuga Horizontal and Richmond Incised were the principal antecedents of Susquehannock pottery. More recently, Niemczycki (1984) challenged the relationship of Witthoft's Seneca/Cayuga to Proto-Susquehannock theory based on a reassessment of Seneca and Cayuga pottery and reopened the search for Susquehannock ancestry (see Gollup, chapter 1 in this volume).

While Witthoft's (1959) treatise is partially based on similarities between Seneca-Cayuga and Proto-Susquehannock pottery motifs, we should also note that he recognized the "slight local variability" in some of the pottery—that is, patterns with Mohawk/Munsee motifs also figured into his equation. Witthoft's (1959) hypothesis—that Proto-Susquehannock (Proto-Susquehannock Incised) pottery is a cognate of Schultz Susquehannock pottery—might be better defended if we replace the Seneca/Cayuga scenario with the motif variations evident in terminal Quiggle phase, West Branch tradition, high-collared, shell-tempered pottery and an amalgam of grit-tempered Cayuga Horizontal / Chance Incised / Garoga Incised wares that are not Seneca (figure 2.10). If this hypothesis can be proven, it follows that the mix of these

ceramic complexes would have had to form prior to the emergence of the Iroquois League, when ceramics over much of northern Iroquoia became more heterogeneous (see MacNeish 1952). We should note here that a central Pennsylvania / eastern Finger Lakes region event involving more geographically localized groups other than the Seneca, as Witthoft (1959) suggested, is a better fit for an ethnogenic tribal model for the Susquehannocks (figure 2.6).

Circumstances leading up to an ethnogenic event in northern Pennsylvania involving local tribal groups must have been, in part, based on periodic conflict impelled by a combination of environmental, ideological, and/or social causes. The calamitous social discord among early sixteenth-century northern Iroquoians changed the cultural landscape of the Iroquoian world forever. As pointed out by Snow (1994:54), "Feuding and warfare, both internal and external, [went into rampant turmoil], leading the [northern Iroquoians] into endless cycles of feuding, where every death led to an act of revenge that would in turn require its own vengeance." These words may well apply to northern Pennsylvania, where the terminal West Branch and North Branch tradition tribal groups evolved into new ones.

It may be posited that as some hostilities between the West Branch and North Branch groups calmed and perhaps even disappeared completely, this encouraged the possibility of trade and mate exchange, eventually leading to the intertribal cooperation and alliances that grew among some groups by the early sixteenth century (figure 2.14). In fact, there is ample evidence in the archaeological record that Quiggle-phase females were potting at Wyoming Valley Chance/Garoga-phase settlements and vice versa by the very early sixteenth century (see Smith 1973:52, 1984:27).

The First Susquehannocks

By the early sixteenth century, the traces of the Quiggle (West Branch tradition) and Wyoming Valley

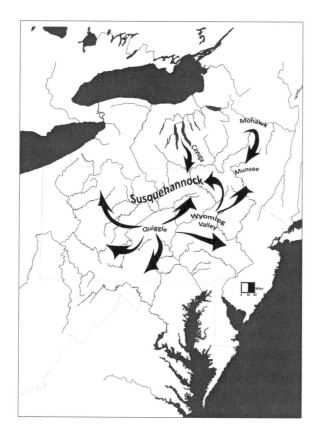

FIGURE 2.14
Terminal Late Woodland and Proto-Contact cultures' interactions in the Susquehanna Valley, AD 1500–1550/1575

Susquehanna, Upper Delaware, and elsewhere (figure 2.14; see Kraft 2001: figure 7.67; Schrabisch 1930; Staats 1979, 1986a, 1986b). These events coincide with a bifurcation involving splintered and displaced communities whose tribal ethnicity remained largely unaffected by the emergent Susquehannocks, who then shifted southward and eastward. The movement is suggested by the very late AMS dates for Quiggle hybrid ceramics from Sheep Rock Shelter, the terminal Quiggle-phase dates from the Kalgren and Bell settlements, and the contemporary-looking Quiggle-phase pottery from rock shelters and a few other village sites in the West Branch headwaters. The depiction of the Jotticas, Capitannesses, and Gachoos on early seventeenth-century Dutch maps (Stokes 1915–28) might suggest a connection with some of these archaeologically obscure groups from the central region of Pennsylvania after the formation of the Iroquois League. Did such groups contribute to the genetic mix of Penn's "Susquehannough Indians" at the Conestoga town some seven decades later?

To be certain, shifting populations left a cultural vacuum in much of the West Branch Valley and parts of the North Branch Valley until the early eighteenth century, when displaced refugee groups from the Chesapeake region briefly settled there before also moving away. A possible explanation for these settlement fragmentations and dispersals is offered in the final section of the chapter.

Although the earliest forms of Schultz Incised, composed of sherds from a few pots, are from the Pepper and Morse Farms on Towanda Creek and the Rockwell Farm on Sugar Creek, the Pepper II site on Pepper's farm is the only site that has been archaeologically investigated (Stowell 1988). Hybridized shell-tempered, incised, collared pottery exhibiting Quiggle and Cayuga-Chance and Garoga motifs and classic Schultz Susquehannock pottery were comingled in a few pits at this small habitation site. Surface collections from three additional sites, also located in the Towanda Creek headwaters near Canton, Pennsylvania, have yielded incised, shell-tempered,

(North Branch tradition) people fade to near obscurity. Some of their grit- and shell-tempered pottery, however, survived at a few dispersed habitation sites in isolated regions of northern Pennsylvania and the Upper Delaware (table 2.1). The trek through the rugged region of the "Dismal Vale" and the Sheshequin Indian path (Wallace 1965) was a difficult one, as lamented by eighteenth-century travelers (see, for example, Bartram 1751). Nevertheless, the route was direct, linking the western headwaters of Towanda and Sugar Creeks near Canton, Pennsylvania, with the central West Branch Valley and the Cayuga territory to the north with the upper North Branch Valley (figure 2.1).

I hypothesize that in the early sixteenth century, the West Branch and North Branch populations, now a multicultural, merged society (the Susquehannocks), spread outward to the rugged headwaters of the Upper and grit-tempered pottery of hybridized terminal Quiggle and Cayuga forms. These ceramics are believed to characterize similar Proto-Susquehannock occupations. None of the Towanda Creek or Sugar Creek sites, however, have yielded objects of the early European trade, nor, because of their small size, do any of them appear to have been palisaded. The pattern generally reflects the settlement archaeology of the earliest Schultz-phase site occupations at and near the Chemung / North Branch Susquehanna confluence as described by Witthoft (1959).

Community pattern data for the descendants of the West Branch and North Branch traditions, who I propose were the Susquehannocks, are astonishingly sparse in stark contrast to that from older native settlements in the Susquehanna Valley. We do not know, for example, whether the earliest Susquehannocks were residing entirely in small, unplanned communities during their tenure in the Susquehanna's North Branch Valley, as postulated by Witthoft (1959), or were living in large palisaded communities like their West Branch and Wyoming Valley predecessors (Herbstritt 2020).

Since Witthoft's summary (1959) on the early Susquehannocks, one site has been explored that adds a piece to the settlement pattern puzzle. After the Agnes Flood of 1972, a Kings College field school salvaged the remains of three semiflexed skeletons along with early Schultz Incised pottery and a few brass objects from the Kennedy (36BR43) site. Later, in 1975, the Pennsylvania Historical and Museum Commission (PHMC) returned to the site (B. Kent 1984:305) and conducted additional investigations that identified another semiflexed skeleton with an early Schultz Incised pot placed on its chest along with three feather quill sheaths of copper (figure 2.15c). In expanding the area around Kings College's excavations, PHMC staff uncovered the post mold pattern of a longhouse (figure 2.12b) that was architecturally like the late Wyoming Valley Chance-Garoga-phase houses at the Schacht-Dundee and Parker sites (see Smith 1973) and was probably the remains of an early Susquehannock dwelling. This suggests that small, single-family

units were probably the norm, supporting Witthoft's (1959) claim that the early Susquehannock houses were placed in a loosely organized fashion on river floodplains.

Earliest European Trade Goods in the Susquehanna Valley

Objects of the European trade were filtering inland from the St. Lawrence Valley by the early sixteenth century (Biggar 1965; Bradley 1987:100–102; Tuck and Grenier 1989). On the earliest proto-Contact Iroquoian sites, these objects are typically little more than nondescript scraps of copper or brass. By the early seventeenth century, the variety of European material increases to include iron tools, glass beads, and other functional items that native groups found useful to possess. Although there could well be exceptions (see Beisaw, chapter 3 in this volume), the general rule is that sites with few trade goods are usually earlier in time than sites with abundant trade goods. Scholars have adopted these basic criteria to gauge the rise in trade goods through time and to develop proto-Contact to Contact period settlement sequences of the tribal groups possessing such objects (Bradley 1987; B. Kent 1984; Pratt 1961; Snow 1995; Wray and Schoff 1953). Applying these criteria to the Upper Susquehanna region (Dunbar and Ruhl 1974; Elliott and Lipe 1970), we can begin to reconstruct a picture of indirect trade in material goods among native groups beginning in the middle to latter decades of the sixteenth century. It may follow, then, that the Susquehannocks, who were already in the Upper Susquehanna region, were also trading in the Upper/Middle Delaware Valleys, as evidenced by the earliest forms of Susquehannock pottery there (Fehr 1967; Forks of the Delaware Chapter 14 1980; Freyermuth and Staats 1992).

Following initial indirect contact with native middlemen, loosely formed trade alliances would have been politically and economically defined—one as favorable, leading to a Huron/Susquehannock alliance, and another in discord, dead-ending with the Five Nations Iroquois. Consequently, the Susquehannock's relocation to the Lower Susquehanna was a solution for avoiding competition and conflict with other northern Iroquoians and their Algonquian neighbors. They were drawn toward the English on Chesapeake Bay after AD 1550 (B. Kent 1984).

The trade in metal objects between interior populations by the early to mid-sixteenth century coincides with the disappearance of terminal Wyoming Valley Complex communities. Smith (1973) and B. Kent (1984) postulated that the Bradford County Susquehannocks, in their southward sweep, were subjugators of the Quiggle-phase people. A reconfiguring of this scenario may now be considered. Could it be that the ethnogenic assimilation of Quiggle and Wyoming Valley groups was the catalyst for further assimilation through aggression? Could it also be that such an event found a place in the oral traditions of remnant Wyoming Valley Garoga-phase Iroquoians from the survivors who fled the valley to other parts of Iroquoia? Certainly, these are possibilities ripe for consideration in what led to war between the Five Nations Iroquois and the Susquehannocks years later (see, for example, Jennings 1968:23). Whatever the case, the aftermath opened a major cultural vacuum in the Susquehanna Valley that lasted about a century, during which time the valley became a principal warpath of the Susquehannocks and other Iroquoians.

Some interior native groups had only limited access to European manufactured goods by the early sixteenth century. Few trade goods made their way into the Susquehanna Valley before the first quarter of the sixteenth century. Two brass beads allegedly found in a cylindrical pit on the Schacht-Dundee site (Smith 1973) are the only objects of metal that may have come from a terminal Wyoming Valley Complex context. Radiocarbon dates from the Parker site and Shawnee Flats site (table 2.2) fit with the Wyoming Valley's terminal Garoga pottery period, which dovetails nicely with the first evidence of trade copper on the eastern margin of Iroquoia (Snow 1995:144).

The terminal West Branch tradition's Quiggle-phase occupations at the Hegarty-Bell, Quiggle-Lapp, and Simmons-Nash sites have each yielded a few copper and brass objects. One long and four short rolled beads of copper at the Hegarty-Bell (a.k.a. Bell) site were associated with two features, and another stray bead was picked up from the surface (Matlack 1986: figure 21). There are two cut brass scraps from Stratum II in the ditch-trench middens at the Quiggle-Lapp (a.k.a. Quiggle) site that also yielded hybridized Quiggle Incised / Schultz Incised and Schultz Incised pottery (Herbstritt 2014b). The scant few objects of copper or brass from the contents of two burials at the Simmons-Nash site consist of a large rolled bead, four smaller rolled beads, and a miniature ring coil (figure 2.15d), all crafted from tightly rolled copper or brass (Herbstritt 2014b). Here again, the antiquity of these objects from terminal West Branch Valley sites appears to be no earlier than the early sixteenth century and, therefore, clearly proto-Contact.

European-derived trade goods—principally, spiral pendants, tubular beads, feather quill sheaths of rolled copper or brass, or rarely, glass beads—are reported from the earliest Shultz-phase Susquehannock settlements centered on the Chemung/Susquehanna confluence, from Athens, Pennsylvania, to the southern end of Tioga County, New York (Herbstritt 2014b; B. Kent 1984: figure 51; Lucy 1950; Stewart 1973; Witthoft 1959:29).

Although few of the Upper Susquehanna Schultz-phase sites had metal trade goods (Crannell 1970), those that did had rolled beads, hoops, spirals (figure 2.15e), and scraps of copper or brass (Dunbar and Ruhl 1974). Type IIa40 glass beads (Crannell 1970) of the Glass Bead Period I are exceedingly rare, as are textiles (figure 2.15a), wrought iron tools (figure 2.15b), and other ferrous objects (Herbstritt 2014c). Taken together, these objects provide only a glimpse of the classes of material that the Susquehannocks desired in the early period of indirect trade with Europeans. Not surprising, these sites are strategically located very near the Susquehannock's hunting and trapping

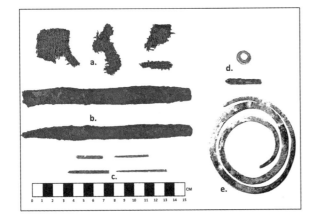

FIGURE 2.15

Organic and metal objects of the terminal Quiggle-phase and early Schultz-phase Susquehannock. a. textile, Queen Ester's Flats; b. two views of a wrought-iron chisel, Queen Esther's Flats; c. copper sheaths and preserved feather quills, Kennedy site; d. ring coil and rolled bead of copper/brass, Simmons-Nash site; e. spiral of sheet-cut copper/brass, Queen Esther's Flats. Courtesy of the State Museum of Pennsylvania, Pennsylvania Historical and Museum Commission.

territory of the Endless Mountains, where they could obtain animal pelts.

Disappearing Shenks Ferrians, Pathogens, and Migrating Susquehannocks

As early as 1525, the Spanish explorer Pedro de Quexos visited the Chesapeake region and may have gone as far as the Delaware estuary (Hoffman 1990), although it is not known how far he probed these waters nor the identities of the native groups he encountered—here the record falls silent. The Spanish established the first Jesuit mission colony in the Chesapeake Bay area in 1570–71 but abruptly ended their mission there after the murder of Father Segura and other Jesuits at the native village of Ajac'an, which is believed to have been situated on the York River in Virginia (Lewis and Loomie 1953; Mallios 2006).

The period of intermittent contact between native peoples and Europeans on the eastern coast of North America threatened death and destruction to large segments of the native population whose settlements dotted the late sixteenth-century landscape. To what degree and extent did short-term droughts (Blanton 2003, 2004) and European-borne pathogens affect virgin soil populations of the Susquehanna-Delaware interior? For now, answering these questions requires more data (see Herrmann 2011; Kelso 2006). We may infer, however, some of the impact by reviewing the account of Englishman Thomas Hariot of the Roanoke Colony (Quinn 1955).

After erecting a fort on Roanoke Island, the English colonists made three visits to native settlements at the tip of the Delmarva Peninsula. These visitations appear to coincide with several outbreaks of disease that ended with the deaths of many natives. North of these settlements, above the fall line at Port Deposit, Maryland, lay the southern boundary of Shenks Ferry territory. These Shenks Ferry peoples might well have witnessed, or experienced firsthand, the effects of pathogenic outbreaks due to their proximity to Chesapeake Bay (figure 2.16). The marine shell trade that had existed for centuries (see, for example, Bradley 2011; Sempowski 1989) likely facilitated the spread of disease along the Susquehanna pathway to the interior at this time. Certainly, the quantity of marine shell associated with terminal Shenks Ferry sites is notable, leading to the hypothesis that by the early sixteenth century, if not earlier, some of the Luray-phase people from the Chesapeake region who were active participants in the marine shell trade were vectors. In fact, some of these non–Shenks Ferry peoples relocated to the Lower Susquehanna Valley, where they were living at some of the Shenks Ferry communities: the Mohr and Locust Grove villages near Bainbridge, Pennsylvania, were two of their resettlements (Graybill and Herbstritt 2014; B. Kent 1984). Shifting populations of Luray-phase people from areas directly or indirectly affected by European-introduced infections would have had an enormous impact on local and regional populations of native peoples such as the Shenks Ferry groups, the Monongahela located farther west, and others north of them who had no previous exposure to the invisible killers (figure 2.16). These upriver transmissions had the potential for contributing significantly to the weakening and/or collapse of native societies in the upper Middle Atlantic and lower Northeast interior. The cultural vacancy thus inadvertently created was later filled by the southward migration of Susquehannocks from northern Pennsylvania.

The Susquehannock's downriver expansion reached the Potomac Valley by the late sixteenth century. Indeed, the archaeology suggests that their settlements there were short-lived and had ended by the first quarter of the seventeenth century (Brashler 1987; see Wall, chapter 5 in this volume). The abrupt presence and later absence of European metal objects and glass beads of the Period 1/2 stage hints at a major systems collapse that ended in the Susquehannock's

dispersal from the South Branch Valley (Kenyon and Kenyon 1983; Wall and Lapham 2003). Interestingly, it was also at this time that the Monongahela, located on the fringe of the lower Upper Ohio Valley, disappeared from the archaeological record. The causative factor again was likely the unexpected introduction of European pathogens onto virgin soil (Herbstritt 2003). Following the "great dispersal" from the Potomac Valley, the remaining Susquehannocks went in various directions, with some relocating northward to resettle at the Schultz / Washington Boro sites on the Lower Susquehanna (figure 2.17).

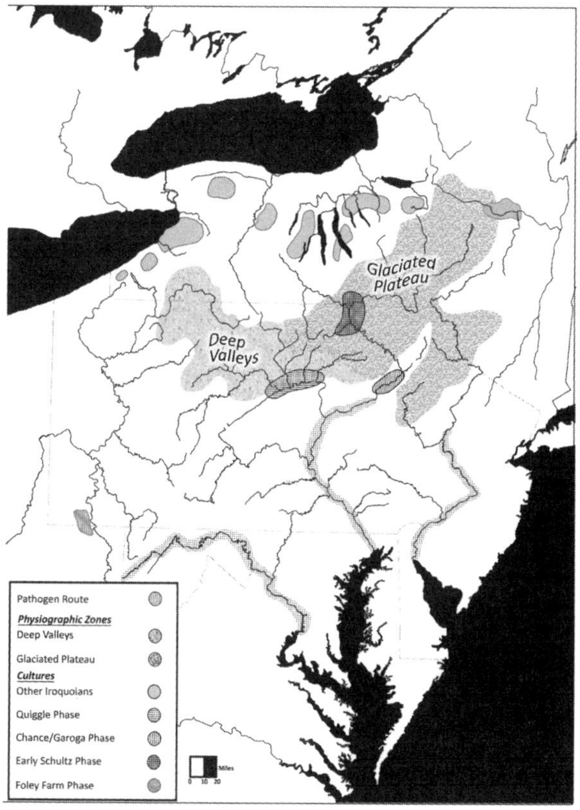

Conclusions

The West Branch and North Branch traditions were parallel cultural developments centered in northcentral and northern Pennsylvania. Beginning in the early thirteenth century and lasting into the early sixteenth century, peoples of both traditions practiced a seasonally scheduled subsistence economy, one principally based on maize-bean agriculture and the hunting and gathering of wild plants and animals. This is a pattern observed over much of Pennsylvania and other

61

FIGURE 2.16
Generalized location of sixteenth-century native groups and hypothesized pathogen routes via Chesapeake and Delaware Bays

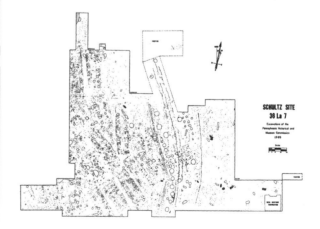

FIGURE 2.17
Schultz site settlement plan, 1969 Pennsylvania Historical and Museum Commission excavations. Schultz-Susquehannock phase, ca. AD 1575–1600. Courtesy of the State Museum of Pennsylvania, Pennsylvania Historical and Museum Commission.

regions of the Middle Atlantic and Northeast at this time (Dent 1995; Funk 1993; Michels 1968).

Punctuated droughts linked to the Little Ice Age from ca. 1350–1550 through the early 1600s affected the growth cycle of maize and other domesticates. In certain regions of Pennsylvania, as elsewhere, the risk factors associated with growing domesticated plant foods over this 300-year period likely determined whether populations coalesced or fissioned. The model presented here suggests two possible scenarios: (1) smaller dispersed groups returned to their parent villages as conditions improved or (2) some groups returned to their parent villages, leaving others to form new villages and thus create the multivillage system of northern Iroquoians.

Settlements of the West Branch and North Branch traditions grew from small unprotected open hamlets composed of a few houses spread out over the landscape (Hatch 1980) to large nucleated settlements with fortified palisades and ditches built in upland and valley settings (Herbstritt 2020). Valley settlements were generally located on or near well-drained soils. Over time, soils depleted through repeated farming were rejuvenated by periodic flooding of the valley. Farmsteads, linked to larger habitation sites located elsewhere, were placed at strategic locations within certain microenvironments to take advantage of longer frost-free growing periods, thereby potentially reducing the risk of crop failures.

On the eastern fringe of the Allegheny plateau, there were village reoccupations within these microenvironments. The earliest Kalgren-Bell-phase sites were located on hilltops overlooking drainage basin divides and wetlands. Small habitations—farmsteads usually composed of one or two houses—were located on the narrow floodplains common to the Deep Valleys section and much of northeastern Pennsylvania's glaciated plateau. Large river confluences and places where smaller tributaries emptied into larger ones were preferred locations for not only farmstead and single-family habitations but also larger, nucleated, and palisaded settlements.

Microenvironments were critical niches to native groups of the Susquehanna Valley for the propagation/ procurement of plant and animal foods and products used in the manufacture of tools and clothing. In northern Pennsylvania and adjacent areas of the Glaciated Low Plateau and the Glaciated Pocono Plateau, lakes and other wetland-related settings were places visited by hunting and gathering parties. Archaeological evidence from rock shelters and small campsites suggests that these activities were shared by males and females. Depending on the activity, an entire nuclear family or groups of nuclear families might participate. The strategy and situation determined who participated in the activity. For example, males might hunt game such as deer, elk, and other large mammals, whereas females might trap, fish, or gather foods, which would require a different strategy. Males and females periodically shared these tasks depending on the situation, such as the participation of individuals of mixed ages and genders in large hunt drives (see, for example, Fenton 1942; Fenton and Deardorff 1943).

In the Susquehanna's North and West Branch Valleys, European trade goods only began to show up at the beginning of the sixteenth century. Exceedingly rare, they were restricted to small scraps of sheet copper or brass. By the mid-sixteenth century, these metals were turned into coils, rolled tubes, and scraps with perforations, all objects of personal adornment. Glass beads and iron tools were even rarer, and there are only two instances where these objects have been identified conclusively as having early Susquehannock associations: several bluish-green glass beads from the Susquehannock cemetery at the Engelbert site and an iron chisel pike from a Susquehannock burial at Queen Esther's Flats.

By the third quarter of the sixteenth century, the Susquehannocks had moved their settlements to the Lower Susquehanna, south of Blue Mountain, and, for a brief period (ca. 1600–1630), to the Potomac Valley.

What happened to the Potomac-bound Susquehannocks after that is unknown. Some surely succumbed to disease or were assimilated into other tribes. Others may have returned north to the Susquehanna Valley, where they remained as part of a larger Susquehannock society. Seventeenth-century English, French, and Dutch maps provide tantalizing hints that tribal groups occupied portions of the Susquehanna Valley north of Blue Mountain, but archaeological confirmation is lacking despite diligent searches (Griffin 1931; Hunter 1983; D. Kent 1976; B. Kent 1984; McCracken 1985; O'Callaghan 1853–87; Sorg 2003, 2004; Stokes 1915–28; Twigg 2005). The bigger question has many facets. Who were these people? Did the mapmakers correctly locate their settlements? Did these obscure peoples and the places named in these documents play any role in Susquehannock culture history?

By the early eighteenth century, the Susquehannocks were collectively known as "Susquehannaugh Indians" or "Conestogas." As refugees drawn together from different parts of the Northeast and Middle Atlantic regions, their fate was determined by their interaction with Europeans and the desire for their material goods. Becoming Susquehannock was an event that began in the clouded history of northern Pennsylvania more than five centuries ago. Their history also shows that their end did not justify their means: as Barry Kent (1984:408; see also Beisaw, chapter 3 in this volume) cogently noted, "These interactions became paramount in directing the course of Susquehannock culture, eventually causing its extinction. By December 27, 1763, the Susquehannock way of life was officially and completely a thing of the past, relegated, as it were, to a few largely forgotten passages of contemporary accounts."

REFERENCES

AD Marble and Company
2003 *Alternative Mitigation to the Interstate Fairgrounds Site (36Br210): Athens Bridge Replacement Project, S.R. 1056, Section 001. Athens Township, Bradford County, Pennsylvania.* 2 vols. Report prepared for the Pennsylvania Department of Transportation, District 3-0. AD Marble and Company, Conshohocken, Pennsylvania.

Bartram, John
1751 *Observations on the Inhabitants, Climate, Soil, Rivers, Productions, Animals, and Other Matters Worthy of Notice Made by Mr. John Bartram in His Travels from Pensilvania to Onondago, Oswego and the Lake Ontario, in Canada.* Printed for J. Whiston and B. White, London.

Biggar, Henry P.
1965 *The Early Trading Companies of New France: A Contribution to the History of Commerce and Discovery in North America.* Argonaut Press, New York.

Blanton, Dennis B.
2003 If It's Not One Thing It's Another: The Added Challenges of Weather and Climate for the Roanoke Colony. In *Searching for the Roanoke Colonies: An Interdisciplinary Collection,* edited by E. Thomson Shields and Charles R. Ewen, 169–76. North Carolina Office of Archives and History, Raleigh.

2004 The Climate Factor in Late Prehistoric and Post-Contact Human Affairs in *Indian and European Contact in Context: The Mid-Atlantic Region.* Edited by Dennis B. Blanton and Julia A. King. University Press of Florida, Gainesville.

Bradley, James W.
1987 *Evolution of the Onondaga Iroquois: Accommodating Change 1500–1655.* Syracuse University Press, Syracuse, New York.

2007 *Before Albany: An Archaeology of Native-Dutch Relations in the Capital Region 1600–1664.* New York State Museum Bulletin 509, Albany.

2011 Re-visiting Wampum and Other Seventeenth-Century Shell Games. *Archaeology of Eastern North America* 39:25–51.

Brashler, Janet G.
1987 A Middle 16th Century Susquehannock Village in Hampshire County, West Virginia. *West Virginia Archeologist* 39 (2): 1–30.

Bressler, James P., and Harry D. Rainey
2003 *Excavations at the Snyder Site (36LY287).* North Central Chapter No. 8 of the Society for Pennsylvania Archaeology and the Lycoming County Historical Society, Williamsport. Paulhamus Litho, Williamsport, Pennsylvania.

Bressler, James P., and Karen Rockey

1997 *Tracking the Shenks Ferry Indians at the Ault Site 36LY120*. North Central Chapter No. 8 of the Society for Pennsylvania Archaeology and the Lycoming County Historical Society, Williamsport. Paulhamus Litho, Williamsport, Pennsylvania.

Brose, Patrick H., Richard P. Guyette, Joseph M. Marschall, and Michael C. Stambaugh

2015 Fire History Reflects Human History in the Pine Creek Gorge of North-Central Pennsylvania. *Natural Areas Journal* 35 (2): 214–23.

Brumbach, Hetty Jo

1975 "Iroquoian" Ceramics in "Algonkian" Territory. *Man in the Northeast* 10:17–28.

Buckley, J. D., and E. H. Willis

1972 Isotopes Radiocarbon Measurements IX. *Radiocarbon* 14 (1): 114–39.

Crannell, Marilyn C.

1970 *Shell Tempered Pottery Vessels from the Engelbert Site, Nichols, New York*. M.S. thesis, State University of New York, Binghamton.

Crawford, Gary W., and David G. Smith

1996 Migration in Prehistory: Princess Point and the Northern Iroquoian Case. *American Antiquity* 61 (4): 35–44.

Dent, Richard J.

1995 *Chesapeake Prehistory: Old Traditions, New Directions: Interdisciplinary Contributions to Archaeology*. Plenum Press, New York.

Dodd, Christine F., Dana R. Poulton, Paul A. Lennox, David G. Smith, and Gary A. Warrick

1990 The Middle Ontario Iroquoian Stage. In *The Archaeology of Southern Ontario to AD 1650*, edited by Chris J. Ellis and Neal Ferris, 321–60. London Chapter, Ontario Archaeological Society Occasional Publications 5, London, Ontario.

Dunbar, Helene R., and Katherine C. Ruhl

1974 Copper Artifacts from the Engelbert Site. *New York State Archaeological Association Bulletin* 61:1–25.

East, Thomas C., Christopher T. Espenshade, Kenneth W. Mohney, Margaret G. Sams, and Bryan C. Henderson

2006 *Phase I/II/III Archaeological Investigations*. Vol. 5, *Losey 1 Site (36TI 129), Losey 4 Site (36TI130) and Losey 3 Site (36TI128)*. Report prepared for the Federal Highway Administration and Pennsylvania Department of Transportation Engineering District 3-0. Skelly and Loy, Monroeville, Pennsylvania.

Elliott, Delores N., and William D. Lipe

1970 *The Engelbert Site*. Triple Cities Chapter, New York State Archaeological Association, Binghamton, New York.

Ellis, Chris J., and Neal Ferris (editors)

1990 *The Archaeology of Southern Ontario to AD 1650*. London Chapter, Ontario Archaeological Society Occasional Publications 5, London, Ontario.

Eshleman, Frank H.

1908 *Lancaster County Indians: Annals of the Susquehannocks and Other Indian Tribes of the Susquehanna Territory from About the Year 1500 to 1763, the Date of Their Extinction*. Express Printing Company, Lancaster, Pennsylvania.

Evans, Lewis

1755 *A General Map of the Middle British Colonies in North America*. J. Almon, London.

Fehr, Elinor R.

1967 *Cultural Interpretations of the Overpeck Site 36Bu5, Bucks County, Pennsylvania*. Unpublished manuscript, Moravian College, Bethlehem, Pennsylvania.

Fenton, William N.

1942 Fish Drives Among the Cornplanter Senecas. *Pennsylvania Archaeologist* 12 (3): 48–52.

Fenton, William N., and Merle H. Deardorff

1943 The Last Passenger Pigeon Hunts of the Cornplanter Senecas. *Journal of the Washington Academy of Sciences* 33 (10): 289–315.

Fenton, William N., and Elisabeth Tooker

1978 Mohawk. In *Northeast*, edited by B. G. Trigger, 466–80. Handbook of North American Indians 15. Smithsonian Institution, Washington, D.C.

Forks of the Delaware Chapter 14

1980 The Overpeck Site (26BU5). *Pennsylvania Archaeologist* 50 (3): 1–46.

Freyermuth, Doris A., and F. Dayton Staats

1992 A Supplementary Report on the Late Woodland Ceramics from the Overpeck Site (36BU5). *Pennsylvania Archaeologist* 62 (1): 53–61.

Funk, Robert E.

1993 *Archaeological Investigations in the Upper Susquehanna Valley, New York*. 2 vols. Persimmon Press Monographs in Archaeology, Buffalo, New York.

Funk, Robert E., and Robert D. Kuhn

2003 *Three Sixteenth Century Mohawk Iroquois Village Sites*. New York State Museum Bulletin 503, Albany.

Gramly, R. Michael

1977 Deer Skins and Hunting Territories: Competition for a Scarce Resource of the Northeastern Woodlands. *American Antiquity* 42:601–5.

Graybill, Jeffrey R.

1989 The Shenks Ferry Complex Revisited. In *New Approaches to Other Pasts*, edited by W. F. Kinsey and R. W. Moeller, 51–59. Archaeological Services, Bethlehem, Connecticut.

Graybill, Jeffrey R., and James T. Herbstritt

2014 The Luray Phase, Mohr (36LA39) and the Protohistoric Period. *Journal of Middle Atlantic Archaeology* 30:25–39.

Griffin, James B.

1931 *Griffin Excavations ms#1*, manuscript on file at the Section of Archaeology, The State Museum of Pennsylvania, Harrisburg.

Guilday, John E., and Paul W. Parmalee

1965 Animal Remains from the Sheep Rock Shelter (36HU1), Huntington County, Pennsylvania. *Pennsylvania Archaeologist* 35 (1): 34–49.

Guilday, John E., Paul W. Parmalee, and Donald P. Tanner

1962 Aboriginal Butchering Techniques at the Eschelman Site (36La12), Lancaster County, Pennsylvania. *Pennsylvania Archaeologist* 32 (2): 9–83.

Guilday, John E., and Don P. Tanner

1961 *Bone Refuse from the Sheep Rock Site Huntingdon County, Pennsylvania: 1961 Excavation by Pennsylvania State Museum*. Unpublished manuscript, Section of Archaeology, The State Museum of Pennsylvania, Harrisburg.

Hart, John P.

1999 Maize Agriculture Evolution in the Eastern Woodlands of North America: A Darwinian Perspective. *Journal of Archaeological Method and Theory* 6:137–80.

Hart, John P., and Hetty Jo Brumbach

2003 The Death of Owasco. *American Antiquity* 68 (4): 737–52.

Hart, John P., and William Engelbrecht

2011 Northern Iroquoian Ethnic Evolution: A Serial Network Analysis. *Journal of Archaeological Theory* 1 (9): 322–49.

2017 Revisiting Onondaga Iroquois Prehistory Through Social Network Analysis. In *Process and Meaning in Spatial Archaeology: Investigations into Pre-Columbian Iroquoian Space and Time*, edited by Eric E. Jones and John L. Creese, 189–214. University Press of Colorado, Boulder.

Hasenstab, Robert J., and William C. Johnson

2001 Hilltops of the Allegheny Plateau: A Preferred Microenvironment for Late Prehistoric Horticulturalists. In *Archaeology of the Appalachian Highlands*, edited by Lynne P. Sullivan and Susan C. Prezzano, 3–18. University of Tennessee Press, Knoxville.

Hatch, James W.

1980 A Synthesis and Prospectus of the Program's Late Woodland Research. In *The Fisher Farm Site: A Late Woodland Hamlet in Context*, edited by James W. Hatch, 320–28. The Pennsylvania State University, Department of Anthropology Occasional Papers 12, University Park.

Herbstritt, James T.

1988 A Reference for Pennsylvania Radiocarbon Dates. *Pennsylvania Archaeologist* 58 (2): 1–29.

2003 Foley Farm: The Importance of Architecture and the Demise of the Monongahelans. *Pennsylvania Archaeologist* 73 (1): 8–54.

2014a *Fortified Villages of the Susquehanna. Field and Laboratory Notes, 1978-2009*. Section of Archaeology, The State Museum of Pennsylvania, Harrisburg.

2014b *Field Notes: Quiggle-Lapp Site (36CN6) Excavations, 2005-2012*. Section of Archaeology, The State Museum of Pennsylvania, Harrisburg.

2014c *Field Notes: Simmons-Nash Site (36CN17) Excavations, 2001-2005*. Section of Archaeology, The State Museum of Pennsylvania, Harrisburg.

2020 Late Woodland Period in the Susquehanna and Upper Potomac Drainage Basins, AD 1100/50–1525/75. In *The Archaeology of Native Americans in Pennsylvania*, edited by Kurt W. Carr, Christopher A. Bergman, Christina Rieth, Bernard K. Means, Roger W. Moeller, and Elizabeth L. Wagner. Pennsylvania Historical and Museum Commission, Harrisburg. In press.

Herrmann, Rachel B.

2011 The "Tragicall Historie": Cannibalism and Abundance in Colonial Jamestown. *The William and Mary Quarterly* 68 (1): 47–74.

Hoffman, Paul E.

1990 *A New Andalucia and a Way to the Orient: The American Southeast During the Sixteenth Century*. Louisiana State University Press, Baton Rouge.

Hranicky, William Jack

1985 Virginia's First European Visitors. *Archaeological Society of Virginia. Quarterly Bulletin* 40 (4): 167–79.

Hunter, Charles E.

1983 A Susquehanna Indian Town on the Schuylkill. *Pennsylvania Archaeologist* 53 (3): 17–18.

Jennings, Francis

1968 Glory, Death and Transfiguration: The Susquehannock Indians in the Seventeenth Century. *Proceedings of the American Philosophical Society* 112 (1): 15–53.

1978 Susquehannock. In *Northeast*, edited by B. G. Trigger, 362–67. Handbook of North American Indians 15. Smithsonian Institution, Washington, D.C.

Johnson, William C.

1998 Chautauqua Cord-Marked, McFate Incised and Conemaugh Cord-Impressed Ceramic Types and the Terminal Late Woodland Period McFate Phase of the Glaciated Allegheny Plateau of Northwestern Pennsylvania. Paper presented in the Northern Ohio's Late Prehistory and Protohistory Symposium, Midwest Archaeological Conference, October 21–24, Muncie, Indiana.

2010 The Kirshner Site (36Wm213): A Preliminary Reassessment of a Multiple Monongahela Component Site. Paper presented at the 77th Annual Meeting of the Eastern States Archeological Federation, October 28–31, 2010, Williamsburg, Virginia.

Kelso, William M.

2006 *Jamestown: The Buried Past.* University of Virginia Press, Charlottesville.

Kent, Barry C.

1974 Locust Grove Pottery: A New Late Woodland Pottery. *Pennsylvania Archaeologist* 44 (4): 1–5.

1984 *Susquehanna's Indians.* Anthropological Series 6. Pennsylvania Historical and Museum Commission, Harrisburg.

Kent, Donald H.

1976 The Myth of Etienne Brule. *Pennsylvania History* 43 (4): 291–306.

Kenyon, Ian T., and Thomas Kenyon

1983 Comments on 17th-Century Glass Trade Beads from Ontario. In *Proceedings of the 1982 Glass Trade Bead Conference,* edited by Charles F. Hayes, 59–74. Research Records 16. Rochester Museum and Science Center, Rochester, New York.

Kinsey, W. Fred, III

1960 Additional Notes on the Albert Ibaugh Site. *Pennsylvania Archaeologist* 30 (3–4): 81–105.

Kinsey, W. Fred, III (editor)

1972 *Archaeology of the Upper Delaware Valley.* Anthropological Series 2. Pennsylvania Historical and Museum Commission, Harrisburg.

Knapp, Tim D.

2009 An Unbounded Future? Ceramic Types, Cultures, and Scale in Late Prehistoric Research. In *Iroquoian Archaeology and Analytic Scale,* edited by Laurie Miroff and Timothy D. Knapp, 101–29. University of Tennessee Press, Knoxville.

Kohler, Dave, and John Orlandini

1985 Chapter Contributions: The Golomb Farm Site. *Pennsylvania Archaeologist* 55 (3): 50–54.

Kraft, Herbert C.

1972 The Miller Field Site, Warren County, New Jersey. In *Archaeology of the Upper Delaware Valley,* edited by W. Fred Kinsey III, 1–54. Anthropological Series 2. Pennsylvania Historical and Museum Commission, Harrisburg.

1975 *The Archaeology of the Tocks Island Area.* Seton Hall University Museum, South Orange, New Jersey.

2001 *The Lenape-Delaware Indian Heritage: 10,000 BC to AD 2000.* Lenape Books, Stanhope, New Jersey.

Lapham, Heather

2004 "Their Compliment of Deer-Skins and Furs": Changing Patterns of White Tailed Deer Exploitation in the Seventeenth-Century Southern Chesapeake and Virginia Hinterlands. In *Indian and European Contact in Context: The Mid-Atlantic Region,* edited by Dennis B. Blanton and Julia A. King, 172–92. University Press of Florida, Gainesville.

Lenig, Donald J.

1965 *The Oak Hill Horizon and Its Relation to the Development of Five Nations Iroquois Culture.* Researches and Transactions of the New York State Archaeological Association, vol. 15, no. 1. n.p., Buffalo.

Lenig, Wayne

2000 In Situ Thought in Eastern Iroquois Development: A History. *The Bulletin of the New York State Archaeological Association* 16:58–70.

Lenik, Edward J.

1999 *Indians in the Ramapos: Survival, Persistence, and Presence.* The New Jersey Highlands Historical Society, Ringwood.

Lewis, Clifford M., and Albert J. Loomie

1953 *The Spanish Jesuit Mission in Virginia.* University of North Carolina Press, Chapel Hill.

Lucy, Charles L.

1950 Notes on a Small Andaste Burial Site and Andaste Archaeology. *Pennsylvania Archaeologist* 20 (3–4): 55–62.

1959 Pottery Types of the Upper Susquehanna. *Pennsylvania Archaeologist* 29 (1): 28–37.

1991a The Owasco Culture: An Update. *Journal of Middle Atlantic Archaeology* 7:169–88.

1991b The Tioga Point Farm Sites 36BR3 and 36BR52: 1983 Excavations. *Pennsylvania Archaeologist* 61 (1): 1–18.

Lucy, Charles L., and Leroy Vanderpoel

1979 The Tioga Point Farm Site. *Pennsylvania Archaeologist* 49 (1–2): 1–12.

MacNeish, Richard S.

1952 *Iroquois Pottery Types: A Technique for the Study of Iroquois Prehistory.* National Museum of Canada Bulletin 124. The Department of Resources and Development, Ottawa.

Mallios, Seth

2006 *The Deadly Politics of Giving: Exchange and Violence at Ajacan, Roanoke, and Jamestown.* University of Alabama Press, Tuscaloosa.

Matlack, Harry A.

1986 *Mystery of the Fort Field: The Bell Site Dig.* Printed by the author.

2000 Notes on the Ryan Site: A Monongahela Village in Clearfield County, Pennsylvania. *Pennsylvania Archaeologist* 71 (1): 69–82.

McCracken, Richard J.

1985 Susquehannocks, Brule and Carantouannais: A Continuing Research Problem. *The Bulletin and Journal of Archaeology of New York State* 91:39–51.

McCracken, Richard J., and Charles L. Lucy

1989 Analysis of a Radiocarbon Date from the Blackman Site, an Early Susquehannock Village in Bradford

County, Pennsylvania. *Pennsylvania Archaeologist* 59 (1): 14–18.

Meginness, John F.
1889 *Otzinachson: A History of the West Branch Valley of the Susquehanna.* 2nd ed., revised. Gazette and Bulletin Printing House, Williamsport, Pennsylvania.

Michels, Joseph W.
1968 Settlement Pattern and Demography at Sheep Rock Shelter: Their Role in Culture Contact. *Southwestern Journal of Anthropology* 24 (1): 66–82.

Miroff, Laurie E.
2009 A Local-Level Analysis of Social Reproduction and Transformation in the Chemung Valley: The Thomas/Luckey Site. In *Iroquoian Archaeology and Analytic Scale*, edited by Laurie E. Miroff and Timothy D. Knapp, 70–100. University of Tennessee Press, Knoxville.

Moeller, Roger W.
1986 Theoretical and Practical Considerations in the Application of Flotation for Establishing, Evaluating, and Interpreting Meaningful Cultural Frameworks. *Journal of Middle Atlantic Archaeology* 2:1–22.

1992 *Analyzing and Interpreting Late Woodland Features.* Occasional Publications in Northeastern Anthropology 12. Archaeological Services, Bethlehem, Connecticut.

Murray, Louise Welles
1921 Aboriginal Sites in and near Teaoga, Now Athens, Penna. *American Anthropologist* 23:183–214.

Oberg, Michael Leroy
2003 Manteo and Wanchese. In *Two Worlds in Searching for the Roanoke Colonies: An Interdisciplinary Collection*, edited by E. Thomson Shields and Charles R. Ewen, 82–91. North Carolina Office of Archives and History, Raleigh.

O'Callaghan, Edmund B. (editor)
1853–87 *Documents Relative to the Colonial History of the State of New York: Procured in Holland, England, and France by John R. Broadhead.* 15 vols. Weed Parsons, Albany, New York.

Payne, Ted
2000 Fifteenth Century Stewart Complex Settlement Practices as Seen at the Piper Airport 1 (36CN210) in Lock Haven, Pennsylvania. Paper presented at the 67th Annual Meeting of the Eastern States Archaeological Federation, November 4–6, Solomons, Maryland.

Pownall, T.
1776 *A Map of the British Colonies in North America.* J. Almon, London.

Pratt, Peter P.
1960 Criticism of MacNeish's Iroquois Pottery Types. *Pennsylvania Archaeologist* 30 (3–4): 106–10.

1961 *Oneida Iroquois Glass Trade Bead Sequence, 1585–1745.* Fort Stanwix Museum, Rome, New York.

1976 *Archaeology of the Oneida Iroquois.* Vol. 1. Occasional Publications in Northeastern Anthropology, Franklin Pierce College, Rindge, New Hampshire.

Prezzano, Susan C.
1992 *Longhouse, Village and Palisade: Community Patterns at the Iroquois Southern Door.* Ph.D. dissertation, Department of Anthropology, State University of New York at Binghamton. University Microfilms, Ann Arbor, Michigan.

Puniello, Anthony J.
1980 Iroquois Series Ceramics in the Upper Delaware Valley of New Jersey and Pennsylvania. In *Proceedings of the 1979 Iroquois Pottery Conference*, edited by C. F. Hayes, 146–55. Research Records 13. Rochester Museum and Science Center, Rochester, New York.

Quinn, David B.
1955 *The Roanoke Voyages.* 2 vols. Hakluyt Society, 2nd ser. Hakluyt, London.

Ritchie, William A.
1929 *An Early Historic Andaste Camp Site at Pine, Clinton County, Pennsylvania.* Unpublished manuscript on file, Section of Archaeology, The State Museum of Pennsylvania, Harrisburg.

1980 *The Archaeology of New York State.* Reprint of 1969 revised edition. Harbor Hill Books, Harrison, New York.

Ritchie, William A., and Robert E. Funk
1973 *Aboriginal Settlement Patterns in the Northeast.* New York State Museum and Science Service Memoir 20. New York State Museum and Science Service, Albany, New York.

Sauer, Carl O.
1971 *Sixteenth Century North America: The Land of the Peoples as Seen by the Europeans.* University of California Press, Berkeley.

Schrabisch, Max
1926 Aboriginal Rockshelters and Other Archaeological Notes of Wyoming Valley and Vicinity. *Proceedings and Collections of Wyoming Valley Historical and Geological Society* 19:47–218.

1930 *Archaeology of Delaware River Valley: Between Hancock and Dingman's Ferry in Wayne and Pike Counties.* Vol. 1. Pennsylvania Historical and Museum Commission, Harrisburg.

Sempowski, Martha
1989 Fluctuations Through Time in the Use of Marine Shell at Seneca Iroquois Sites. In *Proceedings of the 1986 Shell Bead Conference, Selected Papers*, edited by Charles F. Hayes III, 81–96. Research Records 20.

Rochester Museum and Science Center, Rochester, New York.

Smith, Ira F., III

1966 *Raystown Reservoir Archaeological Salvage and Survey Program.* Final Report. The Pennsylvania State University, University Park.

1973 The Parker Site: A Manifestation of the Wyoming Valley Culture. *Pennsylvania Archaeologist* 43 (3–4): 1–56.

1977 The Susquehanna River Valley Archaeological Survey. *Pennsylvania Archaeologist* 47 (4): 27–29.

1984 *A Late Woodland Village Site in North Central Pennsylvania: Its Role in Susquehannock Culture History.* Pennsylvania Historical and Museum Commission, Harrisburg.

Snow, Dean R.

1994 *The Iroquois.* The Peoples of America Series. Blackwell, Cambridge, Massachusetts.

1995 *Mohawk Valley Archaeology: The Sites.* The Institute for Archaeological Studies, State University of New York, Albany.

Sorg, David J.

2003 Linguistic Affiliations of the Massawomeck Confederacy. *Pennsylvania Archaeologist* 73 (1): 1–7.

2004 Lost Tribes of the Susquehanna. *Pennsylvania Archaeologist* 74 (2): 63–72.

Speck, Frank

1931 *A Study of the Delaware Big House Ceremony.* Vol. 2. Pennsylvania Historical and Museum Commission, Harrisburg.

Staats, F. Dayton

1979 Artifact: Susquehannock Schultz Incised Bowl. *Pennsylvania Archaeologist* 49 (1–2): 81–82.

1986a Artifact: A McFate Quiggle Incised Potsherd from the Upper Delaware. *Pennsylvania Archaeologist* 56 (3–4): 57–58.

1986b Artifact: A McFate Incised Pot from the Upper Delaware. *Pennsylvania Archaeologist* 56 (3–4): 6.

Stewart, Marilyn C.

1973 A Proto-Historic Susquehannock Cemetery near Nichols, New York. *New York State Archaeological Association Bulletin* 58:1–21.

Stokes, I. N. Phelps

1915–28 *The Iconography of Manhattan Island, 1498–1909. Reproductions of Important Maps, Plans, Views and Documents in Public and Private Collections.* 6 vols. R. H. Dodd, New York.

Stowell, H. F.

1988 *Pepper II Site: Bradford County, Pennsylvania.* Unpublished manuscript on file, Section of Archaeology, The State Museum of Pennsylvania, Harrisburg.

Sweeney, Jean W.

1966 *The Wyoming Valley Complex: A Ceramic Analysis and Some Cultural Associations.* M.A. thesis, Department of Anthropology, University of Pennsylvania., Philadelphia.

Taber, Thomas T.

1972 *Whining Saws and Squealing Flanges.* Logging Railroad Era of Lumbering in Pennsylvania, bk. 6. Lycoming Printing Company, Williamsport.

1974 *Tanbark, Alcohol and Lumber.* Logging Railroad Era of Lumbering in Pennsylvania, bk. 10. Lycoming Printing Company, Williamsport.

Thwaites, Reuben Gold

1897 *The Jesuit Relations Volume 4 and Allied Documents Travels and Explorations of the Jesuit Missionaries in New France, 1610–1791: The Original French, Latin and Italian Texts, with English Translations and Notes.* The Burrows Brothers Company, Cleveland, Ohio.

Tuck, James A.

1971 *Onondaga Iroquois Prehistory: A Study in Settlement Archaeology.* Syracuse University Press, Syracuse, New York.

Tuck, James A., and Robert Grenier

1989 *Red Bay, Labrador: World Whaling Capital, AD 1550–1600.* Atlantic Archaeology, St. John's, Newfoundland.

Turnbaugh, William H.

1977 *Man, Land and Time: The Cultural Prehistory and Demographic Patterns of North-Central Pennsylvania.* Unigraphic, Williamsport, Pennsylvania.

Twigg, Deb

2005 Revisiting the Mystery of "Carantouan" and Spanish Hill. *Pennsylvania Archaeologist* 75 (2): 24–33.

van den Bogaert, Harmen Meyndertsz

1988 *A Journey into Mohawk and Oneida Country, 1634–1635.* Translated and edited by Charles T. Gehring and William A. Starna. Syracuse University Press, Syracuse, New York.

van Meteren, Emanuel

1909 On Hudson's Voyage, by Emanuel Van Meteren, 1610. In *Narratives of New Netherland, 1609–1664*, edited by J. Franklin Jameson, 6–9. Charles Scribner's Sons, New York.

Wall, Robert D., and Heather A. Lapham

2003 Material Culture of the Contact Period in the Upper Potomac Valley. *Archaeology of Eastern North America* 31:151–77.

Wallace, Paul A. W.

1945 *Conrad Weiser: Friend of the Colonist and Mohawk.* University of Pennsylvania Press, Philadelphia.

1965 *The Indian Paths of Pennsylvania.* Pennsylvania Historical and Museum Commission, Harrisburg.

68

1970   *Indians in Pennsylvania.* Pennsylvania Historical and Museum Commission, Harrisburg.

Webster, Gary S.

1983   *Northern Iroquoian Hunting: An Optimization Approach.* Ph.D. dissertation, Department of Anthropology, The Pennsylvania State University. University Park. University Microfilms, Ann Arbor, Michigan.

Willey, Gordon R., and Philip Phillips

1958   *Method and Theory in American Archaeology.* University of Chicago Press, Chicago.

Witthoft, John

1954   Pottery from the Stewart Site, Clinton County, Pennsylvania. *Pennsylvania Archaeologist* 24 (1): 22–29.

1959   Ancestry of the Susquehannocks. In *Susquehannock Miscellany*, edited by John Witthoft and W. Fred Kinsey III, 19–60. Pennsylvania Historical and Museum Commission, Harrisburg.

Wray, Charles F., and Harry L. Schoff

1953   A Preliminary Report on the Seneca Sequence in Western New York, 1550–1627. *Pennsylvania Archaeologist* 23 (2): 53–63.

Wray, Charles F., Martha L. Sempowski, Lorraine P. Sanders, and Gian Carlo Cervone

1987   *The Adams and Culbertson Sites.* Charles F. Wray Series in Seneca Archaeology. Vol. 1. Research Records 19. Rochester Museum and Science Center, Rochester, New York.

Wren, Christopher

1914   *A Study of North Appalachian Indian Pottery.* The Wyoming Historical and Geological Society, Wilkes Barre, Pennsylvania.

69

PART II

Rethinking Susquehannock Material Culture

3.

Stress and Shifting Identities in the Susquehanna Valley Around the Time of European Arrival

April M. Beisaw

ABSTRACT

Around the time of the Contact period, the Native Americans of the Susquehanna Valley were met with cultural and environmental stresses unlike those they had encountered before. Europeans brought changes in raw materials, health and disease, and social order while the Little Ice Age brought changes in agricultural prospects. These stresses combined to cause significant changes in native lives and in the objects with which archaeologists seek to understand native identities. Through a reanalysis of existing mortuary data from several Susquehanna Valley sites, subtle shifts in native identity are apparent in the positioning of bodies and in the artifacts selected for inclusion in graves. By identifying these shifts and placing them within a larger historical context, we can develop a greater understanding of how Native Americans saw themselves within a changing world.

Introduction

All too often, the stories of Contact period (ca. 1500–1800) Native Americans are those of warfare, death, and/or assimilation. The historical documents that archaeologists mine for "facts" to support their site interpretations are biased accounts of the "disappearing Indian." Such biases are perpetuated when archaeological investigations use counts of European artifacts at Native American sites to create chronologies based on an assumption that more European goods equate to a more recent site, for instance, or when we interpret graves that contain multiple native individuals as mass burials for victims of epidemics

and warfare, even when pathological bone is absent. These approaches take colonization to be the main driving force behind Native American behavior. That assumption robs peoples and cultures of agency, if not dignity, by repressing alternative explanations such as the continuity of community that may be expressed in group burials and the political maneuvering expressed in the adoption and manipulation of trade goods (Cipolla 2017; Ferris 2009).

Since the 1980s, archaeologists and historians have frequently criticized colonial versions of history (e.g., Chilton 2001; Miller and Hamell 1986; Richter 1990; Rubertone 2000; Silliman 2005; Trigger 1991; Veit and Bello 2001), but many continue to perpetuate colonial stories through culture histories that prioritize change over continuity and difference over similarity. Several archaeologists have laid new methodological and theoretical groundwork for seeing and explaining "cultural entanglements" (or mixtures of identity) that characterize the period of earliest European arrival (e.g., Ferris 2009; Scheiber and Mitchell 2010; Silliman 2010). This chapter attempts to complicate the dominant and colonial narrative of the Susquehannocks, a Native American group of what is now central Pennsylvania, by emphasizing the cultural entanglements that are apparent in the archaeological record. Where this chapter differs from similar approaches is in its use of nationality instead of ethnicity to characterize Susquehannock identity.

The recent emphasis on ethnogenesis is not adopted here because such a focus on ethnicity runs the risk of homogenizing the native experience (Griffin 2011:238; see Herbstritt in chapter 2 of this volume). Ethnogenesis, like culture history, requires the discarding of a past in favor of something new. In contrast, a nation-genesis only requires that individuals come together for some common cause and share some basic ways of life to signal their continued membership. Ferris uses the phrase "Aboriginal nation" to refer to collective sociopolitical entities—a "broader-than-village collective" (Ferris 2009:5). Nationality is not the wholesale identity that ethnicity is. It allows for identity to be a complex negotiation of belonging to one or more groups that changes through time and is experienced differently by different members of the nation. Nationality is inherently composed of variation, as members can and do come and go through time. It also allows us to avoid questions of authenticity, for it is often based on an invented or adopted past (Kohl 1998).

If we look at native concepts of nationalism, we can see that they are not so different from our own. We know that in Iroquoian nations such as the Onondaga, members who chose to live within the group were accepted by it regardless of their origins (Bradley 2001:30). Rick Hill, a representative of the Haudenosaunee, the Six Nations Confederacy of Iroquois, defines the membership criteria as agreeing to "act as one people, using one mind to resolve their problems, show affection for each other with one heart, and see themselves as relatives in one family" (Rick Hill, personal communication, March 29, 2009). Nationality is easier to trace because the criteria for inclusion are clearer; members simply need to consider themselves as part of the nation (Kohl 1998:226). Expressions of belonging may differ for immigrants and those who inherited their nationality from "time immemorial." Members may also hold dual or multiple citizenships, formally or informally, and therefore express multiple nationalities simultaneously. This frees us from issues of authenticity, for there is no DNA fingerprint or specific artifact style that makes an individual a member of a nation.

To shift from an ethnicity-based to a nationality-based approach for understanding the Contact period requires us to de-emphasize the trait lists of culture history and the rigid chronologies of the direct historical approach, both of which reduce identity to counts of material goods (Ferris 2009). We also must discontinue our use of the terms "Protohistoric," "Contact," and "Post-Contact," because these are measurements of acculturation, entangled with the assumption that Native Americans abandoned their culture for the presumed superiority of a Euroamerican way of life (Rubertone 2000:436). New research should seek to explain those "problematic" sites and assemblages that never really fit into a culture-history classification scheme (Rubertone 2000:429). New narratives should draw on the pioneering work of archaeologists who have studied acculturation but should also move past those colonial roots.

Barry Kent first published his book *Susquehanna's Indians* in 1984, and it remains in print with only a minor update in 2001. This valuable resource details the archaeology of the region and is an excellent starting point for new research. Kent begins at

74

the presumed beginning, the earliest evidence of the Susquehannock people: their very Iroquoian pottery style that is similar to, but not the same as, pottery from other adjacent groups. The pottery and other traits are traced through the Susquehanna Valley to the ending point near Lancaster, Pennsylvania, where the last of the Susquehannocks were massacred approximately 200 years after their emergence. Oftentimes, this sad ending seems almost justified in Kent's narrative, as the Susquehannocks are depicted as fierce warriors who were focused on controlling trade in their region at any cost—including the presumed massacre of the Shenks Ferry people who preceded them as residents of the valley. Historical sources speak of the Susquehannocks as giants (Smith 1608; see also Becker in chapter 7 of this volume) and cannibals (Alsop 1666).

A new narrative, a second story of the Susquehannocks, starts at this presumed endpoint and moves through space and time in a nonlinear fashion. Instead of building a chronology, I will look at the Susquehannocks thematically, as a nation of native people who are actively negotiating their place among several other nations—including, but not limited to, the Five Nations Confederacy to the north, the Powhatan Confederacy to the south, and several European nations on almost every side. Ferris (2009) has already demonstrated how Iroquoian communities in southwestern Ontario negotiated with colonials through a process of "changed continuities." That work showed how notions of self and community can be maintained while incorporating new peoples and objects into identity. Such an approach can attempt to decolonize the Susquehannock stereotype by

1. rejecting commonly used artifact labels (e.g., native vs. European) that emphasize source over use;
2. rejecting commonly used cultural boundaries (e.g., Susquehannock vs. Shenks Ferry) that are archaeological and/or historical constructs that

may have had little or no meaning to the Native Americans themselves;
3. seeking new ways to see the expression of identity in the archaeological record that are not tied up with ideas of biological inheritance;
4. allowing for variation through time and space in native beliefs about their national identity and desires for inclusion or exclusion with respect to various national groups, native and nonnative; and
5. seeking political explanations for such variation instead of assuming progressive acculturation was at work.

Beginning at the Ending

What better way to start decolonizing a story of Native American demise than with a famous colonist's own account of the massacre of the last Susquehannocks? American history and literature contain numerous accounts of "the last," such as *The Last of the Mohicans* (Cooper 1826) and *Ishi: The Last Yahi* (Riffe and Roberts 1992). None other than Benjamin Franklin penned the story of the massacre that supposedly claimed the last Susquehannocks:

On Wednesday, the 14th of December, 1763, Fifty-seven Men . . . surrounded the small Village of Indian Huts, and just at Break of Day broke into them all at once. Only three Men, two Women, and a young Boy, were found at home, the rest being out among the neighbouring White People, some to sell the Baskets, Brooms and Bowls they manufactured . . . These poor defenceless Creatures [*sic*] were immediately fired upon, stabbed and hatcheted to Death! . . . All of them were scalped, and otherwise horribly mangled. Then their Huts were set on Fire, and most of them burnt down. When the Troop, pleased with their own Conduct and Bravery, but enraged that any of the poor Indians had escaped the Massacre, rode off, and in small Parties, by different Roads, went home. . . . those cruel Men again assembled themselves, and hearing that the remaining fourteen Indians were in the Work-house at Lancaster, they suddenly appeared in that Town . . . armed as before, dismounting, went directly to the Work-house, and by Violence broke open the Door . . . When the poor Wretches saw they had no Protection . . . they divided into their little Families, the Children clinging to the Parents; they fell on their Knees, protested their Innocence, declared their Love to the English, and that, in their whole Lives, they had never done them Injury; and in this Posture they all received the Hatchet! (Franklin 1764:5–6)

This account contains some interesting elements when it comes to assessing Susquehannock identity. First, it claims that a verbal proclamation of loyalty to the English was made, although it was not enough to discourage the attackers from their mission. Such proclamations are usually a part of establishing or maintaining citizenship, and as such, this group may have been claiming an English nationality. Second, the account provides some evidence that this group adopted many English (or proto-American) aspects of life. They were manufacturing baskets, brooms, and bowls and, just as any other English manufacturer would do, went out to sell their wares among the settlers. Lastly, those individuals who survived the first attack took shelter in the workhouse, an institution that catered to the poor and taught them how to become contributing members of Euroamerican society. That they fled there instead of to a church or a Native American village can be interpreted as an expression of loyalty to the nationalistic reform movement. In summary, the "last of the Susquehannocks" were ethnically Native American but expressed a clear Euroamerican nationality in the locations they inhabited, the goods they manufactured, and their verbal proclamation of de facto citizenship; however, it was not enough to save their lives.

Using nationality instead of ethnicity, these Native Americans were not Susquehannock, or not exclusively Susquehannock. The Susquehannock nation had, by this time, ceased to be independent of any other nation. The Iroquois Five Nations Confederacy had adopted the Susquehannocks in the 1680s (Barr 2006), but unlike the Tuscarora who joined in 1722 to create the Six Nations Confederacy, the Susquehannocks did not maintain a distinct national identity within the group. Some Susquehannocks chose to join other non-Iroquoian native nations, and others merged with missionaries or settlers and blended into the new emerging American identity. Historical sources are not clear on the disintegration of the Susquehannock nation because the details were not a matter of European concern.

At the time of this "Susquehannock" massacre, the native victims were known as Conestoga Indians. Conestoga Town was established at the turn of the eighteenth century as a place where Native Americans could live in peace without fear of attack by colonists from either Maryland or Pennsylvania (Jennings 1968). Many Seneca lived at Conestoga Town, and in his narrative, Franklin (1764:3) identifies residents as "the remains of a tribe of the Six Nations." Promises of peace placed the Conestoga firmly within the emerging American political landscape; they had a place and a right of belonging backed up with the paperwork that the Euroamericans were so fond of. This belonging is captured in the title of Franklin's account: "A Narrative of the Late Massacres in Lancaster County of a Number of Indians, *Friends of This Province*" (emphasis added).

To determine if the Conestoga Indians retained their Susquehannock or Six Nations citizenship, we can examine the archaeological record of the Conestoga Indian land. In doing so, we should not look for a specific artifact style that can be traced back to earlier sites. Instead, we should look for evidence of behaviors that reflect loyalty to one or more nations. At Conestoga, multiple loyalties can be seen in the site architecture and in the contents of storage pits and graves.

The following account of the 1972 excavations at Conestoga is taken from Kent's book on the Susquehanna Indians.

Between June and August, 1972, with the aid of a bulldozer and a crew of four, an area of approximately thirty-two thousand square feet was cleared of topsoil, flatshoveled, and mapped . . . The resulting discoveries were about a half-dozen storage pits, three houses, as defined by postmold patterns, and five separate small cemeteries. Total plan dimensions of the two houses at Conestoga could be determined. The larger measured 15 feet by 50 feet, and the other was 15 feet by 35 feet. Both ends of a third house could not be precisely determined . . . *Corners of the houses were very neat right angles.* Obviously the floor plan and the construction (size and spacing of post holes) had changed since the last major Susquehannock town had been built in the lower Susquehanna Valley. Houses at Conestoga were more *cabin-like* . . . Similarly, the spacing of houses had also changed by Conestoga times . . . The archaeology would indicate that the interval between houses was greatly increased, as compared with seventeenth-century towns. . . . Only one or two of the storage pits discovered at Conestoga could definitely be attributed to that occupation. These contained a rare bead or iron scrap of the period. None of the pits had more than a few fragments of bone, an occasional kernel of charred corn, or other garbage; and some contained only a sherd or two of *earlier Shenks Ferry pottery*, which leaves considerable question as to their cultural affiliations. (Kent 2001:382–83; emphasis added)

Based on Kent's description, the Native Americans living at Conestoga had adopted a culture that was neither unchanged from earlier times nor a wholesale adoption of Euroamerican life. Instead, what we see at Conestoga may be comparable to what Silliman (2009) observed on the Eastern Pequot reservation. The native past that is being recalled through daily practice is a recent one that combines elements of old and new in a way that is neither entirely native nor European. Loyalty to the native identity is expressed through continued residence on native lands, but aspirations for inclusion in the Euroamerican system are expressed through cabin use. That the residents of Conestoga continued to be marginalized may be evident in the relative lack of storage pits and the meager contents of those that were identified. Residents did not have enough surpluses to warrant much storage and not enough trash to fill storage pits when they were no longer needed.

The presence of Shenks Ferry pottery on sites that should postdate that "culture" warrants more sophisticated analyses than have been undertaken to date. For example, Silliman (2009) interpreted Terminal Archaic and Early Woodland artifacts at Eastern Pequot cabin sites as having been collected by nineteenth-century native residents, curated for some time, and then disposed of. It is possible that some Shenks Ferry sherds represent an act of commemoration. Recollections of the past are often part of identity formation in the present (Connerton 1989), and in the case of nationality, acts of social memory often work to ensure integration of the multiple ethnicities contained within them. Therefore, the creation of a new pot made in a "traditional" Shenks Ferry style may be recalling a shared past in a way not unlike an Italian-American drinking a pint of green beer on Saint Patrick's Day.

Kent's description of the archaeology of Conestoga supports the details in Franklin's account of the massacre. The Native Americans that lived near Lancaster in the eighteenth century were living a lifestyle that combined old with new and native with nonnative. They were multiethnic Native Americans who likely claimed citizenship in one or more native nations and may have longed for the benefits of English citizenship if they did not claim such loyalty. Additional information on the artifacts recovered from Conestoga provides a means of exploring how the Conestoga may have conceptualized and negotiated these multiple nationalities.

Conestoga Coats

Relationships between nations often revolve around trade for goods or land, and the same was true in eighteenth-century Pennsylvania. Past archaeological studies on trade during this time have transposed a capitalistic culture onto Native Americans when there is little evidence they were focused on acquiring wealth. An alternative approach considers trade as an act that maintains relationships between nations. In this way, trade requires a crossing of national borders, both spatial and cultural. Historical records show that Conestoga was an important place for formal trade between natives and nonnatives (Jennings 1968; Kent 2001), and the recovery of three European coats from Conestoga burial sites supports this.

European coats were used by Native Americans to "transgress boundaries between European and Indian societies" (Johnson 2009:118) by labeling an individual as a headman or interpreter, depending on the elaborateness of the costume. The coats were not simply adopted but modified with Native American elements that reflected the alliances of the wearer. Others created their own versions of clothing that mixed native and nonnative elements. Johnson summarizes the variety of clothing used at Conestoga:

> Natives used cloth and dress acquired from European traders to fashion on their bodies a representation of their roles and actions in colonial society. In most cases these goods were not used in a European manner. Conestogas created their visual identity based on the needs of the day. For daily wear they chose a mixture of European and Indian elements—buttons and broken wineglass stems tied to leather thongs as necklaces or combined leather stockings and a white linen shirt with wampum and a matchcoat . . . intentional creations of dress combinations (as Natives might have seen it) marked their bodies as boundaries, creating a liminal space between "European" and "Native." (Johnson 2009:125)

We could take this interpretation a step further and see the layered clothing as a reflection of their layered identity that retained elements of native identity while showing an acceptance of European identity, as long it was modified to fit within—instead of replacing—native ideals. The three individuals buried at Conestoga with their European-style coats were not wearing them. Instead, the coats were placed within brass kettles. From this, we can assume that the coats reflected a minor portion of their identity and one that was not transferrable to others in death. If these coats were simply costumes, we would expect them to remain among the living, who would take up the trading duties of the deceased. Instead, the European part of their identity died with them and was marked in their burials along with their more dominant native identity. As Ferris (2009:24) argues, "Trade goods are thus less agents of immediate change and more innovations . . . and enhanced economic strategies."

The brass kettles that contained these coats are to thank for the preservation of the fragile textiles. The resiliency of the brass and copper that kettles were manufactured from has resulted in several kettles being recovered from archaeological sites. In many ways, such kettles have come to symbolize the period, for they were one of the earliest products imported for trade with Native Americans (Fitzgerald et al. 1993; Howey 2017). As with the coats and other textiles, Native Americans did not simply adopt the kettles as cookware; they made them fit within the native culture. These kettles reveal the variability through time and space in how Native Americans used goods acquired from Europeans.

Conestoga Kettles and Brass

According to Fitzgerald et al. (1993), banded copper kettles were part of the initial fur trade complex exchanged as early as AD 1580. After AD 1600, kettles had a rolled rim and were made of a cheaper brass. This shift from copper to brass changed the color of the kettles from red to yellow. Red is a powerful symbolic color in native culture, and copper was sometimes coated with red ochre to bring out the red color (Turgeon 1997:9). They were also cut into pieces and used to create new copper objects (Bradley 1987; Bradley and Childs 1991). In these ways, the kettle was transformed into a native object despite its European source.

Howey (2017) argues that European kettles were in demand not because of their newness but because they were made from copper, which had already been used by Native Americans for thousands of years: "During early contact, then, the popularity of trade kettles among indigenous groups was not related to any kind of 'advance' in cooking technology. Rather, the popularity of kettles stemmed in part from copper's preexisting highly charged value among indigenous peoples of the Northeast. Native copper has been used from the Archaic period (ca. 8000–800 BC) onward for highly charged symbolic purposes" (Howey 2017:167). This interpretation is supported by archaeological evidence that earthenware pottery continued to be the main cooking vessel for indigenous groups, regardless of the availability of copper kettles.

That evidence from the Northeast is mirrored in the Susquehanna Valley. While Native Americans accepted the European kettles into their culture, they did not accept the European ideas of how these items were to be used. Kettles and their byproducts are almost exclusively recovered from burial contexts instead of general site refuse. Turgeon sees this pattern of deposition as evidence of appropriation instead of acculturation; burial took these objects out of circulation and put them beyond the reach of their European

creators (Turgeon 1997:21). Perhaps the acceptance of the kettles was more about the desire to be included in trade relations with European nations, while the repurposing of them expressed their loyalty to their native nationality.

Although kettles are relatively common in the burials of Conestoga Town (n = 38) the other sites in the Pennsylvania State Museum's Susquehanna Valley collections don't have many burial kettles. Frey Haverstick has one kettle from the flexed burial of an adult male. Strickler Cemetery has two kettles, one in the burial of an adult male flexed and one with an adult male extended. Byrd Leibhart Cemetery has two kettles, one in the burial of an extended female and one in the burial of a flexed male. Given the complex history of excavations within the valley, the state museum sample does not include kettles in private collections or at other museums. This complicates analysis of the region as a whole.

What are present in the state museum's collections are objects made from kettle brass, such as jinglers and projectile points, from sites with few, if any, complete kettles. This lack of kettles has been used to date those sites as earlier, but if we discard this acculturation assumption, then an alternative interpretation arises: "Implicit in notions of acculturative change is change to something and away from something else. . . . which denies the archaeological fact that change and contact between groups was and is a continuous process . . . [that] marginalizes Indigenous histories and makes them little more than reactive background noise to the main story of European advancement" (Ferris 2009:11–12). If preservation of a kettle in its European form meant the acceptance of the European concept of its best use, then variation in copper and brass assemblages derived from kettles may be reinterpreted as variation in resistance to European ideals. Allowing for diversity in reactions to colonialism is essential to decolonizing narratives (Scham 2001).

Returning to Kent's interpretation of kettles and other European goods at Conestoga, he offers the following: "This preponderance of brass items, particularly at Conestoga Town, is not a reflection of the wealth of the inhabitants; perhaps more than anything it is a product of the town's place in both history and geography. Until about 1725 it was pretty much at the edge of Pennsylvania's frontier, and yet close enough to serve as a convenient place of contact for whites and Indians. Throughout the first quarter of the eighteenth century, *Conestoga Town was the focal point for a very brisk trade as well as numerous land-sale negotiations with many Indians*" (Kent 2001:210; emphasis added). If we see this trading as formal nation-to-nation exchanges, we can understand the Conestoga kettles and brass as further evidence that residents displayed a sort of dual citizenship—native and Euroamerican—that likely aided in their role as traders by literally making them into "middlemen" who had everyone's best interests at heart. The location of Conestoga Town fostered this middle position, as it gave Euroamericans little need to move up the valley for trade and freed other villages from such political responsibilities. Therefore, the artifact assemblage of Conestoga should be different from those at other Susquehanna Valley villages. Counts of brass and kettles do not necessarily equate to change through time or to levels of acculturation but may reveal site function and resident loyalties.

Conestoga Town is an excellent example of how complex questions of native identity can become and how inadequate the concept of ethnicity is for dealing with them. Not only were the residents of Conestoga Town multiethnic, but they were also expressing a European nationality in their choices of clothing and housing. Residents massacred in 1763 declared their English citizenship just before dying. Although this massacre is often cited as the end of the Susquehannocks, more than 100 years later, 200 acres of the former Conestoga Indian land were deeded to six descendants living among the Oneida (Custer 1995). In doing so, these descendants expressed their loyalty to one identity (Conestoga) by working within the system of another (American) and cohabitating

with a third (Oneida). The claimants did not reoccupy the Conestoga land nor did they seek to protect it through preservation. They sold the property. As Conestogas, they had the right to the land, and as Americans, they had the right to profit from it.

Beginning at the Beginning

The established culture history of Pennsylvania has described the pre-Susquehannock occupations of the Susquehanna Valley as the Shenks Ferry. The most recently published definition of that cultural complex (Graybill 1989) divides it into three distinct temporal phases, during which there is a consolidation of populations into larger villages. These phases are the Blue Rock (AD 1250–1400), Lancaster (AD 1400–1500), and Funk (1500–1550). "The best explanation" for this consolidation is ascribed to increasing stress (Graybill 1989:56). Graybill backs away from his own earlier assertion that warfare with the Susquehannocks was the primary reason for the end of the Shenks Ferry. Instead, he argues that epidemics caused their demise: "The reasons for this view are several and include the presence of <u>numbers</u> of multiple interments, suggesting that not all deaths were a product of a single catastrophic event like a village attack; moreover, given the fact that *none* of three triangular arrow points recovered from the mass burial was embedded in bone (and thus, the points are perhaps incidental inclusions), clear evidence for violent deaths is lacking. Additionally, I note that the site's estimated age of ca. AD 1550, by which time European diseases were ravaging numerous other Indian societies throughout Eastern North America" (Graybill 1989:57; emphasis added).

Replacing one colonial story (presumed competitive warfare) with another (presumed epidemic disease) is not necessarily a refinement because the evidence for widespread disease is about as slim as it is for warfare (see "Pathologies" section below). More importantly, this discard of the Susquehannock-on-Shenks-Ferry warfare thesis leaves us with no explanation for the replacement of one group with the other throughout the Susquehanna Valley. If disease wiped out the Shenks Ferry around AD 1550, how could the Susquehannocks have survived in the same place and the same time, especially given their greater involvement in European trade?

Despite his own summary and redefinition of Shenks Ferry, Graybill, like Kent (2001), cannot explain the overlapping and intermixing of the two cultures that is evident in the archaeological record. As he says, "The Shenks Ferry site [36LA2] remains unique for the curious admixture of Shenks Ferry–Susquehannock cultural traits it possesses" (Graybill 1989:57). If warfare and/or epidemic disease doesn't explain the Shenks Ferry–Susquehannock transition, what does? If we give agency to the Native Americans of that time and place, one hypothesis is that they chose to change in response to stresses that included but were not limited to European arrival. Those changes have been interpreted by archaeologists as a replacement of one people with another but the evidence may better fit a model where cultural traits changed because of changes in nationality, not ethnicity.

When Europeans first approached the Susquehanna Valley, the Native Americans who lived there were adjusting to a climate change. The Little Ice Age brought cooler temperatures to the region, which reduced the agricultural season (Anderson 2001) for some. Northern latitudes were more affected than southern ones. At first, shortfalls could be mitigated through existing surplus and trade with neighbors. But surpluses were soon exhausted, and trading partners were unable or unwilling to provide the levels of assistance needed. Where increases in hunting and fishing were insufficient, migration was necessary. The Little Ice Age is part of why sites in the northern and western portions of the Susquehanna Valley differ from those in the much warmer southern portions of the valley (Beisaw 2012).

Native Americans in the Lower Susquehanna Valley had a climate that was more conducive to agriculture, and they had better access to new trading opportunities that alleviated the stresses introduced by the Little Ice Age. In the previous section on Conestoga, we saw how individuals and groups adjusted to support new trade relationships and made a place in their culture for the goods they received, yet there was no wholesale adoption of European life. Perhaps a similar shift in cultural practices explains the admixture of Shenks Ferry and Susquehannock sites and material remains that archaeologists have failed to explain despite decades of research. Maybe the Shenks Ferry did not succumb to colonialism, either by warfare or epidemic. Maybe the Shenks Ferry became the Susquehannock, shifting their identity in response to the stresses of the Little Ice Age and European arrival (see Herbstritt, chapter 2 in this volume).

What follows here is not an attempt to redefine Shenks Ferry and Susquehannock, for that just creates more culture history. Instead, I present evidence of the inadequacy of these categories for understanding change by identifying and describing the "atypical burials" that may be evidence of shifts in native identity. Atypical burials were identified through analyses of grave orientation, the presence and absence of European grave goods, and skeletal pathologies.

Mortuary Patterns of Lancaster Sites

The Lower Susquehanna Valley is where overlapping and adjacent Shenks Ferry and Susquehannock sites can be found. Pottery styles are the fuel of culture history; therefore, I avoid pottery styles in my research as much as possible. All that I will say on the matter is that there are several examples of atypical pottery that can be seen as evidence of shifting identities. At Schultz, there are Susquehannock designs on pottery constructed using "Shenks Ferry paste" (Kent 2001:313). At Frey Haverstick, the opposite occurs: Shenks Ferry designs on an otherwise Susquehannock pot in an otherwise Susquehannock burial. This pot was found with a woman and child with flexed body positions and oriented toward the northwest, an orientation preferred by the Susquehannocks (see the "Orientation and Grave Goods" section below). The field notes by Kent and Warfel describe it as "a shell tempered Susquehannock form with crude, Shenks Ferry-like incised designs on collar." A grave identified as Shenks Ferry was adjacent to this one.

Throughout the Lancaster area, burials have been assigned to one culture or the other based on the "site" it was deemed associated with, the position of the body/bodies, and the types of grave goods found (Janet Johnson, personal communication, 2008). The assumption is that Susquehannocks buried individuals in a flexed position and with a variety of grave goods, especially one or more items of European origin. Shenks Ferry burials are usually those of extended individuals with sparse grave goods. My review of burial data compiled by Boza Arlotti (1997) and original excavation field notes for these burials has convinced me that body position and grave goods are too variable for this Shenks Ferry–Susquehannock distinction to hold true (Beisaw 2008). Mortuary data from the Schultz, Funk, Ibaugh, Frey Haverstick, Strickler, and Byrd Leibhart sites (table 3.1) reveal similarities in orientation, pathologies, and even grave goods that suggest these native identities were fluid, if a distinction existed at all. Where possible, I have used Boza Arlotti's burial numbering system to identify specific examples. These numbers appear in brackets throughout the section below.

TABLE 3.1 Shenks Ferry and Susquehannock burials by site

Site	Date	Susquehannock	Shenks Ferry
Schultz	1575–1600	72	49
Funk	1600	185	14
Ibaugh	1600–1625	58	2
Frey Haverstick	1625–45	39	7
Strickler	1645–65	157	0
Byrd Leibhart	1665–80	52	0
Conestoga Town	1690–1763	80	0
Total		*643*	*72*

Pathologies

Both environmental and cultural stresses can leave their marks on bone. Five types of skeletal pathologies are evident in the Lancaster mortuary data. These are dental pathologies (periodontal disease and tooth abscesses) linked to the consumption of carbohydrates and poor dental health, cranial pathologies (porotic hyperostosis and cribra orbitalia) linked to poor nutrition (specifically anemia), and long bone pathologies (periostitis) linked to a variety of infections. Smallpox and many other contagious diseases do not leave distinctive skeletal pathologies and therefore are difficult to diagnose from the archaeological record.

Although the Lancaster skeletal sample available for pathological assessment is biased by collection techniques and differential preservation, a pattern is obvious; Shenks Ferry burials show evidence of general health and nutritional stress, whereas Susquehannock burials show very high rates of dental disease with few instances of general stress. If the Susquehannock culture was actually a shift in behaviors intended to reduce stresses brought on by the Little Ice Age and European arrival, then the pathology data suggests it was relatively successful. One pathology is particularly prevalent in Shenks Ferry burials: periostitis of the tibia. Before I classify tibial periostitis as a Shenks Ferry characteristic, however, we must look at the atypical burials. There are three cases of tibial periostitis within graves typed as Susquehannock—one at Schultz (49.0010) and two at Strickler (64.0002, 64.0003). The Strickler cases of tibial periostitis are those of an individual buried in the extended position with one European grave good (a metal hoe) and a female with no grave goods oriented toward the southeast. The southeast orientation may be significant given that all Shenks Ferry cases of tibial periostitis at Ibaugh and Frey Haverstick all have the same orientation. Although these burials were assigned to different cultures by one set of criteria, another suggests that they have much in common.

Orientation and Grave Goods

Burial orientation is often cited as a relatively unbiased measure that reveals specific patterns. For example, a recent master's thesis on Shenks Ferry mortuary patterns contains the following assertion: "Shenks Ferry burials exhibit one predominate [sic] type of internment that is present throughout all the cultural phases and that is composed of the following characteristics: an adult individual in a shallow, elongated trench with an east-west orientation, lying in an extended, supine body position with one or both hands often resting over the abdominal region and the head often tilted to one side as many graves tend to be just slightly too short to comfortably accommodate the corpse" (Glah-Donahue 2010:13).

This pattern of east-west orientation does not hold true in the Lancaster area mortuary data. There, the majority of Shenks Ferry burials are oriented toward the north (n = 16) or the southeast (n = 16). Approximately one quarter are oriented to the east (n = 11), and one is toward the northwest. Interestingly, the Susquehannock-typed burials that predate Conestoga Town show a strong preference for a northwest orientation (n = 144), but all orientations are used, including north (n = 81), southeast (n = 16), and east (n = 9).

When burial orientation is examined by site, different patterns emerge (figure 3.1). For example, southerly oriented Lancaster area burials occur only at Funk and Ibaugh, and all have few grave goods. At Funk, these southerly burials are all very similar to each

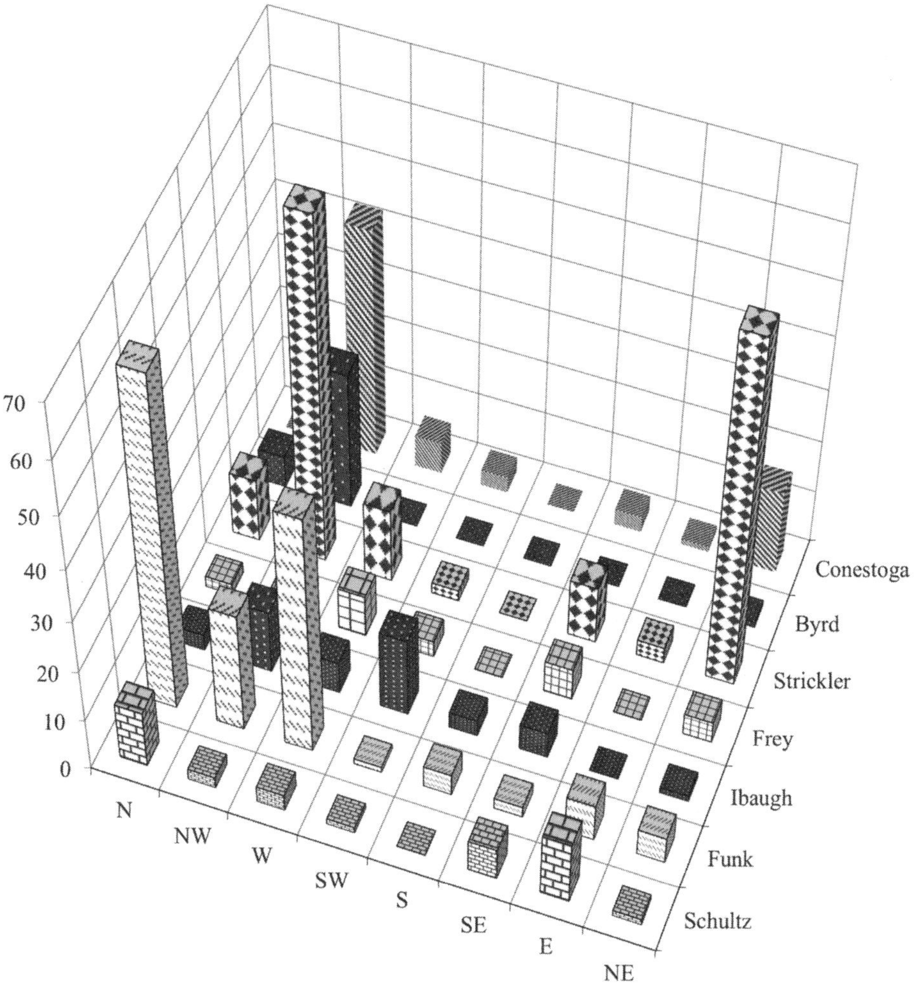

83

FIGURE 3.1
Burial orientation by site

other and include one adult male and three children. South-oriented burials at Ibaugh contain items unique to that site. For example, one double burial of two adults contains the only metal projectile points, and the other, a flexed adult of unknown sex, contains the only wampum bead from the site. Both metal projectile points and shell wampum are artifacts associated with European trade. The Susquehannock-preferred northwest orientation includes graves with objects of both native and European origin. However, at least one northwest-oriented burial with grave goods contains an individual laid out in an extended position and was typed as Shenks Ferry. This adult male (49.0024) was buried at the Shultz site with two ceramic sherds, two shell beads, three bone pendants, and 365 bone beads. This is the only Schultz burial with more than one bone bead and the only Shultz burial oriented to the northwest. With almost 400 grave goods, it also far exceeds the average of 1.65 grave goods in Shenks Ferry burials at Shultz. This certainly seems like a strong case for blurring cultural boundaries.

Individually, any of these or other, atypical burials are insignificant, but together they reveal the inability of culture history to address variation. How do we explain a Susquehannock burial with a Shenks Ferry position and orientation? Or burials with unusual orientations *and* unusual artifacts? When we start to focus on this variation, new patterns emerge. For example, southerly and easterly oriented burials occur in frequency only at sites that were occupied simultaneously or consecutively and therefore may be evidence of a cultural shift that failed to take hold. Alternatively, they may be indicative of interaction with other cultures that prefer such orientations like the Seneca, who had a strong relationship with the historic Susquehannock.

Adoption of European Goods

The inclusion of European goods in native burials is another way to examine shifting identities. Recent research has shown that European goods were not used by natives to replace their own goods. Instead, European goods were repurposed, with a focus on the qualities of the raw materials and the symbolism of those qualities, especially color (Brenner 1988; Johnson 2009; Miller and Hamell 1986; Trigger 1991; Turgeon 1997; Veit and Bello 2001).

We have already identified atypical burials at Ibaugh that contain the only wampum and metal points for that site. At the Schultz site, glass beads were found in only two burials (49.0017 and 49.0019). These burials may be atypical only in their presence of glass beads, which became common at other sites, but they

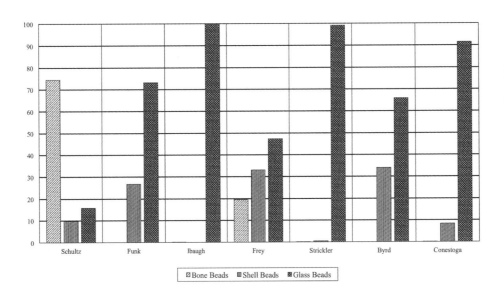

FIGURE 3.2
Frequency of bead materials by site

84

are nonetheless evidence of culture change. Although glass beads increased in numbers, they did not replace shell or bone beads (figure 3.2), and all three types were common in burials at Frey Haverstick. Similarly, kettles first appeared at Funk, but they did not replace ceramic pots (figure 3.3), which continued to be found in burials until Conestoga. Ceramic pots outnumbered kettles by three to one at Stickler and Byrd Leibhart. Interestingly, all kettles at Funk occurred with children and within multiple burials.

The repurposing of European goods for native use is evident in the Lancaster burial assemblage, where metal bracelets, points, and spirals manufactured from kettles were more numerous than the kettles themselves (figure 3.4). This was especially evident at Ibaugh, where metal spirals were present but kettles were absent. Kettles represented about 25% of the European copper and brass at Byrd Leibhart, but metal points composed 55% of that same assemblage.

European trade goods were not numerous at Schultz (1575–1600), Funk (1600), Ibaugh (1600–1625), or Frey-Haverstick (1625–45). They increased in frequency at Strickler (1645–55) and Byrd Leibhart (1665–80) and were very common at Conestoga

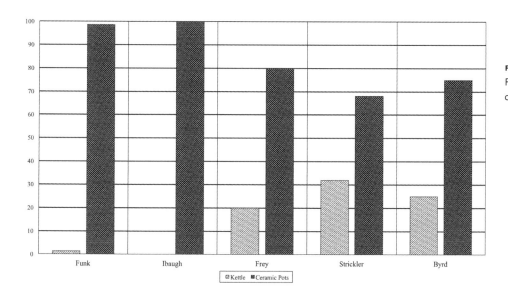

FIGURE 3.3
Frequency of kettles and ceramic pots by site

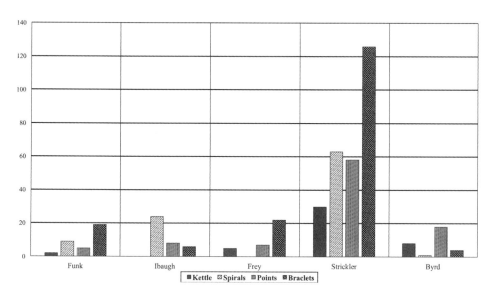

FIGURE 3.4
Frequency of kettles, metal spirals, metal points, and bracelets by site

(1690–1763). However, native goods and customs persisted, even at Conestoga. There, despite the use of coffins, preferences for burial orientation were similar to the previous Susquehannock pattern for the region.

This mortuary analysis has attempted to reveal the variation that is evident in the archaeological record of the Lancaster region of the Susquehanna Valley. A large set of mortuary data was used to challenge the perceived norms for typologies based on grave orientation, grave goods, and health. By focusing in on otherwise atypical burials, we can see the exceptions that problematize the culture-historical classification of the Shenks Ferry and Susquehannock. It is in atypical burials that the first instances of European trade goods appeared at several sites. Therefore atypical burials speak to moments of culture change whether it relates to Shenks Ferry–Susquehannock or Susquehannock-Conestoga.

Creating a New and Less Colonial Narrative

Native Americans residing in the Susquehanna Valley before AD 1625 are often categorized as either Shenks Ferry or Susquehannock. After 1625, the Shenks Ferry had "disappeared," and Susquehannock warriors are usually blamed, although there is no evidence of such violence in the archaeological record. It is probably no coincidence that 1625 is also when Europeans established a significant presence in the valley (Richter 1990). Native nations would have been forced to react, and the unification of the Shenks Ferry and Susquehannock into one nation may have followed. As a result, new native traditions evolved from a combination of old and new—Shenks Ferry, Susquehannock, and European—as economic and political alliances shifted.

Around 1635, Native Americans from the neighboring Monongahela moved east to join those residing in the Susquehannock Valley (Richardson, Anderson, and Cook 2002). At this same time, the Lenape were moving in from the west but were expelled by the Susquehannocks (Sugrue 1992). Conflict with the Five Nations Iroquois to the north began to build as a smallpox epidemic spread. That the Susquehannock nation successfully managed this time of great change is suggested by a bioarchaeological study by Gagnon (2004). When individuals from seven different Susquehannock sites were analyzed, Gagnon found no overall increase or decrease in health or change in patterns of stress. As a nation, the Susquehannocks were able to integrate to a multiethnic citizenship while managing both trade relations and political conflict with several other nations at once. Uniformity in material culture was likely the least of their concerns.

Becker (2013) provides us with an osteological assessment of Susquehannock and Piscataway health during the 1600s using collections from the National Museum of Natural History in Washington, D.C. She found more evidence of venereal syphilis in Susquehannock males than in Piscataways but less premolar tooth loss: "Overall, I expected that Susquehannock health would have been worse because of greater accounts of violence and disruptions to their traditional way of life. My findings were not the straightforward pattern expected . . . the most puzzling of the results was the lack of interpersonal violence on any of the skeletal remains" (Becker 2013:726). Colonialism is a kind of violence, but warfare and epidemics are not the only mechanisms for culture change.

Interactions between nations are often rooted in trade. Long before the arrival of Europeans, Native Americans engaged in trade, and those who inhabited the Susquehanna Valley traded with groups as far away as the Rocky Mountains for items of ritual use and personal adornment (Richter 1990). Early trade with Europeans followed similar patterns, where cultural metaphors were more important that the intended use of the objects (Miller and Hamell 1986). The arrival of new trading partners altered Native American trade networks, and realignments of loyalties occurred.

Citizens who disagreed with the decisions of their nation shed that identity while others took up the role of middlemen, which required the adoption of a new identity(s) that expressed multiple loyalties.

Nationality is not experienced or expressed uniformly among the citizenship of a nation. The homes and bodies of politicians and patriots express higher levels of national pride than do those of ordinary citizens, detractors, or dissidents. Ambassadors—or, in this case, professional traders—must express loyalty to the nation they represent but should also express acceptance of, if not loyalty, to the nation on which their work relies. Archaeology of nationality allows for this variation without declaring that some individuals are authentically members while others are not.

The archaeological record is ripe with unstudied and understudied variation that can provide us with an opportunity to examine issues of interaction and identity in greater detail (Rubertone 2000:439). The differences in artifact assemblages from sites throughout the Susquehanna Valley may be evidence of change through time or of variation in levels of patriotism felt by the members of each site. Perhaps sites with a relative lack of trade goods were inhabited by those who did not support the move toward increased interaction with nonnatives. Perhaps those with large amounts of trade goods were simply trying to maximize trade relationships by putting European traders at ease when they visited their village. Perhaps some individuals or villages took on a dual identity or even a dual citizenship to free others from trade relations, allowing them to practice a more traditional way of life while benefiting from the political work of others. If those in the northern Susquehannock territory handled relations with the Iroquoian groups, we would expect them to display more of a combined Susquehannock-Iroquois material culture. If those in the southern Susquehannock territory handled relations with nonnatives, we would expect them to display more of a combined Susquehannock-European material culture.

Conclusions

This chapter attempts to provide a starting point for decolonizing our story of a single Native American group, the Susquehannock, by

1. rejecting the idea that the source of an artifact is more important than how its owners chose to use it,
2. rejecting commonly used cultural boundaries (e.g., Susquehannock, Shenks Ferry, Conestoga, European), since these terms are a mixture of historical and archaeological ideas that probably had little or no meaning for the individuals we study,
3. using nationality instead of ethnicity as a way of understanding the complexity of identity that is evident in the archaeological record of the sixteenth to eighteenth centuries in order to free ourselves from the limitations of biological inheritance,
4. allowing for variation through time and space in expressions of national identity, and
5. seeking the underlying political motivations for expressing inclusion in or exclusion from a specific national identity.

The concept of nationality may be especially useful for understanding indigenous culture around the time of European arrival because the creation of a monolithic Native American past has itself been a nationalist undertaking. The American narrative uses Native America as its own starting point, the beginning of American identity. Although there are no artifacts that identify any of us as members of an American nation, we insist that Native American identity is readable through pottery styles and other tangible cultural traits. In doing so, American history makes more sense; the wilderness of North America could not have existed if hundreds of nations already occupied it. Nations do not simply die off, but individuals and ethnic groups die all the time. Burials may be evidence of shifts in native identity brought about by environmental and cultural changes occurring around the time of European contact. Additional research is needed to fully understand these shifts.

Acknowledgments

Many thanks to Paul Raber for bringing together new scholars and scholarship on Pennsylvania archaeology. Much of this work could not have been undertaken without the extensive research conducted by Ana Boza Arlotti; the support of the Pennsylvania Historical and Museum Commission, which granted me the Scholar in Residence fellowship; and the work of many other archaeologists who excavated these sites and curated their collections. My research assistant, Glynnis Olin, helped with the assembly of this manuscript.

REFERENCES

Alsop, George
1666   *A Character of the Province of Maryland.* 1902 reprint. The Burrows Brothers Company, Cleveland, Ohio.

Anderson, David G.
2001   Climate and Culture Change in Prehistoric and Early Historic Eastern North America. *Archaeology of Eastern North America* 29:143–86. doi:10.2307/40914449.

Barr, Daniel P.
2006   *Unconquered: The Iroquois League at War in Colonial America.* Praeger, Westport, Connecticut.

Becker, Sara K.
2013   Health Consequences of Contact on Two Seventeenth-Century Native Groups from the Mid-Atlantic Region of Maryland. *International Journal of Historical Archaeology* 17:713–30.

Beisaw, April M.
2008   *Untangling Susquehannock Multiple Burials.* Scholar in Residence Final Report: FC#4100045134, ME#20801. Report submitted to the Pennsylvania Historical and Museum Commission, Harrisburg.

2012   Environmental History of the Susquehanna Valley Around the Time of European Contact. *Pennsylvania History: A Journal of Mid-Atlantic Studies* 79 (4): 366–76.

Boza Arlotti, Ana M.
1997   *Evolution of the Social Organization of the Susquehannock Society During the Contact Period in South Central Pennsylvania.* Ph.D. dissertation, Department of Anthropology, University of Pittsburgh, Pittsburgh. University Microfilms, Ann Arbor, Michigan.

Bradley, James W.
1987   *The Evolution of the Onondaga Iroquois: Accommodating Change, 1500–1655.* Syracuse University Press, Syracuse, New York.

2001   Change and Survival Among the Onondaga Iroquois Since 1500. In *Societies in Eclipse: Archaeology of the Eastern Woodland Indians, AD 1400–1700,* edited by D. S. Brose, C. W. Cowan, and R. C. Mainfort Jr., 27–36. Smithsonian Institution, Washington, D.C.

Bradley, James W., and S. Terry Childs
1991   Basque Earrings and Panther's Tails: The Form of Cross-Cultural Contact in Sixteenth-Century Iroquoia. *MASCA Research Papers in Science and Archaeology* 8 (2): 7–17.

Brenner, E. M.
1988   Sociopolitical Implications of Mortuary Ritual Remains in 17th-Century Native Southern New England. In *The Recovery of Meaning: Historical Archaeology in the Eastern United States,* edited by Mark P. Leone and Parker B. Potter Jr., 147–82. Smithsonian Institution, Washington, D.C.

Chilton, Elizabeth S.
2001   The Archaeology and Ethnohistory of the Contact Period in the Northeastern United States. *Reviews in Anthropology* 29:337–60. doi:10.1080/00988157.2001.9978265.

Cipolla, Craig N. (editor)
2017   *Foreign Objects: Rethinking Indigenous Consumption in American Archaeology.* University of Arizona Press, Tucson.

Connerton, Paul
1989   *How Societies Remember.* Cambridge University Press, Cambridge, England.

Cooper, James Fenimore
1826   *The Last of the Mohicans.* H. C. Carey and I. Lea, Philadelphia.

Custer, Jay.
1995   An Unusual Indian Land Claim from Lancaster County. *Pennsylvania Archaeologist* 65 (2): 41–47.

Ferris, Neal

2009　*The Archaeology of Native-Lived Colonialism: Challenging History in the Great Lakes.* University of Arizona Press, Tucson.

Fitzgerald, William R., Laurier Turgeon, Ruth Holmes Whitehead, and James W. Bradley

1993　Late Sixteenth-Century Basque Banded Copper Kettles. *Historical Archaeology* 27 (1): 44–57.

Franklin, Benjamin

1764　*A Narrative of the Late Massacres in Lancaster County of a Number of Indians, Friends of This Province, by Persons Unknown, with Some Observations of the Same.* Franklin and Hall, Philadelphia.

Gagnon, Celeste Marie

2004　Stability in a Time of Change: Contact Period Health in the Lower Susquehanna Valley. *Archaeology of Eastern North America* 32:101–21.

Glah-Donahue, Lisa

2010　*The Role of Pottery in Shenks Ferry Mortuary Features at the Mohr Site.* Unpublished M.A. thesis, Department of Anthropology, Temple University, Philadelphia.

Graybill, Jeffrey R.

1989　The Shenks Ferry Complex Revisited. In *New Approaches to Other Pasts*, edited by W. Fred Kinsey and Roger W. Moeller, 51–59. Archaeological Services, Bethlehem, Connecticut.

Griffin, Patrick

2011　A Plea for a New Atlantic History. *The William and Mary Quarterly* 68 (2): 236–39.

Howey, Meghan C.

2017　Sympathetic Magic and Indigenous Consumption of Kettles During Early Colonial Encounter in the Northeast. In *Foreign Objects: Rethinking Indigenous Consumption in American Archaeology*, edited by Craig N. Cipolla, 162–83. University of Arizona Press, Tucson.

Jennings, Francis

1968　Glory, Death, and Transfiguration: The Susquehannock Indians in the Seventeenth Century. *Proceedings of the American Philosophical Society* 112 (1): 15–53.

Johnson, Laura E.

2009　"Goods to Clothe Themselves": Native Consumers and Native Images on the Pennsylvania Trading Frontier, 1712–1760. *Winterthur Portfolio* 43 (1): 115–40. doi:10.1086/597283.

Kent, Barry

2001　*Susquehanna's Indians.* Revised edition. Anthropological Series 6. Pennsylvania Historical and Museum Commission, Harrisburg.

Kohl, Philip L.

1998　Nationalism and Archaeology: On the Constructions of Nations and the Reconstructions of the Remote Past. *Annual Review of Anthropology* 27:223–46.

Miller, Christopher L., and George R. Hamell

1986　A New Perspective on Indian-White Contact: Cultural Symbols and Colonial Trade. *Journal of American History* 73 (2): 311–28.

Richardson, James B., David A. Anderson, and Edward R. Cook

2002　The Disappearance of the Monongahela: Solved? *Archaeology of Eastern North America* 30:81–96.

Richter, Daniel K.

1990　A Framework for Pennsylvania Indian History. *Pennsylvania History* 57 (3): 236–61.

Riffe, Jed, and Pamela Roberts (directors)

1992　*Ishi: The Last Yahi.* Film. Rattlesnake Productions, Berkeley, California.

Rubertone, Patricia E.

2000　The Historical Archaeology of Native Americans. *Annual Review of Anthropology* 29:425–46. doi:10.1146/annurev.anthro.29.1.425.

Scham, Sandra Arnold

2001　The Archaeology of the Disenfranchised. *Journal of Archaeological Method and Theory* 8 (2): 183–213.

Scheiber, Laura L., and Mark D. Mitchell (editors)

2010　*Across a Great Divide: Continuity and Change in Native North American Societies, 1400–1900.* University of Arizona Press, Tucson.

Silliman, Stephen W.

2005　Culture Contact or Colonialism? Challenges in the Archaeology of Native North America. *American Antiquity* 70 (1): 55–74. doi:10.2307/40035268.

2009　Change and Continuity, Practice and Memory: Native American Persistence in Colonial New England. *American Antiquity* 74 (2): 211–30.

2010　Crossing, Bridging, and Transgressing Divides in the Study of Native North America. In *Across a Great Divide: Continuity and Change in Native North American Societies, 1400–1900*, edited by L. L. Scheiber and M. D. Mitchell, 259–76. University of Arizona Press, Tucson.

Smith, John

1608　*A True Relation of Occurrences and Accidents in Virginia, 1608.* Document No. AJ-074, American Journeys Collection, Wisconsin Historical Society Digital Library and Archives, http://www.americanjourneys.org/pdf/AJ-074.pdf.

Sugrue, Thomas J.

1992　The Peopling and Depeopling of Early Pennsylvania: Indians and Colonists, 1680–1720. *The Pennsylvania Magazine of History and Biography* 116 (1): 3–31.

Trigger, Bruce G.

1991　Early Native North American Responses to European Contact: Romantic Versus Rationalistic

Interpretations. *The Journal of American History* 77 (4): 1195–215.

Turgeon, Laurier

1997 The Tale of the Kettle: Odyssey of an Intercultural Object. *Ethnohistory* 44 (1): 1–29.

Veit, Richard, and Charles A. Bello

2001 Tokens of Their Love: Interpreting Native American Grave Goods from Pennsylvania, New Jersey, and New York. *Archaeology of Eastern North America* 29:47–64.

90

4.

Public Kettles, Private Pots

THE MATERIALITY OF

SEVENTEENTH-CENTURY

SUSQUEHANNOCK COOKING VESSELS   Lisa M. Lauria

ABSTRACT

This chapter seeks to redress the ways that colonialism and its intellectual legacy have shaped our understanding of Susquehannock history and cultural change. Changes in Susquehannock ceramic style during the seventeenth century have commonly been understood as a reflection of Susquehannock acculturation and consequent indigenous cultural decline. All but the smallest-volume Susquehannock ceramic vessels were made for purposes surrounding the preparation and consumption of food. Over the course of the seventeenth century, brass and copper kettles were integrated into existent patterns of food preparation and consumption. As kettles replaced the highly public and visible ceramic family cooking pot, the remaining ceramic vessels produced were increasingly limited to private use. The makers of ceramic pots changed production for their own reasons and to meet their changing needs. The changing decorative and technical choices of Susquehannock women do not reflect an adoption of European cultural values or patterns or the loss of indigenous ones but rather the narrowing of ceramic production. Susquehannock women continued to craft vessels in the manner of their ancestors, but as the social context of the ceramic cooking vessel shifted from both public and private spaces to exclusively private ones, the technical and decorative functions of large pots no longer served a purpose. The changing materiality of cooking vessels therefore reflects sensible adaptations to the new materials introduced by Europeans but not acculturation or cultural or artistic decline.

Introduction

The elaborate incised decorations on some Susquehannock pots make those vessels aesthetically beautiful, just as the carefully molded human effigy faces of others make them symbolically compelling. As folk art, Susquehannock pottery exhibits local variations in an overall style within the larger traditions of indigenous pottery of the Middle Atlantic and Northeastern regions of sixteenth- and seventeenth-century North America. Susquehannock pots have captured public and academic interest for well over a century. In 1903, William Henry Holmes published photographs of a fractured Susquehannock effigy pot and several effigy and incised sherds in his annual report to the Bureau of Ethnology. Archaeological exploration of the Susquehanna River Valley in the early twentieth century led to further documentation and description of Susquehannock effigy vessels and their connection to other Iroquoian pottery traditions (Cadzow 1936; Skinner 1938:45–67). It is telling and significant that the effigy pot was first associated with the native peoples of the Lower Susquehanna River Valley, identified as Susquehannocks. The Washington Boro Incised effigy pot was then seen as the hallmark of Susquehannock identity and culture, supposedly its "highest" point. Archaeologically speaking, the distinctiveness and artistic brilliance of the pots became conflated with the distinctiveness and brilliance of the people that made them.

In the 1960s and 1970s, the Pennsylvania Historical and Museum Commission and various colleges and universities began large-scale excavations that often began by stripping the plowed topsoil off sites with backhoes. These machine-powered excavations uncovered vast portions of the sites, including many graves and refuse pits. The ceramics recovered from those features greatly expanded the ceramic database that professional archaeologists used to create seriated ceramic typologies and to build chronological cultural histories. These histories told a tale of a unified "Susquehannock" people, who left the Haudenosaunee homeland and migrated south toward the Lower Susquehanna Valley. Once in their new home, the story goes, their culture flourished and developed more elaborate ceramic decorations, including effigies, before European trade led to "decline" due to the Susquehannocks becoming "dependent" on European-made goods and "acculturated" to European ways, losing their distinctive ceramic (and hence cultural) identity. Their story supposedly ended in Conestoga, where European-made objects prevail and where they were extinguished in a series of genocidal massacres by the "Paxton Boys," a group of Scots-Irish from the frontier zone that is now the Harrisburg area.

In 1984, Barry C. Kent's publication of *Susquehanna's Indians* became the definitive statement on Susquehannock cultural history. At the time, it was notable for including detailed archaeological and extensive documentary evidence to support the overall narrative of migration, efflorescence, dependency, and decline. The pattern of ceramic change from highly decorated vessels to minimally decorated vessels, coupled with the rapidly increasing numbers of copper and brass kettles, seemed to Kent to be clear evidence of Susquehannock craft deterioration, cultural decline, and "acculturation" over the course of the seventeenth century. From his perspective, Susquehannocks became dependent on European goods, like kettles, which displaced their distinctive handmade items and especially the highly decorated pots that had identified them archaeologically as distinctively "Susquehannock." The eighteenth-century settlement of Conestoga was barely distinguishable from colonial and other native sites from the time period, chock-full of European-made objects. Susquehannocks disappeared archaeologically well before they were extinguished as a distinct people.

The Susquehannock ceramic typology is a useful tool for constructing chronologies of ceramic types, but they should not be equated with the history and life of the peoples that made them. When shifts within and between types are tied to historical narratives based on European sources and perspectives on history, colonialist forms of knowledge, such as ceramic typologies, reify colonialist ways of constructing the past. However, changes in Susquehannock ceramic vessel style do not necessarily indicate that the "real" Susquehannock narrative adhered to the mid-twentieth-century anthropological models of dependency, acculturation, and cultural "decline" or "loss." Poststructuralist and postcolonial perspectives have challenged this high-modernist, high-colonialist way of understanding the relationship between the colonized and colonialism as well as the difference between dependency and adaptive cultural change. Subaltern and indigenous perspectives must be integrated fundamentally into scholarly analysis. Real people made real choices under unbearably stressful circumstances, during a horrific period of history. Living people understood themselves, their choices, and their worlds without later anthropological models shaping those understandings to our present purposes. Under colonialism, narratives of decline are produced about the peoples that colonialism attempted to dominate, even if that is not the intent of the scholars who write them.

In this chapter, I attempt to redress some of the ways that colonialism and its intellectual legacy have shaped our understanding of Susquehannock history. I shift to a postcolonial perspective when examining the archaeological evidence, to see these objects (ceramic vessels and kettles) as entangled in the changing colonial worlds in which they were made and used. This study challenges the prevailing Susquehannock narrative of cultural decline and explains changes in Susquehannock ceramic vessel arts as the result of individual choices made within the contexts of social life and women's agency. By explicitly engaging with gender and examining ceramic vessel production and use within social contexts and by viewing artifacts as entangled in the lives and worlds of the people who manufactured and consumed them, the alleged shift from pots to kettles seems less like a loss of cultural integrity than a sensible response to the properties of new materials made available through trans-Atlantic trade. As European-made kettles were incorporated into Susquehannock society, Susquehannock women adapted decorative and technological elements of ceramic vessel production in response to a narrowing of ceramic vessel use in food preparation and consumption in private rather than public spaces. Changes in Susquehannock ceramics during the seventeenth century do not signal cultural loss, dependency, decline, or passive acculturation to allegedly "superior" European wares. Later ceramic vessels do not indicate the loss of technological skill but rather its improvement in several respects, even as they are less ornate. The gradual incorporation of kettles and shifts in ceramic use

and production tell a story of human adaptation and intelligent decision-making in a changing world, one in which Susquehannock women made choices and exerted agency over the tools they made together and used to prepare meals and offer hospitality, just as they had done for hundreds of years.

Overview of Susquehannock "Culture History" and Ceramic Analyses

Throughout the seventeenth century, European and colonial governments interacted with people whom they named "Sasquesahannough," "Andaste," and "Minqua," and yet no one recorded a name by which these communities self-identified. Other native peoples, colonial representatives, and later historians and archaeologists linked these various names under "Susquehannock." The Susquehannocks, as commonly understood, are a colonial construction. While there were very real and vibrant communities of people in the Lower Susquehanna River Valley during the sixteenth and seventeenth centuries, they were scattered in the native-colonial wars and turmoil of the 1670s. A small remainder, along with natives from other areas, coalesced at Conestoga in the eighteenth century, but colonists massacred them in 1763. The idea of a single, unified "Susquehannock" people emerged from colonial documents. Scholars have assumed that they shared the core cultural traits that the other speakers of Northern Iroquoian languages did. Archaeologists reified this historical and ethnographic model when they matched the historically known "Susquehannocks" to archaeological sites in the Lower Susquehanna Valley, creating an archaeological "Susquehannock" cultural taxon that could be traced farther back in time and space (see Beisaw, chapter 3; and Herbstritt, chapter 2 in this volume).

Twentieth-century archaeologists drew on both documentary and archaeological evidence to tell a story about the migration of the Susquehannocks down the river that bears their name. The Susquehannock figures present in the seventeenth-century documentary record were men, described as giants, warriors, traders, and diplomats (see Becker, chapter 7 in this volume). Historical accounts of Susquehannock encounters with John Smith and other English, Swedish, Dutch, and French colonists overwhelmingly documented the men's activities, speeches, and actions. While the archaeological artifact that signaled "Susquehannock" more than any other was pottery that was produced by Iroquoian women, twentieth-century archaeologists did not explicitly analyze that pottery with respect to gender (Engelbrecht 2003; Lauria 1999; Witthoft 1959). Presumably everyone used pottery, but women crafted the ceramic vessels and farmed, gathered, and prepared the foods that were cooked and served in those vessels. By studying Iroquoian ceramics, we get a glimpse into a portion of Iroquoian women's work. Barbara Mann (2000:207) writes that among the Haudenosaunee Iroquois, "both men and women worked cooperatively in collective units focused on community-centered tasks." Iroquoian women were rarely isolated from one another because their socioeconomic lives centered on cooperation and communal sharing (Mann 2000:205), suggesting that women commonly worked together even if they did not live together in a single longhouse. Explicit consideration of the gendered context of Susquehannock production and use of ceramic vessels could help us better understand the roles, values, and decisions of Susquehannock women, both before and during colonization.

The archaeological similarities between the Susquehannocks and Haudenosaunee Iroquois settlements are unmistakable, including the central importance of longhouse architecture, which suggests that Susquehannock social organization was similar to that of other Iroquoian peoples, for whom fuller ethnographic and historical evidence exists. Seventeenth-century documents suggest a Susquehannock clan system and a sexual division of labor linking women to cultivation and the household and men to hunting, trading, diplomacy, and war (Jennings 1978). Matrilineal descent or matrilocal residence patterns

are not clearly documented for the Susquehannocks but are well-documented for other Iroquoian groups and appear to be closely tied to longhouses. The interpretation that follows proceeds on the assumption that matrilineages were the single most important organizational pattern in Susquehannock society during the seventeenth century and that related women and children frequently assembled in work groups bigger than a single hearth or longhouse. The precise living arrangements of related and nonrelated women are not essential for my analysis, as I assume that women did gather together to produce pottery, just as Iroquoian women gathered to perform other types of work (Chilton 1999; Engelbrecht 2003; Mann 2000).

Throughout this analysis, I use the term "Susquehannock" to refer to the people living in the nucleated villages of the Lower Susquehanna River Valley, ca. 1575 to 1675. My use of Susquehannock does not presume a unitary political-economic group over time. I use it to refer to the people who lived, worked, and died in these villages and also to refer to the pottery made, used, and deposited in these villages (regardless of typological identification).

The Susquehannock ceramic typology evolved during the middle of the twentieth century. The main ceramic typology reference guide through the 1960s and 1970s was W. Fred Kinsey's (1959) summary in *Susquehannock Miscellany*. Kinsey described three major Susquehannock pottery types, each named for the associated Lower Susquehanna village site where it was most abundant (see table 4.1 and figure 4.1). In chronological site order, they were Schultz Incised, Washington Boro Incised, and Strickler Cord-Marked. The Schultz Incised type included a "Low-Collar Subtype," meaning that the ceramics at the Schultz site did not neatly fall into a single, uniform "type." The Washington Boro Incised type included three subtypes: Complex-Banded, Multiple-Banded, and Simple-Banded—indicating a range of decorative variation in the ceramics from this time period. The Strickler Cord-Marked type included the Rounded-Collar and Flared-Rim subtypes to account

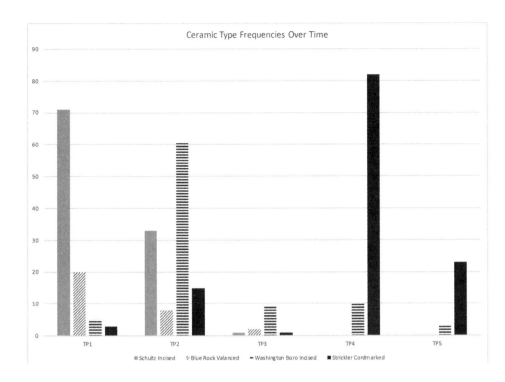

FIGURE 4.1
Susquehannock ceramic type population over time (TP = temporal period, as defined in Table 4.1)

for variation in vessel shape without distinguishing these "undecorated" vessels from one another. Kinsey (1959:63) explains the purpose of subtypes as a way to further define clustered groups of pots without over-refining types. Basically, subtypes make types easier to describe in terms of patterned variation. Several years later, Heisey and Witmer (1962) reclassified the Schultz Incised Low-Collar subtype as Blue Rock Valanced, making it the fourth Susquehannock pottery type. Kent (1984) followed the same four-type division of Schultz Incised, Blue Rock Valanced, Washington Boro Incised, and Strickler Cord-Marked types in *Susquehanna's Indians*.

The ceramic analyses of scholars from Witthoft (1959) and Kinsey (1959) to Kent (1980; 1984) focused on creating and refining ceramic histories that were equated with cultural histories. Statements of cultural relationship, change, and continuity within Susquehannock communities were based on transformations within and between ceramic types. Both Kinsey (1959) and Kent (1984) interpreted the shift from the elaborately decorated Schultz and Washington Boro pottery types to the minimally

TABLE 4.1 Pottery analyzed

Period name	Period rank	Sites studied	Vessel Count
Schultz	1	**36LA7 Schultz**	20
		36LA9 Funk	83
Washington Boro	2	**36LA8 Washington Boro Village**	4
		36LA54 Ibaugh	15
		36LA4 Keller	92
		36LA12 Eschelman*	2
Transitional	3	**36LA1 Roberts**	6
		36LA6 Frey-Haverstick	7
Strickler	4	**36LA3 Strickler**	106
Byrd Leibhart	5	**36YO170 Byrd Leibhart**	29
		Other	5
		Total	369

Village sites are shown in bold, while cemetery sites are in regular font.

* Eschelman is a smaller portion of the Washington Boro village.

decorated Strickler types as a degeneration in ceramic arts. Kinsey wrote, "This tremendous change in pottery style was no doubt facilitated to a large extent by the influence of the brass kettle. The swift adoption of the European kettle produced a profound effect upon the potter's craft. In the process of acculturation, with the resulting break-up of native culture, as patterns changed radically in a short time span, so did the pottery. Strickler Cord-marked reflects these changes" (Kinsey 1959:97). The Strickler Cord-Marked ceramic type became an artifact of acculturation and was described as a "product of ceramic degeneration" (Kent 1984:138). If the Washington Boro Incised effigy pot represented the apex of Susquehannock culture, then the Strickler Cord-Marked pot represented its deterioration. The complete disappearance of an indigenous ceramic tradition at Conestoga Town represented the extinction of Susquehannock culture many years before the massacre of its descendant peoples. Kinsey describes "the final chapter of the story of the Conestoga-Susquehannocks" as "feeble attempts to maintain themselves after their defeat and dispersal in 1675 [as] reflected in a poor material culture, lacking any native pottery" (1959:98).

A new direction in Susquehannock pottery studies seeks to examine vessel morphology and use it rather than decoration to evaluate function or cultural meaning. Alyssa Strauss (2000) exemplified this approach in her analysis of Susquehannock vessel form and function. While she utilized the four Susquehannock pottery types as defined in *Susquehanna's Indians*, her purpose was to identify and study emic pottery classes presumed to have cultural meaning to the producers of the pottery and not simply meaning created by the archaeologist. Strauss proposed that Susquehannock peoples classified their ceramic vessels on the basis of function rather than decorative style and that functional classes were based on total vessel volume independent of the decorative style or manufacturing process. Her classification was a new sort of ceramic typology, though it was still based on parameters designed by the researcher—in this case, metric volume. Drawing on ethnohistorical and ethnoarchaeological evidence for vessel use and an examination of total vessel volumes in her sample, Strauss defined six Susquehannock vessel classes—extrasmall, small, medium, medium-large, large, and extralarge. Based on an examination of the contexts of deposition

and residues associated with food preparation, she argues that all but the very smallest ceramic vessels were produced for food preparation and consumption, not storage or mortuary use.

While ceramic variation assists in the formulation of ceramic types, once types are defined, type-based analyses tend to suppress the observation of variation in ceramics. Ceramic attribute analyses are a means to examine that variation by exploring difference rather than similarity. By turning the focus of analysis from ceramic type assignment to attribute measurement, variation can be documented and examined across both space and time (Engelbrecht 1980). Attribute analysis permits a more fine-grained comparison between individual vessels and between individual sites and site components. Ceramic attribute analyses have the potential to reveal patterns in social relationships between individual potters and social units within and beyond the village unit. By moving away from a study of subjective ceramic types and focusing on measurable ceramic attributes—variation introduced by and shared among Susquehannock women—archaeological analysis can illuminate individual choices made by those women during ceramic production. Interpreting individual production choices can then be attempted by looking at the social contexts of ceramic vessel use within Susquehannock communities.

During the seventeenth century, the indigenous peoples of the Lower Susquehanna River Valley became entangled in a colonial world of diverse people and objects. Some of these objects were locally manufactured (ceramic vessels), but others were manufactured in places unknown to their consumers (e.g., kettles). The point is that all of these objects existed in the same communities at the same time. In the analysis that follows, I explore change in Susquehannock ceramic vessel production and use alongside changes in the use of brass kettles. My research builds on the work of Strauss (2000) by examining the social contexts of vessel use for vessels of different volumes. Drawing on the work of Chilton (1998, 1999) and Wonderley (2007), I also consider the decorative and technical styles of these vessels. It is a women-centered look at cooking vessels (ceramic and metal), food preparation, ceramic production, and the patterned relationships between these objects and actions between 1575 and 1675. During this century, the Susquehannock family cooking pot, central to sustenance and central in public view, changed from a handcrafted and highly decorative ceramic vessel to a shiny metal kettle. The replacement of some, but not all, ceramic vessels with kettles narrowed the role of ceramic vessels in the daily lives of Susquehannocks. Women continued to craft ceramic vessels, but the production choices they made in terms of technical and decorative style changed. These choices reflect innovation and utility rather than acculturation and dependency. My analysis offers a new interpretation of an old question: Why did Susquehannock ceramics change so dramatically in the middle of the seventeenth century? To answer this question, I examine changes in the decorative and technological attributes of ceramic vessels within the social contexts of their production and use. By viewing ceramic production and use as entangled with Atlantic trade economies and the supply of metal kettles, the overall narrative of Susquehannock history between 1575 and 1675 changes from one of decline to one of adaptation.

Data Collection and Recording

Data for this analysis were derived from an examination of collections of ceramic vessels and ceramic sherds housed in the Archaeology Section of the State Museum of Pennsylvania.[1] These collections are not the only Susquehannock collections available for inspection by outside scholars, but they are the largest and most spatially and temporally diverse of such collections.

The ceramic artifacts examined for this study came from five Susquehannock village sites and five distinct Susquehannock cemeteries believed to represent five periods of culture history (Kent 1984). The Roberts (36LA1), Strickler (36LA3), and Byrd Leibhart (36YO170) sites included cemetery and village contexts but did not distinguish these as separate archaeological sites. I also looked at pottery vessels from four sites for which site size, type, and temporal period were not determined. Table 4.1 (above) shows the numbers of ceramic vessels examined from each archaeological collection. In total, I examined 12,264 pottery sherds and 369 whole or nearly whole pottery vessels from these collections.

In order to best examine individual choice in ceramic production, I recorded decorative, morphologic, and technologic attributes for each ceramic vessel and sherd. Pratt (1980:31) notes that researchers should pay attention to what a particular attribute actually measures as well as to the difficulty, observational error, and time expended in recording the chosen attributes. I recorded 34 ceramic attributes for vessels and 31 attributes for sherds (see tables 4.2 and 4.3 for a summary). My research interests, at the onset of data collection, centered on variation in ceramic decoration over time, so my selected attributes emphasized the measure of decorative style (table 4.3) rather than morphological or technological style (table 4.2), which speaks more to vessel form and function. Strauss (2000) suggested that vessel decoration and vessel size were unrelated and that vessel function was directly connected to vessel volume. I chose to record vessel height and vessel opening diameter as rough estimates of overall vessel size and volume to account for vessel morphology. Strauss (2000) calculated an estimated vessel volume for incomplete vessels for which she had vessel-lip opening diameter recorded. These formulae were specific to Susquehannock ceramic type and subtype and could not be applied more generally, though I did apply her formulae to the Washington Boro Incised vessels in my study. While I recorded primary and secondary inclusion types (temper) for all vessels and sherds, temper size was recorded for only

TABLE 4.2   Ceramic vessel attributes: technological and morphological

Surface finish	Exterior surface finish of the vessel
Interior finish	Interior surface finish of the vessel
Paste texture	Overall feel of the baked ceramic in cross section when possible
Paste color	Color was identified using Muncell color charts. This attribute was somewhat problematic because the color of the clay varied throughout the vessel.
Temper	Primary and secondary inclusion type
Lip treatment (rounded, flattened, pointed, thickened, undetermined)	Shape of the cross section of the vessel lip
Collared (yes, no, undetermined)	Presence or absence of a distinct vessel collar
Collar height	Measured in centimeters
Vessel opening diameter	Measured in centimeters
Rim shape (flattened, flared, rounded, thickened, plain, undetermined)	The shape of the vessel above the neck in profile. A plain rim shape indicates the absence of a vessel neck.
Castellations (notched, rounded, pointed, flared point, descending point, none, undetermined)	A castellation is the highest part of the vessel rim. A pot can have none or several but generally no more than four. Castellations can be marked with notching or can be rounded or pointed. The castellation can then remain upright, can be flared out from the rest of the collar, or in some cases, can be flared out to an extreme and then turned down to become more parallel with the collar.
Lobes (molded, impressed, notched, none, undetermined)	Lobes may appear on the bottom of a vessel collar, giving it a "scalloped" edge effect.
Decorated (presence/absence)	Presence or absence of decorative elements

some of the sherds and vessels in my study. Inclusion density, a technological attribute, was not recorded for each vessel or sherd, but general observations were noted for different sites.

Dating of Susquehannock archaeological deposits is generally done at the level of the site, based on a variety of factors. The Susquehannock chronology is built on a seriation of ceramics and other artifact types from village and burial deposits. Dates of occupation for each village are based on glass bead chronologies, the presence of other datable objects of European manufacture, and references to historical documentation of village features or locations. With the publication of *Susquehanna's Indians* in 1984 (Kent 1984), Susquehannock ceramic types became associated with specific temporal periods and were used by archaeologists to assist in the dating of archaeological deposits where those ceramic types occurred. By extension, this created a framework within which Susquehannock cultural history was written. I chose to record temporal period as a ranked variable. Table 4.4 lists the Susquehannock occupation periods as presented by Kent (1984) and White (2000) alongside my ranked values. The Oscar Leibhart (1665 to

1674) period is not given a rank because no ceramic data from this period were available for analysis in the collections at the State Museum. Use of a ranked value for time period allows for an examination of change over time and variation across space. I begin my analysis with an overview of attribute variation in the ceramic study population over time.

The Susquehannock ceramic vessel population does show clear shifts in attribute use over time (table 4.5). While some of these shifts are suggested, and therefore expected, by the relative shift in Susquehannock pottery-type prevalence over time (figure 4.1), these changes are more noticeable when measured in terms of attributes. Both Kent (1984:136–40) and Kinsey (1959:97) note the overall decrease in decorated pottery over time and the lack of elaborate decoration in the Strickler Cord-Marked type as compared to other Susquehannock types. While decorated vessels became less frequent at sites in the Lower Susquehanna Valley over time, this observation does little to describe the processes influencing individual potters' choices during this time period. A closer examination of ceramic decorative attributes over time indicates a decreased use of several specific decorative attributes, including

TABLE 4.3 Ceramic vessel attributes: decorative

Lip decoration (smoothed, notched, scalloped, undecorated, undetermined)	Any surface modification to the vessel lip after it was shaped
Impressed decoration (presence/absence)	Any decorative technique that involves pushing something into the clay.
Applied decoration (presence/absence)	Any decoration that is formed from a separate piece of clay and then attached to the clay vessel
Molded decoration (presence/absence)	Any decoration that is formed by pinching and shaping the clay of the vessel itself
Incised line (presence/absence)	This type of impressed decoration involves dragging a sharp or blunt instrument across the surface of the wet clay to form a line.
Cord impression (presence/absence)	This type of impressed decoration is formed by pushing a piece of cordage or an instrument wrapped in cordage into the surface of the wet clay.
Stamped impression (presence/absence)	This type of impressed decoration is formed by pushing a raised relief into the surface of the wet clay to form a noncontinuous decoration. Stamps can then be repeated.
Punctates (presence/absence)	This type of impressed decoration is formed by pushing a small blunt instrument into the surface of the wet clay to form a dot. Punctates usually appear in series to form dotted lines.
Parallel lines (presence/absence)	Any decorative technique that is applied in a way that creates parallel lines as part of the decoration
Perpendicular lines (presence/absence)	Any decorative technique that is applied in a way that creates perpendicular lines as part of the decoration
Right triangles (presence/absence)	Any decorative technique that is applied in a way that creates right triangles as part of the decoration
Isosceles triangles (presence/absence)	Any decorative technique that is applied in a way that creates isosceles triangles as part of the decoration
Neck decoration (smoothed, gashed, cord, punctation, incised line, none, undetermined)	This can be any decoration that encircles the neck (or narrowest part) of the ceramic vessel and differentiates it from the rest of the vessel, most commonly a single horizontal band of impressed decoration encircling the neck. A vessel that has a nonsmoothed exterior surface can also have the neck smoothed as a form of decoration.
Shoulder decoration	Any decoration appearing on the shoulder portion of the vessel
Body decoration	Any decoration appearing on the body of the vessel
Effigy	Face or body of a human or less commonly an animal figure
Effigy technology	This refers to how the effigy was created. An applied effigy is made of clay and then attached to the vessel. A molded effigy is formed directly from the clay of the vessel where it appears. It can be formed by pinching the clay on the exterior of the vessel or by pushing on the interior surface of the vessel to create a lump that is then molded. An incised effigy is simply a two-dimensional incised relief on the surface of the vessel.
Horizontal banding	This is any unit of elements that encircle the vessel horizontally. Most commonly seen as one or more horizontal and parallel lines that have been incised, gashed, or punctated.

TABLE 4.4 Susquehannock site chronology and ranked temporal periods

Period name	Ranked period	Kent	White
Early Schultz Migration	0	1550–75	
Schultz	1	1575–1600	1590–1615
Washington Boro	2	1600–1625	1615–40
Transitional	3	1625–45	1640–50
Strickler	4	1645–65	1650–65
Oscar Leibhart	NA	1665–74	1665–74
Byrd Leibhart	5	1676–80	1676–80

Adapted from White (2001:238)

horizontal banding, parallel lines, triangular elements, castellations, incised lines, cordage impression, and punctates. Effigies, which were infrequent in the first temporal period, rose in frequency during the second and third temporal periods and then declined in frequency rather dramatically but did not disappear.

Written descriptions of the defined Susquehannock types do indicate extensive use of incised lines, parallel lines, and punctation in Schultz Incised (Kinsey 1959:68–69; Witthoft 1959:47–49) and note these attributes as infrequent for Strickler Cord-Marked pottery (Kinsey 1959:88–89). One might predict an outcome similar to that observed in the study population, where frequencies of these three attributes dropped off between the second and fourth temporal periods.

TABLE 4.5 Comparison of attribute frequencies over time for Lower Susquehanna Valley pottery vessels

	AD 1575–1600	AD 1600–1625	AD 1625–45	AD 1645–65	AD 1665–80
Smoothed surface	.398	.345	.750	.208	.172
Cord-marked surface	.602	.655	.250	.792	.828
Rounded vessel base	.973	1.00	1.00	1.00	1.00
Elliptical vessel body	.773	.816	.700	.352	.500
Globular vessel body	.213	.184	.300	.648	.500
Powdery paste	.864	.947	.769	.667	.690
Smooth paste	.087	.018	0	.305	.276
Gritty paste	.049	.035	.231	.029	.034
No horizontal banding	.030	.089	.231	.702	.857
≥2 horizontal bands	.750	.795	.692	.106	.071
Collar presence	.941	.938	.769	.440	.517
Decoration present	.961	.929	.846	.385	.241
Smoothed neck	.140	.218	.077	.040	.034
No neck decoration	.634	.691	.923	.921	.931
Undecorated shoulder	.966	.972	1.00	.970	1.00
Flattened lip	.556	.541	.538	.093	.069
Rounded lip	.404	.450	.462	.897	.897
Undecorated lip	.596	.824	.923	.753	.586
Notched lip	.374	.176	.077	.124	.172
Flat rim	.860	.832	.727	.184	.250
Flared rim	.070	.093	.182	.531	.429
Rounded rim	.040	.037	.091	.214	.250
Castellation present	.634	.670	.692	.605	.241
Lobes present	.616	.336	.077	.080	.172
Effigy present	.050	.241	.417	.081	.103
Impressed decoration	.942	.929	.846	.346	.207
Applied decoration	.097	.090	.077	.058	.034
Molded decoration	.204	.188	.462	.067	.138
Incised line	.835	.830	.846	.163	.103
Cord impressions	.573	.170	.154	.029	0
Punctated decoration	.505	.518	.462	.240	.172
Parallel lines	.912	.866	.846	.173	.103
Perpendicular lines	.710	.629	.700	.107	.071
Right triangles	.490	.210	0	0	0
Isosceles triangles	.350	.238	.200	.029	0

However, the frequency pattern for cord-impressed decoration (figure 4.2) is less likely to be noted on the basis of the written typology descriptions. Interestingly, this is one decorative attribute shift that could not be predicted by a ceramic type-based study. In defined type descriptions, cord-impressed decoration tends to get lumped with incised line decoration (as linear impressions). A type-based analysis masks the variation in this particular decorative attribute—one that requires a different crafting tool

(cordage or a cord-wrapped stick) from other forms of incising.

The decreases in frequency of these four attributes over time are clear in graphic form but are only moderately significant, statistically. Since the frequency pattern for cord-impressed decoration was the most dramatic, I chose to test the hypothesis that the presence of cord-impressed decorations is not temporally sensitive. In other words, time period and the presence of cord-impressed decorative elements

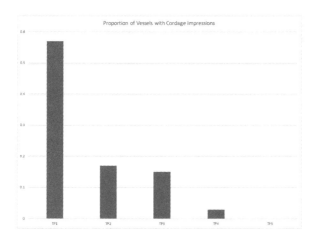

FIGURE 4.2

Frequency of cord-impressed decoration over time (TP = temporal period, as defined in Table 4.1)

are independent variables. Because my sample size for the period AD 1625–45 was so small (n = 13 vessels), I excluded it from my test. Few nonparametric tests are available for use with nominal data. I used the chi-square statistic and concluded that cord-impressed decorative elements do appear to be moderately temporally sensitive.[2]

Since its formulation, the Susquehannock ceramic vessel typology has served as a means to order Susquehannock sites in a temporal sequence (Kinsey 1959; Witthoft 1959). Cord-impressed decorations appear on about 75% of all ceramic vessels from the first temporal period. These vessels are variously typed as Schultz Incised, Blue Rock Valanced, and Washington Boro Incised. For all three of these types, cord-impressed decorations become less common in the second temporal period and infrequent after. If treated independently as a time-sensitive variable (e.g., Braun 1980; Klein 1994), this one decorative attribute might serve as a more accurate measure of temporality in Susquehannock ceramic vessels and sherds than ceramic type (Plog 1990:69). While other decorative attributes do appear to be temporally sensitive (presence of horizontal banding, impressed decoration, incised lines, punctates, parallel lines, right triangles, and isosceles triangles), cord-impressed decoration is

the only decorative attribute that does not clearly correspond to a shift in observed Susquehannock ceramic types over time.

The clearest examples of temporal variation in vessel morphology are evident in mean vessel size, the treatment of vessel lips, and the shape of vessel rims. Vessel lips are frequently either rounded or flattened in profile, although they can also be pointed (Kinsey [1959] calls this "thinned"). The study population indicates a shift in preference from flattened lips to rounded lips over time. Vessel rims can come in several different forms, which are named for their shape in cross section. The three most common rim shapes present in the study population are flat, flared, and rounded. An early preference for flat rims seems to give way to a preference for either flared or rounded rims over time (table 4.5). This temporal shift in rim shape is not unexpected in a type-based analysis, since Schultz Incised, Blue Rock Valanced, and Washington Boro Incised types generally display flat rims while the Strickler Cord-Marked type is subdivided on the basis of rim shape with flared and rounded rim subtypes.

Mean vessel size also decreases over time. Strauss (2000) observed a similar pattern but argues that total vessel volume is the best measure of Susquehannock vessel size as different stylistic types take different forms. Strauss (2000:117) found "lip diameter" to be the best predictor of vessel volume and calculated separate curves and measures of correlation strength for each Susquehannock ceramic type and the Strickler ceramic subtypes. Strauss (2000) argues that the average vessel volume of the overall Susquehannock assemblage decreased over time as brass kettles came to replace the functional role of the ceramic vessels belonging to her larger vessel volume categories (medium and medium-large pots). My argument builds on this observation of Strauss and explores the relationship between vessel volume, decorative style, and social contexts of vessel use. Ceramic typologies, whether based on decorative or morphologic styles, do not address the social contexts of both the production and the use of those vessels. It is only through an examination of social and historical contexts that human agency and subaltern perspectives can be examined. This brief examination of temporal variation in decorative and morphologic attributes demonstrates that inspection of individual attributes can provide information about human choice during production. In order to interpret those choices, it is necessary to situate ceramic production and use in social and historical contexts. In the discussion that follows, I explore these contexts and examine stylistic choice within these contexts.

The Significance of Public Pots and Kettles

Here, I explore the technomic, sociotechnic, and ideotechnic functions of Susquehannock cooking vessels (Binford 1962). Technomic functions are utilitarian—a ceramic vessel used to cook a meal. Sociotechnic functions are informed by the social context of objects—using one's "fine china" to serve a meal when the everyday dishes can perform the same task communicates something to the diners about the host's intentions for the evening, social status, or wealth. Ideotechnic functions reflect religious or ideological meaning. Think of the wine chalice used to serve wine during a Christian communion—this vessel could easily hold any beverage to quench one's thirst, but it is only used for this one specialized purpose and is treated with great care and ceremony. Moving beyond the basic technomic function of different ceramic vessels for cooking, I examine the social and symbolic potential of ceramic cooking vessels during use and manufacture by focusing on rituals of hospitality and feasting, the proliferation of human effigy faces on Susquehannock ceramic vessels, and the adoption of metal kettles. I argue that all of these contexts and adaptations provide opportunities for symbolic expression.

Iroquoian family cooking vessels had a visually prominent place in the longhouse, whether they were made of clay or metal. According to Engelbrecht (2003:87), cooking vessels "stood as symbols of family and hospitality." Food was shared within and between longhouses. Barbara Mann observes, "Treating with guests was an ancient duty of the *gantowisas* [Iroquoian women]" that required women to keep "a large pot of *sagamité* (a sort of corn stew) . . . simmering near a pot of herbal tea" at all times (2000:107–8, 229). Iroquoian hospitality meant that visitors were promptly fed and family could help themselves to food at any time (Engelbrecht 2003; Mann 2000). The constant availability of food and tea meant that cooking vessels were always in public view. Chilton paints a vivid image of the Iroquoian ceramic cooking pot and its place within the longhouse: "Pots were used for cooking on the hearth in the center of each longhouse compartment and were visible to everyone on a daily basis. Because maize stews were cooked for long periods of time, pots would often sit on the hearth for many hours. With the base of the pots either sitting in or dangling over the fire, pronounced, geometrically incised collars on the vessels were a prominent, central icon for anyone entering the longhouse compartment" (Chilton 1999:59).

These highly visible family cooking vessels generally were medium sized except when cooking for larger numbers, which demanded larger vessels. Snow (1994:107) suggests a typical family cooking vessel held about 7.5 liters, which is consistent with Strauss's "medium" category of volumes ranging from 3.01 to 10 liters. These medium-volume vessels were the family cooking pots that Susquehannock women used to prepare daily boiled meals for their family unit within the longhouse (see Chilton 1999). Medium-large vessels (10.01–32 liters) served the same purpose as the medium vessels but were used for larger family groups, when more people needed to be fed. Large (32.01–59 liters) and extralarge (more than 59 liters) vessels were used for preparing food for feasts and so were not used daily (volume categories come from Strauss 2000, modified by this author to encompass continuous ranges). Larger vessels served the same purposes of hospitality as medium family vessels but on a larger scale that could include the wider community.

During the seventeenth century, ceramic family and feasting vessels disappear from the Susquehannock artifact assemblage (table 4.6). Large and extralarge vessels, which account for 23% of the sample at the Schultz site (first temporal period), account for only 3% of the sample at the Washington Boro site (second temporal period). There is only one Washington Boro–type large vessel recovered from the Strickler village (fourth temporal period). Communal-use vessels of these volumes were associated with feasting. There is no other preserved vessel form in the archaeological record of this region that could replace these large feasting vessels. The decline of the larger vessel volume classes between the first and fourth temporal periods (between ca. AD 1575 and 1650) signals a change in communal feasting events between peoples beyond the family longhouse unit. It appears that Susquehannock social patterns surrounding feasting changed early in the seventeenth century, a time that predates sustained interactions with Europeans and their commodities.

Both family and feasting vessels held prominent places in public view during use, so it is important to consider the social contexts and the sociotechnic functions of these vessels. A ceramic vessel resting over the fire in the center of a longhouse would be seen by everyone, whether guest or kin, on entering the structure and whenever obtaining food or tea from the vessels. The woman who crafted a vessel was also the woman responsible for providing hospitality to guests and family. It was her handcrafted vessel that presented and represented the hospitality of her family, her longhouse, her matrilineage, and her clan. The vessel also demonstrated her artistic skills. She likely gave careful thought to the production of such a vessel, because she knew it needed to serve her family while also providing a visual representation of her social obligations to others. The social contexts of ceramic vessel use impacted the choices made by Susquehannock women during ceramic vessel production. The discussion that follows will build on two assumptions: (1) that Susquehannock ceramic production was a socially situated part of female life and (2) that Susquehannock ceramic vessels were a medium for symbolic messaging.

The social contexts of Susquehannock ceramic vessel production are not directly observable in the archaeological record, nor are they described in the ethnohistorical record. However, we can attempt to reconstruct these contexts by drawing on ethnoarchaeology and ethnographic analogy. Among the Haudenosaunee, pottery production was undertaken by "groups of related women. . . . and shared within and between lineages and clans" (Chilton 1998:157). The same was likely also true among the Susquehannocks. Chilton (1998:157) calls Iroquoian vessel manufacture a "household industry" that was "characterized by part-time production for group use." She argues that the social contexts of use and production presented opportunities for nonverbal communication between the users and producers of Iroquoian ceramic vessels. High-collared Iroquoian vessels were visually prominent when resting over the fire inside a longhouse, so the elaborate designs on those collars had the potential to communicate to other users who understood the symbolism embedded in the decorations. Chilton (1999:59) argues further that the process of manufacture itself was encoded with social messaging: "The slab-building of pots of consistent size and shape and the repetitive incising of decorations on collars provide the potential for pots to embody messages about group membership, the role of

TABLE 4.6 Occurrence of Susquehannock ceramic vessel classes over time

Vessel class	Rank 1	Rank 2	Rank 4	All three ranks
Extrasmall	32	62	71	165
Small	64	122	84	270
Medium	23	31	8	62
Medium-large	25	8	0	33
Large	18	2	1	21
Extralarge	25	4	0	29

Adapted from Strauss (2000:147).

women, social integration, and the egalitarian ideal of Iroquois society." When Susquehannock women gathered to craft ceramic vessels, their work group embodied Susquehannock ideas surrounding group membership, women's roles, social integration, and egalitarian ideals. The pots they crafted in these groups were the results of individual actions in a social group environment. The repetitive building or decorating of vessels could reinforce those ideals, and the pots themselves embodied those ideals.

The variety of incised decoration on Susquehannock pots, both in type of incising and in motif patterning, decreases over time (for a more elaborate explanation, see Lauria 2012). As settlements grew larger, women began to make decorative choices that were meaningful to larger groups of women. The great variety of decorative attributes and decorative motifs evident on ceramic vessels during the first temporal period occupation of the Schultz village reflects a settlement of once dispersed family groups coming together in a settlement larger than most had ever lived in before. By the second temporal period occupation of the Washington Boro village, women were active participants in much larger social groups. The choice of decorative elements of a more limited sort and the more uniform assembly of those attributes into repetitive motifs suggests increased interaction between women's work groups.

The population change of Susquehannock settlements and the resulting changes in women's work groups and ceramic production can be explored through another example—the organization of feasts. Large and extralarge vessels, common in the first temporal period, were not produced during the fourth or fifth temporal periods (Strauss 2000). These vessels were used for feeding larger numbers of people and were not used daily. Like their medium and medium-large counterparts, they too would have rested prominently over a large, communally visible fire. These larger vessels were very much at the center of public view when in use. The disappearance of large and extralarge vessels by the middle of the seventeenth century raises the question, Why did feasting become less common over time in Susquehannock villages?

The presence of large- and extralarge-volume feasting vessels during the late sixteenth and early seventeenth centuries suggests they functioned as a means of bringing people from different matrilineages, longhouses, or even different settlements together in the preparation and sharing of food. In his examination of Susquehannock longhouses, David Anderson (1995:58) argues that the shift in use of below-bench storage pits from within the longhouse (common during the first temporal period) to storage outside the longhouse (more common by the fourth temporal period) "shows a change in longhouse unit membership and a shift toward greater social cooperation at the supra-longhouse unit level." Perhaps the same shift is also reflected in the Susquehannock ceramic vessel complex. If we accept the interpretation of Susquehannock history that says the Schultz village was the first time all "Susquehannock" peoples settled together in a single large village (see Kent 1984; Witthoft 1959), then communal feasts would have served to bring these previously dispersed family units (longhouses or clans) together. If, by the fourth temporal period, "greater social cooperation at the supra-longhouse unit level" had been achieved, then perhaps communal feasts, hosted by single matrilineages or longhouses, were no longer common events and large communal feasting pots were no longer maintained by each longhouse or matrilineage.

* * *

Susquehannock effigy vessels are both visually and artistically compelling, but while Washington Boro–type effigy vessels are distinctive in execution, effigy vessels are not uniquely Susquehannock. While the discussion above begins to explore the sociotechnic functions of ceramic vessels used in communal settings where others could readily see them, Chilton (1999) recognizes the potential for the elaborate geometric patterning on these vessels to serve a role in symbolic communication between the makers and users

104

of the pots. This raises the question of whether or not ceramic cooking vessels also embodied ideotechnic functions in Susquehannock society. Kent and his forerunners generally considered the Washington Boro Incised–type effigy pot as the apex of Susquehannock ceramic vessel arts. As Kinsey put it, "Face and full-figure effigies may possibly be expressions of religious, ceremonial, or clan symbolism. The fact that they are nonexistent on Strickler Cord-marked, which is of the later historic period when trade goods are most abundant, suggests that their absence may be related to *the deterioration of native arts and crafts and the disruption of older tribal culture patterns*" (Kinsey 1959:85; emphasis added). While the symbolic potential of human effigy figures makes these vessels compelling to archaeologists, the symbolic potential of undecorated ceramic vessels is far more difficult to acknowledge. Less-decorated or undecorated Susquehannock vessels were interpreted by archaeologists as the deterioration of cultural patterns and shared systems of symbolic belief. However, the disappearance of one decorative attribute, the face effigy, does not signal the deterioration of ceramic vessel arts or the disruption of Susquehannock cultural patterns regarding food preparation and hospitality. The persistence of the effigy vessel beyond other "decorative" vessel forms indicates a continuation rather than a disruption of cultural patterns in the third quarter of the seventeenth century.

The data in this study indicate that Susquehannock effigy vessels were a part of a wider ceramic complex associated with food preparation. Effigy vessels are associated with archaeological contexts across a good portion of the Northeast, including southern New England, the Upper Delaware River Valley of Pennsylvania and New Jersey, and eastern and upstate New York up through the St. Lawrence Valley in Canada. These effigy traditions appear in contexts as early as the fifteenth century and continue through the seventeenth century. Wonderley places Oneida effigy vessels firmly within the domestic/utilitarian ceramic complex. He calls them "the material correlates

of women's activities in the home and, especially, of cooking corn" and argues, "If the symbolic meaning of an object is in any way appropriate to its context and use, then an Oneida effigy probably is linked to corn and food preparation in a realm of domesticity and femaleness" (Wonderley 2007:363). The same argument applies to Susquehannock effigy vessels. Similar to the Oneida effigy tradition (Wonderley 2007:360), the Susquehannock effigy tradition followed patterns for effigy placement and associated decoration (table 4.7). All effigy vessels in the study population (n = 47) were decorated with incised parallel lines. These vessels generally had an undecorated lip (91.3%) or, in rare cases (n = 4), a notched lip. The lips of these vessels were more often flattened (65.2%) than rounded. The shape of effigy vessel rims was flat or, infrequently (n = 3), flared. In all but two cases in the study population,

TABLE 4.7 Effigy and noneffigy Washington Boro–type vessels: attribute frequencies

	Noneffigy Washington Boro Incised vessels	Effigy Washington Boro Incised vessels
Smoothed surface	.514	.413
Cord-marked surface	.486	.587
Elliptical vessel body	.941	.744
Globular vessel body	.059	.256
Flattened lip	.472	.644
Rounded lip	.528	.356
Undecorated lip	.944	.911
Notched lip	.056	.089
Flat rim	.865	.932
Flared rim	0	.068
Rounded rim	.135	0
Castellations present	.611	.956
Lobes present	.243	.239
Impressed decoration	1.00	1.00
Applied decoration	0	.261
Molded decoration	.081	.587
Incised line	.973	1.00
Cord-impressed decoration	.081	.130
Punctate decoration	.378	.565
Parallel lines	1.00	1.00
Perpendicular lines	.629	.773
Right triangles	.086	.114
Isosceles triangles	.229	.159

effigies were placed on a castellation, which was most frequently notched (68.9%) or rounded (24.4%). The 12 effigy sherds from the study population followed these patterns as well.

Susquehannock effigy vessels are associated with all five temporal periods in this analysis. Effigy vessels in the sample population demonstrate a temporal shift from mostly cord-marked surfaces in the first two temporal periods to mostly smooth surfaces. The preference for flattened vessel lips shifted to more rounded lips in the fourth and fifth temporal periods. The few notched-lip effigy vessels were from the first (n = 3) and second (n = 1) temporal periods only. In the first temporal period, all effigy vessels had rounded (n = 4) or pointed (n = 1) castellations. Beginning in the second temporal period, notched castellations became the dominant form, with rounded castellations disappearing altogether by the fifth temporal period. Cord-impressed elements appeared on the earliest effigy vessels but disappeared completely by the fourth temporal period. Punctate attributes were present in all temporal periods on effigy vessels, while impressed neck decorative elements only appeared in the first two temporal periods. The five effigy vessels from the first temporal period were all atypical when compared with those from later temporal periods. One of these was typed as a Schultz Incised vessel. The other four effigies are illustrated in figure 4.3.

It seems that the majority of Susquehannock effigy vessels were made for use in preparing food for either personal or family consumption. Vessel size/use categories based on Strauss (2000) were calculated for 35 of the 47 effigy vessels in the study population. Vessel-opening diameter was not recorded for the other effigy vessels (n = 12), so size/use categories could not be assigned. Of the 35 categorized effigy vessels, 14.3% (n = 5) were medium, 74.3% (n = 26) were small, and 11.4% (n = 4) were extrasmall. Three of the four extrasmall vessels had opening diameters close to the division for extrasmall and small vessels and may, in actuality, have been large enough for preparing an individual serving of food.

FIGURE 4.3
First temporal period effigy vessels

My ceramic vessel study population suggests that most effigy vessels were made by women for individual rather than communal use. We cannot know for certain if women were the exclusive users of effigy vessels, but an examination of the distribution of effigy vessels in burials suggests that may have been the case. Ethnohistorical sources indicate that objects that were buried with the deceased were intended for that person's use in the afterlife (Alsop 1666). Sixteen of the 47 effigy vessels in the study population were clearly associated with 15 burials for which information on the individuals interred is known. Five of those 16 effigy vessels are buried with an adult female, 3 with children, 5 with adults of unknown sex, and 1 in a multiple burial of a child and adult of unknown sex. There are no examples of an adult male buried with an effigy vessel, which suggests that women were the primary users of effigy vessels. The effigy vessels recovered from the graves of children were likely filled with food and placed there by mothers. Children may not have necessarily used small individual pots prior to death.

Whether or not Susquehannock women were the exclusive users of effigy vessels, they were the ones who made them. Wonderley's (2007) examination of Oneida effigies proceeds according to Wiessner's (1990:110) second level of stylistic analysis, in that he tries "to understand the meaning of the symbolism behind [effigy] style to grasp the underlying nature of social relationships." Wonderley believes effigy vessels represented an active role in communication and that the effigies themselves referred directly to corn-husk people. He proposed that "Oneida effigies may be the surviving material correlates of a specifically human female obligation. The effigies bespeak silent invocation, a form of thanksgiving offered in fulfill-ment of ritual contract by Oneida food-providers to non-human beings responsible for making possible agricultural harvests" (Wonderley 2007:346). It is cer-tainly possible that Susquehannock effigies embod-ied a specific symbolic relationship between human women and spirit beings, but it is also possible that they signified a more general social relationship between the women who made and used them. While the Oneida effigy tradition appears to have origi-nated in the second half of the fifteenth century, the Susquehannock tradition began in the early seven-teenth century. Curiously, Oneida effigies from the Beecher/Blowers and Thurston sites, dating to ca. 1595–1625 and ca. 1625–37, respectively, most closely resemble Susquehannock effigies from the period of the Washington Boro village occupation, ca. 1615–30 at its full range. Whether or not Susquehannock women were interacting with Oneida women at this point in time is beyond the scope of this chapter, but the similarities might suggest a shared symbolic sys-tem beyond the village.

As noted above, the earliest examples of Susquehannock effigy vessels from the first temporal period are different than those that become more com-mon during the second temporal period. Beginning in the second temporal period, effigy faces became more formulaic and the decorative attributes that accom-panied them became more consistent (figure 4.4).

Above, I suggested that the decreased presence of communal feasting vessels and the decrease in decora-tive attribute variation by the fourth temporal period may represent a more cohesive Susquehannock com-munity. Here, I propose that the manufacture of effigy vessels by Susquehannock women may have been an early representation of a community of women com-ing together beyond the matrilineal unit. Crafting effigy vessels in the presence of other Susquehannock women would have been a socially integrative expe-rience. Adoption of a common decorative element, regardless of its symbolic meaning, suggests a degree of solidarity between women, even as it is variably executed with individual skill and choice.

Effigy vessels continued to appear in burials through the third, fourth, and fifth temporal peri-ods, even when the majority of pottery was no longer decorated in the fourth and fifth temporal periods. If these vessels were indeed symbolic of social relation-ships between women or between women and spirits, then it is fitting that they would be well cared for and would follow their makers/users in their journey to the afterworld.

The attribute frequencies for effigy vessels are much like those for the Washington Boro Incised type as a whole, but there are some differences in attri-bute patterning between the Washington Boro vessels with effigies and those without (see table 4.7). While an elliptical vessel body shape was most common for all Washington Boro–typed pots, a globular body shape was used in about 25% of the effigy vessel sample. Effigy vessels also seem more likely to have had a flat-tened lip than a rounded lip. There is a strong correla-tion between effigies and castellations. More than 95% of effigy vessels were castellated, but only 61% of the noneffigy Washington Boro–type vessels were castel-lated. All castellated Washington Boro–type vessels also had incised parallel line decorations. Applied and molded decorative attributes were nearly absent from Washington Boro Incised vessels without effigies.

Applied decorations did appear on or near the castellations of noneffigy vessels during the fourth

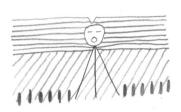
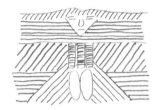

FIGURE 4.4
Second temporal period effigy vessels

temporal period on some Strickler Cord-Marked vessels. Kent described "ladders" that were horizontally gashed and applied vertical clay strips that appeared at the castellation. Kent (1984:144) proposed that these ladders were "very stylized representations of full-figure effigies," and Wonderley (2007:358–60) agreed. He suggested that "if only a single location is appropriate to the humanoid effigy, any other image at that position might reasonably bear some conceptual link to the human-like figure or figural theme" (Wonderley 2007:358–59). Kent (1984:144) noted the appearance of a few ladder motifs (applied or incised) under the castellation of some ceramic vessels from the first temporal period. Another common decorative element on Schultz-typed Susquehannock ceramics (74.2% of study sample) was the placement of a rectangular element of incised parallel vertical lines below the castellation. Perhaps the same patterns related to the placement and decoration accompanying an effigy applied to the earlier decorative pattern.

The increased presence of the European metal kettle corresponds with the decreased presence of the ceramic family cooking vessel (table 4.8). During the earliest temporal period, medium vessels made up 12% and medium-large vessels accounted for 14% of the assemblage. By the second temporal period, medium and medium-large vessels made up 14% and 3% of the assemblage, respectively. Medium-class ceramic vessels made up only 5% (8 of 164 vessels) of the ceramic vessel assemblage at the Strickler site (fourth temporal period), and there were no medium-large vessels. Both Strauss (2000:148) and Kent (1984:204) argue that the majority of brass kettles from Susquehannock sites have vessel volumes that place them firmly in the

TABLE 4.8 Estimated number of ceramic pots and brass kettles in burial contexts over time

Temporal period	Village name	Number of ceramic pots	Number of brass kettles*	Ratio of kettles to pots
First TP	Schultz	210	1	.005
Second TP	Washington Boro	200	4	.010
Third TP	Roberts	29	4	.138
Fourth TP	Strickler	169	145	.858
Fifth TP	Byrd Leibhart	45	25	.556
18th century	Conestoga Town	0	42	

Adapted from Kent (1993:292) and Strauss (2000:6).

* Kettle counts refer to unmodified kettles from burial contexts that may have been used for food preparation/consumption before burial or in the afterlife.

family cooking vessel class. It appears that during the middle of the seventeenth century, the brass kettle replaced the medium ceramic cooking vessels as the vessel central to family hospitality. Replacing locally made vessels with foreign-made vessels does not, in itself, indicate any alteration of Susquehannock daily food preparation or consumption patterns. Brass kettles were used to prepare stews and corn mush over the central fire in the longhouse. What this pattern does suggest, however, is that Susquehannock women chose to replace their handcrafted, highly decorated, and highly visible ceramic cooking pots with vessels that they did not manufacture themselves.

Brass kettles had material qualities that likely made them more appealing to Susquehannock women than ceramic cooking vessels. Metal kettles are more durable and lighter than ceramic vessels of the same size. The metal conducted heat far more efficiently, reducing the need for firewood, which women collected. Metal kettles had built-in, fire-resistant handles that made them easier to handle and that also allowed them to be hung over the fire instead of nestled in the coals. Metal kettles were well-suited for daily boiling of foods and liquids over a fire and offered several compelling material advantages over ceramic pots. Each of these material qualities speaks to the utilitarian use of metal kettles as cooking vessels. But just as ceramic vessels served sociotechnic and, perhaps, ideotechnic functions, the same can be argued for a brass or copper kettle (see Turgeon 1997).[3]

Susquehannock women chose to incorporate European kettles into their existing rituals of hospitality for guests and their families. The choice to trade for metal kettles and use them to prepare family meals reveals a preference on the part of Susquehannock women for cooking in those kettles instead of handmade ceramic vessels of the same vessel volume. This is agency, not dependency. The adopted kettles replaced highly decorative communal-use vessels that had the potential to communicate symbolically to others. But as Turgeon (1997) argues, ethnohistoric accounts document both the social and ideological value that copper and brass kettles held within and beyond the realm of food preparation/consumption. Having food and drink ready for guests and kin was itself a symbol of hospitality, regardless of the vessel used to prepare those items. In the mid-seventeenth-century Atlantic world, Susquehannock women's access to metal kettles and the use of those kettles in long-standing rituals of hospitality were symbolic of the increasingly entangled social networks in which these women and their matrilineages engaged. In other words, displaying a kettle over the central longhouse fire communicated that this woman was an active participant in the social networks of the changing world beyond her village.

Private Pots in Social Contexts

Between the late sixteenth century and the middle of the seventeenth century, Susquehannock women chose to replace some ceramic vessels with metal kettles. Kettles replaced ceramic family cooking pots and some smaller individual cooking pots. These choices narrowed the social contexts of ceramic vessel use from public and private contexts to more exclusively private contexts. As a result, ceramic production shifted from producing vessels for both individual and communal use to producing of vessels for individual use only. As ceramic vessels moved out of public view during use, their communicative role changed from an active to a passive role (Sackett 1990). Similarly, as kettles became more widely available and commonly used by more Susquehannock women, their symbolic role may also have become increasingly passive. According to Wiessner (1990:107), "Passively used style is not subject to frequent or intensive comparison and thus social boundaries reflected by it may not keep up with changing social relations." When brass kettles replaced ceramic vessels as the family cooking pot in Susquehannock households, ceramic vessels no longer served as a means for public social messaging in their use during food preparation. However, women continued to gather to craft ceramic vessels. I argue that as the sociotechnic functions of ceramic vessels shifted from both public and private settings to private settings only, Susquehannock women adapted their decorative and technical attribute choices to reflect this shift in ceramic vessel use. As the sociotechnic (or communicative) role of Susquehannock ceramics shifted, Susquehannock women made different stylistic decisions during ceramic production. These decisions are reflected in temporal shifts in the decorative and technical attributes of some ceramic vessels. These private pots were not central to the rituals of hospitality, but they were technologically improved for their intended use.

The decrease in elaborately decorated pottery led twentieth-century scholars to argue for Susquehannock cultural deterioration. These archaeologists had depended so heavily on the decorated pottery types that, to them, it looked like the distinctiveness of a people disappeared along with their decorated pottery. Decorative attributes, more than technical attributes, defined the Susquehannock ceramic types, but an "attribute analysis of technical choice" (Chilton 1998) requires an examination of a very different set of attributes. In Chilton's (1998) examination of Iroquoian and Algonquian ceramic traditions in the Northeast, she focused on four technical attributes: primary inclusion type, inclusion density, wall thickness, and vessel size. The majority (94.9%) of ceramic vessels in my study population had crushed shell as the primary inclusion type. Crushed burned shell was an "optimal inclusion type for cooking vessels" (Chilton 1998:149) because of its low thermal expansion coefficient (Rice 1987:229). In regard to inclusion density, both Kinsey (1959:88) and Kent (1984:138) remarked that the Strickler Cord-Marked vessels, most common during my fourth and fifth temporal periods, have a lower density of shell temper. I observed the same pattern but did not record inclusion density for all vessels in the population. Kent (1984:138) and I both observed some Strickler-typed vessels that seemed to have no visible inclusions at all. A densely tempered paste can present more problems when heated and cooled repeatedly (Braun 1983, 1987), but it is usually strong. Thus earlier temporal period Susquehannock ceramics with greater densities of shell temper were strong vessels but likely had a short use life when heated and cooled regularly. Vessel wall thickness also affected a pot's resistance to thermal shock, as thinner walls were "less apt to crack when used for cooking" (Chilton 1998:151). Susquehannock ceramic sherds in my study population have a mean thickness between 5.4 millimeters and 6 millimeters, and this was consistent through all temporal periods. Surface treatment is commonly considered a decorative attribute, but it "can be an artifact of manufacturing technique, or purposeful 'finishing' for either technical or decorative purposes" (Chilton 1998:153). If Susquehannock potters were using a cord-wrapped paddle to form their vessels, then a cord-marked surface would have been a default end result of forming the pot. However, some Susquehannock pots have been purposely smoothed, whereas some later pots have very pronounced cord-marking. According to Chilton (1998:154), a cord-marked surface "can increase thermal shock resistance and reduce thermal spalling," making it advantageous for cooking and easier to transport due to a less slippery surface. The unsmoothed surfaces of these later vessels were a deliberate choice that had useful benefits.

In the second half of the seventeenth century, Susquehannock women were crafting pots more exclusively for private, individual use. These women may have made different choices when crafting their pots—maximizing technical attributes for cooking and portability. In his discussion of later period Susquehannock ceramics, Kent explained, "A majority of Strickler Cord-marked examples . . . are in fact technologically fairly good pottery. The type is usually quite symmetrical in outline—generally more so than the preceding types—and overall it is slightly harder and more durable than other Susquehannock types" (1984:138). Kent's mention of Strickler-typed vessels as "harder and more durable" suggests that Susquehannock potters may have perfected their ceramic pastes over time to better account for both thermal and mechanical stresses. If surface cord-marking and decreased inclusion density both improved a vessel's ability to endure thermal stress, then Strickler Cord-Marked vessels were a technological improvement on an already strong cooking vessel. If these same vessels were also more symmetrical in shape, perhaps Susquehannock women chose to invest more time in shaping the vessels they crafted as they invested less time in crafting elaborate incised decorations on their vessels. Shaping a symmetrical vessel without the use of a potting wheel requires great skill. If later temporal period vessels were indeed more symmetrical than preceding vessels and technologically better designed to endure thermal stress and transport, then I would argue that these vessels further demonstrate the continuance, if not the improvement, of Susquehannock women's technical and artistic skills, not craft deterioration.

The predominance of small- and extrasmall-volume ceramic vessels on Susquehannock sites during the second half of the seventeenth century and the increasing numbers of kettles belonging the medium cooking vessel class demonstrate a continuation of Susquehannock cultural patterns surrounding food preparation and burial ritual. Unlike medium- and larger-volume vessels, extrasmall (up to 0.5 liter) and small vessels (0.51–3 liters) were used by individuals—young and old, male and female—and were not commonly in public view. Small vessels were used for the preparation of individual meals while away from the village and/or the family cooking area of the longhouse (Strauss 2000). Snow (1994:107) estimates an individual serving size of food at 1.5 liters, making small-volume vessels ideal for serving one or two people. Susquehannock women, like Haudenosaunee women, likely cooked individual meals for themselves during their monthly menses (Engelbrecht 2003:85; Snow 1994:107). Everyone old enough to be away from the family cooking area might have a vessel that he or she could use when needing to prepare an individual meal. Strauss (2000) and I both observed that small ceramic vessels were the most frequently occurring vessel class in the Susquehannock archaeological collections *and* the most frequently occurring vessel class recovered from Susquehannock burials. Both patterns make sense if it is assumed that many Susquehannock people owned a personal cooking pot.

While some extrasmall vessels were used for food preparation, others were manufactured for purposes other than cooking food. Some extrasmall vessels appear to have been made by children and were likely used by children as toys. The high proportion of extrasmall vessels accompanying child burials seems to validate this interpretation and strengthens the interpretation that individuals were buried with items of personal use and significance. Adults also used extrasmall vessels for the preparation of paints or medicines (Strauss 2000). Some extrasmall burial vessels have evidence of pigment staining or dried pigment residues in them (personal observation; also noted in Strauss 2000). Whether used for cooking food, preparing medicines, or childhood play, extrasmall vessels were designed for individual use.

Ceramic vessels end up in the archaeological record through three different means—as refuse disposal, in situ abandonment, or symbolic deposition in the ground. Susquehannock sites have no documented in situ abandonment of ceramic vessels, so the collection available for study was either discarded as refuse or intentionally buried as grave offerings. Strauss (2000) found that small and extrasmall vessels were the most common vessel-use classes accompanying burials. In *Susquehanna's Indians*, Kent (1984:139–40) proposed that Strickler pottery was a debased ceramic type manufactured solely for inclusion in burials, but Strauss (2000:144–45) demonstrated that even these small vessels had been used for cooking before burial. Therefore, the nearly exclusive use of small ceramic vessels in mortuary contexts was a continuation of the Susquehannock ritual practice of burying individual possessions and provisions with the deceased. An examination of identified male and female burials suggests continuity in ritual behavior related to death over time (see Lauria 2012 for a full analysis). While not all individuals were buried with personal objects (including small personal vessels), this practice is evident in all five temporal periods from the late sixteenth century through the third quarter of the seventeenth century. Moreover, the burial of vessels of "older" typed decorative styles with women in the first and fifth temporal periods demonstrates the care with which women handled their handmade vessels over their lifetimes and strengthens the interpretation of these vessels as personal items of significance to the deceased.

I have argued that Susquehannock ceramic vessel production narrowed as family cooking pots were replaced with metal kettles. While the common decorative and technical attributes of Susquehannock ceramic vessels shifted between AD 1575 and 1675, the patterns observed in the study population demonstrate a continuation of Susquehannock traditions surrounding food preparation and burial rituals.

The continued production of smaller ceramic vessels offered a mechanism for continued female interaction beyond the longhouse. However, as the social contexts of ceramic vessel use narrowed from visually prominent hospitality rituals and individual private use in food preparation or burial to only the latter uses, the choices made during the production of ceramic vessels also changed, but those choices continued to reflect the role of ceramic vessels in Susquehannock daily life.

Summary

The introduction of metal kettles into Susquehannock life did not inevitably transform Susquehannock cultural traditions and beliefs. While ceramic vessel production changed, these transformations were the result of conscious decisions on the part of Susquehannock women. Their craft skills did not deteriorate. These women, like their ancestors, chose to elaborate specific stylistic attributes, utilizing different but equally artistic ones. The socially integrative activity of crafting ceramic vessels in groups did not end when metal kettles were incorporated into the food production complex. Women continued to gather and craft vessels, but as kettles became entangled in Susquehannock food production, women developed different visions for their pottery.

In the late sixteenth and early seventeenth centuries, high-collared, ornately incised family cooking vessels were prominently displayed over the central hearth of the longhouse for all to see while the hard corn cooked down to an edible mush. By the middle of the seventeenth century, the then widely available brass kettle replaced the medium ceramic vessel as the family cooking pot. Now it hung over the central fire. The manufacture and use of small and extrasmall ceramic vessels continued as it always had in Susquehannock villages. These vessel categories were never as prominently displayed as the medium and larger vessels. While ceramic vessels no longer served as symbols of hospitality across Susquehannock society, their manufacture still offered an opportunity for communication between Susquehannock women. If the great variety of combinations of decorative elements on sixteenth-century ceramic vessels demonstrated a Susquehannock community composed of matrilineal longhouses acting as individual units, then the crafting of effigy vessels in the early to mid-seventeenth century and the less decorated but technologically optimized vessels in the second half of the seventeenth century demonstrates a Susquehannock community of women united beyond the level of the longhouse. The very fact that effigy vessels continued to appear at Susquehannock sites after noneffigy forms fell out of use suggests a continuation of the social mechanisms responsible for their appearance in the first place. Seventeenth-century Susquehannock ceramic vessels do not document acculturation. Rather, the observed changes in these vessels over time reflect innovation

on the part of Susquehannock women, who altered their manufacturing techniques for crafting vessels for individual use. Metal kettles replaced the pots that once held the potential to communicate through symbolic expressions like effigies and complex geometric designs while they rested on the central cooking fire in the longhouse. Kettles were not locally made, so they did not communicate local knowledge in the way that ceramic vessels could. However, they could still reflect shared beliefs regarding hospitality and human obligations to one another. Kettles, like ceramic pots, were both utilitarian and symbolic. The choice to convey hospitality through a ceramic pot or a brass kettle was precisely that—a choice. Individual women, at different points in time, chose to adopt the kettle into their routines of hospitality. A kettle hanging over the central fire in the longhouse became the visual embodiment of entanglement in a rapidly changing world.

REFERENCES

Alsop, George

1666   A Small Treatise on the Wild and Naked Indians (or Susquehanokes) of Mary-Land, Their Customs, Manners, Absurdities, and Religion. In *A Character of the Province of Mary-Land*, edited by John Gilmary Shea, LL.D., 71–81. 1869 reprint. T. F. for Peter Dring, London.

Anderson, David

1995   *Susquehannock Longhouses and Culture Change During the Contact Period in Pennsylvania*. M.A. thesis, University of Pittsburgh, Pittsburgh.

Binford, Lewis R.

1962   Archaeology as Anthropology. *American Antiquity* 28 (2): 217–25.

Braun, David P.

1980   Experimental Interpretations of Ceramic Vessel Use on the Basis of Rim and Neck Formal Attributes. In *The Navajo Project: Archaeological Investigations*, edited by D. C. Fiero, R. W. Munson, M. T. McClain, S. M. Wilson, and A. H. Zier, 171–231. Research Paper 1, Museum of Northern Arizona, Flagstaff.

1983   Pots as Tools. In *Archaeological Hammers and Theories*, edited by J. A. Moore and A. S. Keene, 107–34. Academic Press, New York.

1987   Coevolution of Sedentism, Pottery Technology, and Horticulture in the Central Midwest, 200 B.C.–A.D. 600. In *Emergent Horticultural Economies of the Eastern Woodlands*, edited by W. F. Keegan. Center for Archaeological Investigations Occasional Paper 7. Southern Illinois University, Carbondale.

Cadzow, Donald A.

1936   *Archaeological Studies of the Susquehannock Indians of Pennsylvania*. Safe Harbor Report No. 2. Pennsylvania Historical Commission, Harrisburg.

Chilton, Elizabeth S.

1998   The Cultural Origins of Technical Choice: Unraveling Algonquian and Iroquoian Ceramic Traditions in the Northeast. In *The Archaeology of Social Boundaries*, edited by Miriam T. Stark, 132–60. Smithsonian Institution, Washington, D.C.

1999   One Size Fits All: Typology and Alternatives for Ceramic Research. In *Material Meanings: Critical Approaches to the Interpretation of Material Culture*, edited by Elizabeth Chilton, 44–60. University of Utah Press, Salt Lake City.

Engelbrecht, William

1980   Methods and Aims of Ceramic Description. In *Proceedings of the 1979 Iroquois Pottery Conference*, edited by Charles F. Hayes III, 27–29. Research

Records 13. Rochester Museum and Science Center, Rochester, New York.

2003 *Iroquoia: The Development of a Native World.* Syracuse University Press, Syracuse, New York.

Heisey, Henry W., and J. Paul Witmer
1962 Of Historic Susquehannock Cemeteries. *Pennsylvania Archaeologist* 32 (3–4): 99–130.

Jennings, Francis
1978 Susquehannock. In *Northeast*, edited by Bruce G. Trigger, 362–67. Handbook of North American Indians 15. Smithsonian Institution, Washington, D.C.

Kent, Barry C.
1980 An Update on Susquehanna Iroquoian Pottery. In *Proceeding of the 1979 Iroquois Pottery Conference*, edited by Charles F. Hayes III, 99–103. Research Records 13. Rochester Museum and Science Center, Rochester, New York.

1984 *Susquehanna's Indians.* Anthropological Series 6. Pennsylvania Historical and Museum Commission, Harrisburg.

Kinsey, W. Fred, III
1959 Historic Susquehannock Pottery. In *Susquehannock Miscellany*, edited by J. Witthoft and W. Fred Kinsey, 61–98. Pennsylvania Historical and Museum Commission, Harrisburg.

Klein, Michael J.
1994 *An Absolute Seriation Approach to Ceramic Chronology in the Roanoke, Potomac and James River Valleys, Virginia and Maryland.* Ph.D. dissertation, Department of Anthropology, University of Virginia. University Microfilms, Ann Arbor, Michigan.

Lauria, Lisa M.
1999 *Defining Susquehannock: An Evaluation of the Archaeological Construction.* Unpublished M.A. thesis, Department of Anthropology, University of Virginia.

2012 *Defining Susquehannock: People and Ceramics in the Lower Susquehanna River Valley, AD 1575 to 1690.* Ph.D. dissertation, Department of Anthropology, University of Virginia.

Mann, Barbara Alice
2000 *Iroquoian Women: The Gantowisas.* Peter Lang, New York.

Plog, Stephen
1990 Sociopolitical Implications of Stylistic Variation in the American Southwest. In *The Uses of Style in Archaeology*, edited by Margaret Conkey and Christine Hastorf, 61–72. Cambridge University Press, New York.

Pratt, Marjorie K.
1980 The St. Lawrence Iroquois Conference: Some Lessons to Be Learned. In *Proceedings of the 1979 Iroquois Pottery Conference*, edited by Charles F. Hayes III, 31–32. Research Records 13. Rochester Museum and Science Center, Rochester, New York.

Rice, P. M.
1987 *Pottery Analysis: A Sourcebook.* University of Chicago Press, Chicago.

Sackett, James R.
1990 Style and Ethnicity in Archaeology: The Case for Isochrestism. In *The Uses of Style in Archaeology*, edited by Margaret Conkey and Christine Hastorf, 32–43. Cambridge University Press, Cambridge.

Skinner, A. Alanson
1938 The Andaste. In *A Report of the Susquehanna River Expedition*, edited by Warren K. Moorehead, 45–67. Andover Press, Andover, Massachusetts.

Snow, Dean R.
1994 *The Iroquois.* Blackwell, Oxford.

Strauss, Alisa N.
2000 *Iroquoian Food Techniques and Technologies: An Examination of Susquehannock Vessel Form and Function.* Ph.D. dissertation, Department of Anthropology, The Pennsylvania State University, University Park. University Microfilms, Ann Arbor, Michigan.

Turgeon, Laurier
1997 The Tale of the Kettle. *Ethnohistory* 44 (1): 1–29.

White, Sharon
2001 *To Secure a Lasting Peace: A Diachronic Analysis of Seventeenth-Century Susquehannock Political and Economic Strategies.* Ph.D. dissertation, Department of Anthropology, The Pennsylvania State University, University Park. University Microfilms, Ann Arbor, Michigan.

Wiessner, Polly
1990 Is There a Unity to Style? In *The Uses of Style in Archaeology*, edited by Margaret Conkey and Christine Hastorf, 105–12. Cambridge University Press, Cambridge.

Witthoft, John
1959 Ancestry of the Susquehannocks. In *Susquehannock Miscellany*, edited by John Witthoft and W. Fred Kinsey III, 19–60. Pennsylvania Historical and Museum Commission, Harrisburg.

Wonderley, Anthony
2007 Oneida Ceramic Effigies: A Question of Meaning. In *Archaeology of the Iroquois: Selected Readings and Research Sources*, edited by Jordan E. Kerber, 343–69. Syracuse University Press, Syracuse, New York.

NOTES

1. Support for 12 weeks of research at the State Museum of Pennsylvania came in the form of a Pennsylvania Historical and Museum Commission Scholar in Residence Grant.

2. I selected a significance level of $\alpha = .05$. In this case $X^2 = 102.207$ with $n = 348$ and $df = 3$. The phi measure of association calculates a value of .542 for this relationship—a moderate strength of relation.

3. The argument presented in this chapter is imbalanced in regard to ceramic pots and metal kettles. The evidence I present here was recognized after my museum collection analysis of Susquehannock ceramics was completed. I have not had the resources or opportunity to conduct independent research on Susquehannock use of and access to European kettles. My discussion of these objects relies heavily on the work of others (Kent 1984; Strauss 2000). To that end, my conclusions are preliminary, and I would encourage anyone with resources and interest to pursue the argument further.

115

PART III

New Studies and Data

5.

The Nature of Susquehannock Community Patterns in the Upper Potomac

LONGHOUSES OR SHORT-TERM
STRUCTURES? SUSQUEHANNOCK
ARCHAEOLOGY IN THE UPPER
POTOMAC RIVER VALLEY

Robert D. Wall

ABSTRACT

The presence of Susquehannock peoples in the Upper Potomac Valley has been explored more fully at several new sites in the last few decades, indicating that Susquehannock settlements can no longer be considered as anomalies in Upper Potomac prehistory. Their brief but intense presence in the region is evidenced by the existence of early Susquehannock sites in both the North and South Branch Valleys, which abruptly ended ca. 1620, based on glass trade bead and ceramic analyses from Potomac Valley sites. There is no evidence of late Susquehannock sites in the region that are comparable to Strickler and other mid-seventeenth-century sites of the Susquehannock heartland in the Lower Susquehanna Valley. The brief presence of Susquehannock peoples in the Upper Potomac region is also manifested in the community patterns of these settlements, the lack of longhouse structures suggesting the transient nature of most or all of these settlements.

Introduction

The presence of Susquehannock peoples in the Upper Potomac Valley in the early seventeenth century has been explored more fully in the last few decades, though their settlements had been recorded previously in the Potomac Valley, southwest of their traditional territory in the Susquehanna River Valley. Susquehannock sites have been known since the 1940s, when the Herriott Farm site was excavated (MacCord 1952; Manson and MacCord 1941, 1944). Their settlements are no longer considered to be anomalies in Upper Potomac prehistory. Rather, they represent a brief but pervasive presence in the region for approximately two decades. This short period, evidenced by early Susquehannock sites in both the North and South Branch Valleys, abruptly ends ca. 1620, based on glass trade bead and ceramic analyses from Potomac Valley sites. There is no evidence of late Susquehannock sites in the region that are comparable to Strickler and later seventeenth-century sites of the Lower Susquehanna Valley. However, Schultz and initial Washington Boro phases appear to be well represented (Cadzow 1936).

The brief appearance of Susquehannock peoples in the Upper Potomac Valley also appears to be manifested in the community patterns of these settlements. The lack of longhouses may reflect the transient nature of most or all of these settlements. Perhaps sites were used for the short term due to the uncertainty of existence in these new lands or they fulfilled a specific need (e.g., fur trade) that was met over the course of just a few decades. Whatever the reason may have been, the lack of enduring settlements is reflected in the brief chronological and community pattern data from Upper Potomac region sites (figure 5.1). Most of the community pattern data are too limited to derive any conclusions, though the Barton site has been more comprehensively surveyed by geophysical (magnetometer) instruments to discern patterning in the Late Woodland through Susquehannock occupations (figure 5.2). Limited block excavations have also been conducted at the Barton site, some as a follow-up to the geophysical investigations.

Several questions arise about the number, distribution, size, function, and duration of these Upper Potomac Valley sites, compared to the villages and cemeteries recorded in the Lower Susquehanna Valley, Pennsylvania, the heartland of seventeenth-century Susquehannock settlements. Were these Potomac Valley sites cemeteries, villages, or both? Or were they large base camps or hamlets used for short-term activities related to the fur trade? Trigger (1976:220) has noted that coastal trade originating with early colonization may have stirred the interest of Susquehannock peoples in trading for European goods before the beginning of the seventeenth century.

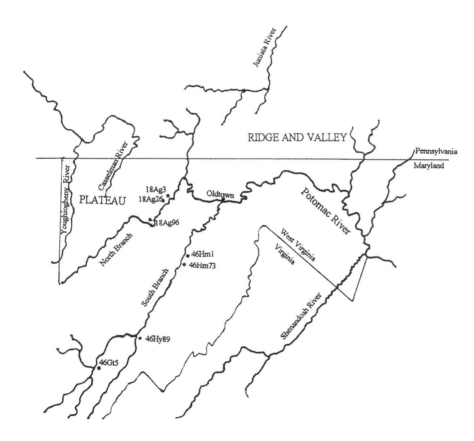

FIGURE 5.1
Susquehannock sites of the Upper Potomac region

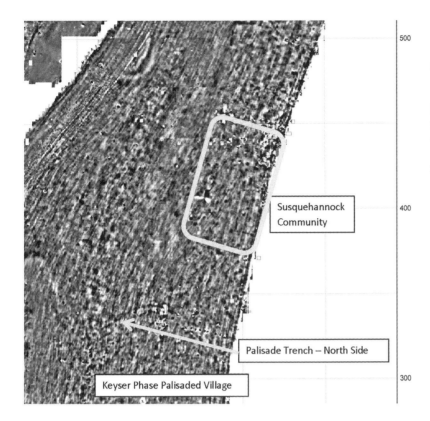

FIGURE 5.2
Magnetometer survey of Barton site (18AG3), showing the Keyser palisade line and the Susquehannock community north of the Keyser village (after Horsley and Wall 2010). Courtesy of the Maryland Historical Trust, Office of Research, Survey, and Registration.

Susquehannock Community

Palisade Trench – North Side

Keyser Phase Palisaded Village

Hunter (1959) further notes that the Susquehannocks informed Captain John Smith that they were obtaining trade goods from the Maritimes. This is about the same time that the Upper Potomac region settlements were being established. If these Upper Potomac region settlements were built right after their contact with John Smith, the Schultz–Washington Boro transition elements in their material culture would fit well within an estimated time frame of ca. 1610–20.

There were already established trade networks used by the Susquehannocks and other contemporary groups in the region at the time of contact. The marine shell trade (esp. marginella beads) predates the Contact period in the Upper Potomac region by several centuries. Shell beads of various types are found in burials associated with the pre-Contact, Late Woodland, Keyser, and Mason Island cultures. Both the Barton (18AG3) and Cresaptown (18AG119) sites in the North Branch Valley evidence very diverse shell bead assemblages. At the time of the Contact period,

the introduction and distribution of European manufactured trade goods simply followed established networks. Trade in native copper came later, also prior to European contact, evidenced by finds of copper beads in Keyser house structure contexts in the mid-fifteenth century on the Barton site. The raw material from the Barton site's Keyser component most likely comes from New Jersey sources, based on data derived from laser ablation studies conducted by Lattanzi (2008) of the New Jersey State Museum.

Environmental Background

The North Branch of the Potomac River flows out of the Appalachian Plateau physiographic province, where it may be described as little more than a shallow and swift-flowing stream. It achieves much greater volume at the base of the Allegheny Front, where large alluvial floodplains develop from the vicinity of Keyser,

West Virginia, and north to Cumberland. It is within this area that several of the larger Late Woodland and Contact period villages are known, including 18AG3 (Barton site), 18AG119 (Cresaptown site), and 18AG26 (Llewellyn site).

The South Branch of the Potomac River encompasses a much larger drainage basin and lies entirely within the Ridge and Valley physiographic province. The river course stretches just over 100 miles northeast from the headwaters to the confluence with the North Branch. Within the South Branch Valley are several other Susquehannock sites dating from the end of the 1500s through the first quarter of the 1600s. As in the North Branch Valley, the Susquehannock occupations along the South Branch immediately follow the Luray phase of the Late Woodland period, which is represented by small villages, some of which are palisaded (figure 5.1).

The Sites

North Branch Valley

There are four substantial Susquehannock sites in the Upper Potomac Valley and several other sites that have produced Susquehannock artifacts but have not been fully investigated via subsurface testing. The four definite Susquehannock sites include Pancake Island (46HM73; Anonymous 1889; Brashler 1987), Herriott Farm (46HM1; MacCord 1952; Manson and MacCord 1941, 1944), Moorefield (46HY89) in the South Branch Valley (Maymon and Davis 1998), and the Barton site (18AG3) in the North Branch Valley (Wall 2004; Wall and Lapham 2003). None of these sites have so far produced any evidence of longhouses of any kind. Longhouses do, however, typify Susquehannock sites of the Lower Susquehanna Valley (see Wyatt, chapter 6 in this volume).

Other sites in the North Branch Valley (e.g., Llewellyn, 18AG26) have produced brass, copper, and iron artifacts; early seventeenth-century (Kidd type II and IV) glass trade beads; and small amounts of Susquehannock (Schultz and Washington Boro) ceramics from surface collections (Wall 2004). This indicates a widespread though sparse distribution of Susquehannock settlements in the first few decades of the seventeenth century. No other early historic period native cultures are known for the region at this time—at least none that have been documented through archaeological investigations. Keyser-phase, Late Woodland cultures may have been present up until the late sixteenth century, but the majority of dates reflect a slightly earlier presence. For example, on the Barton site, the Keyser-phase village has been radiocarbon dated to the mid-1400s.

The Llewellyn Site (18AG26) is located about one mile upstream from the Barton site at the confluence of a small creek and the Potomac River. The site has produced a surface collection containing a possible Washington Boro–phase rim sherd and star chevron glass trade beads. The site has only been surface collected. The glass beads include predominantly Kidd type II and IV varieties, which date to the first half of the seventeenth century (Wyatt, chapter 6 in this volume). Similar bead assemblages have also been recovered from early historic period Monongahela sites in nearby southwestern Pennsylvania. Preliminary analysis by Heather Lapham (personal communication, 1999) of a collection of 95 beads from the site show a predominance of monochrome light-blue, dark-blue, and brick-red beads (table 5.1). Those that are most distinctive are the barrel-shaped star chevron beads similar to Kidd's Type IV and estimated to date to the period between 1575 and 1625. These bead types have been found on Susquehannock sites as well as Monongahela sites of southwestern Pennsylvania such as Foley Farm in Greene County (James Herbstritt, personal communication, 1998). Also recovered from the site are copper and brass ornaments, shell-tempered pottery, a Washington Boro Incised rim sherd, and triangular projectile points.

Sites such as Llewellyn and Barton are multicomponent and were utilized by Late Woodland groups

TABLE 5.1 Glass trade bead descriptions from the Llewellyn site (18AG26)

Kidd bead type	Count	Description
Ia5	1	Large, tubular, opaque white
IIa1	1	Large, round, opaque redwood
IIa2	6	Medium, circular, opaque redwood
IIa13	1	Medium, round, opaque white
IIa15	1	Medium, oval, opaque white
IIa40	26	Small to medium, round Semitranslucent/opaque robin's egg blue
IIa46	4	Small, round, opaque shadow blue
IIa51	1	Small, circular, translucent dark shadow blue
Iva	1	Small, circular, translucent navy-blue bead with two glass layers
IVa1	1	Large, round, redwood bead with either an opaque black core (IVa1) or a translucent apple-green core
IVa6	7	Small, circular, redwood beads with a translucent apple-green core
IVa7	1	Medium, oval, redwood bead with a translucent apple-green core
IVa12	2	Small, circular, cerulean beads with three layers
IVa19	5	Large, round, opaque light-aqua bead
IVb33	3	Large, round, three-layered navy-blue bead
IVb34	1	Large, round, three-layered navy-blue bead with 16 opaque white stripes
IVk4	9	Medium to large, round, four- or five-layered navy-blue chevron bead

as well as by earlier Archaic period populations. The location of an early historic period Susquehannock site is consistent with the locations of a long sequence of hamlets and villages in this area. Another point about the Llewellyn and Barton sites is that they are only about a mile apart, and both face the Potomac River. Though probably not large enough to be classified as villages, they were probably occupied sequentially.

Surface collections from the Flanigan site (18AG96), located about six miles upstream from the Llewellyn site, have also produced glass trade beads (e.g., star bead Type IVk4, IIa40, and IIb56 or 57) and a few sherds of incised shell-tempered pottery consistent with thinly constructed Susquehannock ceramics. The glass beads all date from ca. 1600 to the 1630s. No subsurface testing has been done on this site either. It is located in a small floodplain area that could

accommodate a moderately sized hamlet or small village.

South Branch Valley

In the South Branch Valley of the Potomac River, Pancake Island (46HM73), Herriott Farm (46HM1), and the Moorefield (46HY89) site make up the triad of Susquehannock sites recorded there, although surface finds of early seventeenth-century glass trade beads have also been collected from the surface of a few sites in the valley.

Moorehead's late nineteenth-century exploratory excavations at Pancake Island revealed burials with grave associations, ceramics, triangular points, and miscellaneous animal bones (Anonymous 1889:186). Moorehead also excavated a site about 12 miles downstream from Pancake Island that is likely the location of the Herriott Farm site. There, he recovered glass trade beads, ceramics, and items of metal. The ceramics were illustrated in Holmes's comprehensive ceramic study (1903:164–65, plate CXLIII), and the site was also described in 1894 by Fowke (1894:66), who noted evidence of hearths, human remains, and European-manufactured artifact items such as iron hatchets, glass beads, and brass ornaments. Moorehead's collection has essentially disappeared except for a single ceramic vessel and ledgers listing artifacts curated at the Ohio Historical Society in Columbus.

About 100 years after Moorehead's work at Pancake Island, severe flood erosion in 1985 revealed the location of what may be part of the same site he excavated. Excavations conducted by Brashler on the Pancake Farm (46HM73) revealed a site area measuring approximately one acre in size, including 25 features, 12 burials, a palisade enclosure, and a sheet midden, but there were no house patterns (Brashler 1987). The pit features include 4 bell-shaped pits filled with refuse and 2 cylindrical pits. Both of these feature types are also represented in the Susquehannock component of the Barton site. Grave associations included a cluster of bear claws, a pottery vessel, quartz biface, antler pipe, and beaver incisors. Burials are scattered throughout the roughly 9-by-12-meter block area and its extensions. The presence of burials and a palisade suggest a longer occupation.

The large area inside the double palisade, which appears to curve inward toward the river, contains some post patterns but no obvious longhouses (Brashler 1987:5). The double palisade does not at all appear to accommodate a village expansion, as at the Schultz site. Rather, it provides a sturdier defense structure or is simply an element in defining the boundaries of the community. The distance from the palisade to the levee is only about 20 meters, which means much of the site (estimated to be as much as 10–20 m) may have been eroded away, with about 0.75 acre left, according to Brashler (1987:10). The length of the exposed palisade, approximately 40 meters, implies the presence of a village. Its lack of curvature, however, also implies a more linear settlement, positioned close to the river. It may reflect a pattern similar to those seen at both Barton and Herriott Farm, where the sites are very close to the river and appear to lack occupation areas farther from the river.

Aside from the palisade, features (n = 25) at Pancake include cylindrical-shaped pits (n = 4), burials, and sheet middens, all comparable to those recorded at the Schultz site. The burials are scattered throughout the exposed excavation block area and do not appear to represent a distinct and separate cemetery area, as at Schultz. Post molds were also recorded, but no distinct houses and—again—specifically, no longhouses (Brashler 1987:9).

Pottery from Pancake Island exhibits traits common to Shultz-phase ceramics—that is, it is thin and shell tempered, with incised, inverted triangular plats (Brashler 1987:23). Bone tools include beamers and awls, and items of European manufacture include metal but no glass beads. The lack of glass beads may simply be due to the small sample, but Brashler suggested it may be an indication of the early date of the occupation, an inference supported by the presence of the typically early brass spirals. Other metal objects include brass cones, a brass gorget, brass fragments, and an iron axe and metal hasp.

The Herriott Farm site, originally described by Moorehead in the 1880s, was still found to be eroding into the river in 1940. Excavations conducted at that time encountered bell- and basin-shaped pit features and post molds exposed in the cut bank, along with numerous burials (Fowke 1894:65; MacCord 1952; Manson and MacCord 1941, 1944). This is probably the same location as an eroding site described much earlier by Kercheval (1833) in his *History of the Valley of Virginia*. As with the Pancake Island site, there has been a significant amount of erosion at Herriott Farm, so there may be little left of the site. Fifteen graves were recorded, with associations including bone beads, shell beads, a bone awl, a ceramic vessel, a perforated copper plate, a cluster of quartz flakes, around 300 glass beads (blue and chevron or star beads), an iron axe, and items of copper (tubular beads, earring, spirals or coils, cones, and spear tip; Anonymous 1889:187). The burial data can be summarized as follows: Burial 1 contained an adult interment and was associated with a clay pipe and a tubular copper bead. Burial 2 held a child estimated to be about seven years of age and was associated with 123 blue and black glass beads, 5 tubular copper beads, 16 tubular shell beads, 23 large disk shell beads, 2 copper coils (Basque earrings), a single broken shell gorget, 1 copper pipe, and 25 small tubular shell beads. Burial 3 was associated with a single copper bead. European-manufactured trade items included glass beads (table 5.2), an iron axe, brass spirals, cones and tubes, and bear molar pendants similar to those recovered from the Washington Boro site. In an early analysis of the ceramics from these sites, Holmes (1903:164–65) noted the prevalence of Iroquoian pottery and illustrated examples from Moorehead's excavations (Holmes 1903: plate CXLIII). The pottery has attributes of Schultz Incised with its characteristic triangular geometric plats bordered by parallel incising.

TABLE 5.2 Herriott Farm site (46HM1) glass trade beads

Kidd bead type	Count	Description
IIa40	5	Small to medium, round, semitranslucent/opaque robin's egg blue
IIa46	7	Small, round, opaque shadow blue
IIa51	7	Small, circular, translucent dark shadow blue
IIa55	4	Large, round, redwood bead with either an opaque black core (IVa1) or a translucent apple-green core
IIa56	5	Small, circular, redwood beads with a translucent apple-green core
IIb9	1	Medium, oval, redwood bead with a translucent apple-green core
IVa12	23	Small, circular, cerulean beads with three layers
IVa18	21	Small, circular, translucent navy-blue bead with two glass layers
IVa19	4	Large, round, opaque light-aqua bead
IVb	47	Large, round, three-layered navy-blue bead
IVb14	1	Large, round, three-layer navy-blue bead with 16 opaque white stripes
IVb33	8	Large, round, three-layer navy-blue bead with 8 pairs of opaque white stripes
IVk4	1	Medium to large, round, four- or five-layer navy-blue chevron bead

Keyser-phase, Late Woodland ceramics were also recovered from the Herriott Farm site, indicating, like the Barton site, use of the same location for a settlement. The Susquehannock component ceramics are similar to Schultz Incised, and the low numbers of glass beads on these sites are comparable to sites like Schultz, where most of the beads are from nine graves. Kinsey (1959) notes that trade objects from the Schultz site were not abundant and included 39 pieces of metal, particularly brass cones, beads, an arrow point, and iron axes and knives. Kinsey (1959) concludes that the South Branch sites such as Herriott Farm may represent a transitional occupation between the Schultz and Washington Boro phases.

The third principal Susquehannock site in the South Branch Valley was revealed through excavations by Goodwin and Associates in Moorefield, West Virginia, about 20 miles from Romney, where the remains of burials associated with European trade goods and Susquehannock ceramics were recorded. The male burials were associated with ceramic vessels, triangular points, and pipes. Infant graves contained most of the glass trade beads, which included mostly Kidd type IIa and IVa beads but no star chevron beads comparable to those recovered from North Branch Valley sites (Goodwin and Associates 1996; Maymon and Davis 1998). Glass beads recovered from the excavations also commonly included Kidd type IVa11, IVa14, IVa18, and IIa7. They include small seed beads and beads of various colors, including robin's egg blue, cobalt blue, black, white, red-white-blue striped, and brick red. Metal objects included hawk's bells, iron tools, and copper cones, but there were no copper or brass spirals, a common association with early Susquehannock sites (Bradley and Childs 1991). Perhaps this indicates a slightly later Susquehannock occupation. The ceramics associated with these burials include Schultz pottery with some sherds exhibiting decoration very typical of Susquehanna Valley Schultz pottery and other vessels exhibiting a mixture of styles with attributes such as piecrust impressions (exaggerated Keyser-like attributes) on vessel lips and variations in cord-roughened exterior surfaces. Although elements in the ceramic assemblage appear to be Schultz, much of the trade material appears to date to the Washington Boro period. Items of native material recorded on the site included goose effigy beads and drilled elk or bear teeth (L-shaped and plain), comparable to Herriott Farm site finds.

Other sites in the South Branch Valley containing evidence of European trade goods of likely Susquehannock affiliation included the Crites site (46HY25) near Moorefield on the South Branch, an isolated Schultz Incised vessel (Nat. Mus. No. 391694) from a rock shelter near the headwaters of the South Branch west of Petersburg, and isolated incised shell-tempered sherds in stratified contexts in Petersburg, West Virginia, also along the South Branch (Wall 1993).

Barton Site

The most recent data on Susquehannock community patterns in the Upper Potomac region comes from ongoing excavations at the Barton site. This is the principal information used here to evaluate Susquehannock community patterns in the region. The Barton site lies at the foot of the Allegheny Front on a broad Pleistocene terrace overlooking the North Branch of the Potomac River. The river flows along the base of the mountain in a northeasterly direction before trending east near Cumberland, Maryland. The characteristic sharp relief of the uplands causes constrictions at several points along the Potomac. In the floodplain area surrounding the Barton site, there is a broad bottomland section comparable in size to only a few other settings in the North Branch Valley. The Juniata Valley can be accessed from this area of the Potomac via Wills Creek, the headwaters of which lie near the Juniata River. The area is also accessible to the Upper Ohio Valley on the west side of the Allegheny Front, thereby making the North Branch Valley a strategic crossroads between the Upper Ohio Valley to the northwest, the Susquehanna Valley to the north, and the lower reaches of the Potomac River Valley and the Chesapeake. This may have been a suitable location for the control of regional trade networks.

The Barton site was initially tested by Henry Wright in 1960 with a small stratigraphic cut in the edge of the terrace, with subsequent work involving surface surveys and test excavations (Wall 1981; Wall and Curry 1992; Wright 1963). In 1993, test excavations near the edge of the Keyser-phase village were initiated. Based on the review of extensive surface collections, the site became known as a Late Woodland village site composed of several occupations spanning the Late Woodland and Contact periods. Test excavations continued along the margins of the site from 1993 to 1995 to ascertain the extent of the various components represented on the site. A substantial Susquehannock component was revealed in 1995, and work has progressed in this area of the site from

1996 to the present. Work has also been undertaken on the fifteenth-century Keyser-phase village, revealing a complete house pattern within the confines of the encircling palisade. The Keyser village is about 50 meters south of the edge of the Susquehannock settlement and is clearly delineated by a double palisade. It is possible that some remnant of the Keyser village existed when the Susquehannocks first arrived. Other Keyser-phase sites in the Upper Potomac and Shenandoah drainage basins are much later in age and their inhabitants may have directly interacted with the Susquehannocks when they moved into the Upper Potomac Valley. Whether any Keyser-phase villages are contemporaneous with early Susquehannock settlements in the Upper Potomac is possible but uncertain. On the Barton site (18AG3), the Keyser and Susquehannock settlements are in close proximity but the artifact assemblages show no overlap or mixing.

Most of the artifacts recovered from the Susquehannock component of the Barton site lie within the plow zone and in features and adjacent contexts in the upper portion of the B horizon. Feature contexts have produced a broad range of radiocarbon dates and associated ceramic assemblages that are consistent with the radiocarbon dates. Botanical evidence from the Susquehannock component of the Barton site includes predominantly hickory and maize with trace amounts of beans, squash, knotweed, grape, and acorn (Furgerson 2007). The cultivated and wild plants represented are not unlike those used by the Susquehannock's Late Woodland predecessors.

What defines the period of occupation of the Susquehannock component of the site, aside from Schultz Incised ceramics, are surface and feature recoveries of glass trade beads (table 5.3). The beads date primarily from two time periods—first, the early seventeenth century and, second, the late seventeenth to early eighteenth century. The former is assumed to relate to the Schultz-phase Susquehannock occupation, and the latter is affiliated with the Shawnee settlement, documented in early seventeenth-century maps

TABLE 5.3 Barton site (18AG3) glass trade beads

Kidd bead type	Count	Description
Ia5	1	Large, tubular, opaque white bead
Ia19	1	Tubular, navy
Ibb*	1	Tubular, striped
If*	1	Faceted
IIa6	1	Round, opaque black
IIa7	1	Round, opaque black
IIa13	2	Medium, round, opaque white bead
IIa14	1	Circular, opaque white
IIa40	2	Small to medium, round Semitranslucent/opaque robin's egg blue
IIa41	3	Small, circular, opaque robin's egg blue
IIbb*	1	Medium, round, translucent navy-blue bead with one stripe made of three lines of red, white, and red glass (no Kidd variety available)
IIb26*	1	Medium, oval, opaque white with navy stripes
IIb67	1	Large, oval, clear navy blue with white stripes
IVa1	1	Large, round, redwood bead with opaque black core
IVb24*	1	Medium, round, opaque shadow-blue bead with five red stripes and a translucent blue core
IVb34	1	Large, round, three-layer navy-blue bead with 16 opaque white stripes
IVk4	4	Medium to large, round, four- or five-layer navy blue
WIb*	1	Large, round, opaque black bead (no Kidd type available)
WIb1	1	Large, round, clear gray
WIb2	1	Large, round, translucent white
WIb5	2	Large, round, translucent pale blue (opal/alabaster)
WIb6	1	Large, round, translucent light gold
WIb10	2	Large, round, opaque light aqua
WIb11	1	Large, round, opaque robin's egg blue
WIb15	2	Large, round, translucent ultramarine
WIb16	2	Large, round, translucent navy blue
WIc*	1	
WId1	1	Large, donut-shaped, translucent amber
WId6	1	
WIIc2	1	Medium, circular, five-sided faceted transparent light gray
WIIc11	1	Large, five-sided, pressed, faceted, translucent bright copen blue
WIIc12	2	Large, five-sided, pressed, faceted, translucent amethyst
WIIIb	1	Very large, tubular, translucent white

* Kidd type classification is uncertain.

of the North Branch of the Potomac and designated as "Shawnee Old Fields" (Fry and Jefferson 1755).

The Schultz Incised ceramics recovered from the site can be described as follows. Rim (collar) profiles are very slightly inverted, forming a convex exterior surface where the thin collar adheres to the vessel wall. The collared area averages a little more than 5 millimeters thick, and the vessel bodies are typically only 4 millimeters thick. Lips of vessels are undecorated and rounded. On many rim sections, just below the lip on the exterior, are two horizontal grooves that parallel the lip of the vessel and sweep upward into the castellations, which are notched with short, parallel grooves. Below the castellations, inverted triangular patterns bounded by intersecting oblique incisions mark most of the collar surfaces. The incised patterns also demarcate an equilateral triangular zone defined by horizontal grooves made with final S-twist cordage impressions. The base of the collar where it meets the body of the vessel is marked by slightly oblique cord-wrapped stick impressions. The bodies of vessels exhibit fine cord-marked (final Z-twist) impressions.

The Susquehannock component at the Barton site is estimated to be about 70 meters long and is found only about 60 meters from the Potomac riverbank to the rear of the settlement. The settlement rests on a broad Pleistocene terrace that is underlain by deeply stratified Holocene deposits. The Susquehannock community is estimated to be about half the size of the adjacent Keyser-phase village, which measures 110 meters across and is clearly defined by palisade trenches with associated post alignments. There has likely been little erosion of the site due to riverbank cutting, a more common occurrence in the South Branch Valley, where bank erosion has seriously damaged the Pancake Island and Herriott Farm sites. This is evident in the magnetometer survey data from Barton, which show relatively complete palisade enclosures on habitation areas much older than the Susquehannock settlement (figure 5.2). What the magnetometer imaging does not show are obvious patterns of structures or linear arrangements of features that would represent longhouses (Horsley and Wall 2010). Similar studies of Susquehannock sites in Pennsylvania using geophysical methods have identified large features associated with houses but not necessarily post patterns (Rubino 2013; Wyatt, chapter 6 in this volume).

A series of two-meter test units and larger block excavations covering about 250 square meters have been undertaken on the Susquehannock area of the Barton site. Post mold patterns have so far not produced any evidence of longhouses. Instead, the post mold patterns suggest smaller circular structures not unlike the earlier Keyser and Mason Island structures used from ca. AD 1000–1500. There are no overlapping Keyser-phase occupations in this area of the site nor are there any shell-tempered ceramics of Keyser-phase affiliation. Keyser ceramics are easily distinguishable from shell-tempered Schultz pottery by construction and cordage impressions in spite of the fact that both types are shell tempered. Mason Island artifacts and features, however, are found throughout the Susquehannock habitation area. This also includes house patterns, at least one of which has been established as a Mason Island structure, as evidenced by diagnostic artifact associations in post mold fill.

The recorded post patterns associated with Susquehannock ceramics or near concentrations of Susquehannock pit features include arcs and short lines of posts as well as small posts in shallow trenches and larger posts in deep trenches. The latter suggests a palisade trench, but the feature is discontinuous and not linked to similar linear patterns. The smaller posts in trenches are unusual for the region but appear to represent some variant of a house wall with a shallow trench excavated for the posts. A similar feature was found in the Keyser-phase village with much smaller posts and a clear association with Keyser ceramics. None of these patterns represent what is more typical of longhouses. Rather, they appear to represent smaller structures that mimic what is more common in the region—that is, round to oval house patterns measuring about 6 meters in diameter. They may also

have been the imprint of more temporary or short-term structures.

Susquehannock pit features on the Barton site are consistent with those recorded on other early Susquehannock sites (figure 5.3). These include silo-shaped pits, some with a slight flare outward at the base; basins; middens; and hearths. There have been no human remains or distinct cemeteries associated with the Barton site's Susquehannock occupation. Susquehannock features tend to be most concentrated near the riverbank. This is where a linear pattern of silo-shaped pits, around one meter deep, are distributed in a loosely linear alignment, some paired, within 10 to 15 meters of the riverbank and about 10 meters apart. These are not clearly associated, externally or internally, with any house patterns, though many incomplete arcs of posts are found in the same area. It is likely that these silo-shaped pits and their nearby post associations document separate households, albeit incompletely represented in the archaeological record. The linear spacing of the silo-shaped pits may reflect more of a linear community plan along the river, though elements of other structures are found farther away. Not enough area has been exposed to determine a more complete community pattern. Hearths located near the silos likely represent interior hearths for the structures. The remaining features recorded in the larger block excavations are basins and middens, which served as general repositories for camp debris.

Close to the levee edge, excavations have revealed a greater density of Susquehannock camp debris within feature contexts, though Mason Island features have been located there as well. Dense clusters of post molds indicate the presence of an intensively utilized habitation area that extends to the existing riverbank. Additional tests in this area have encountered similar densely occupied surfaces and large sections of Schultz Incised Susquehannock vessels. This suggests either that the greatest density in site activities occurred in the riverbank area or that riverbank erosion may

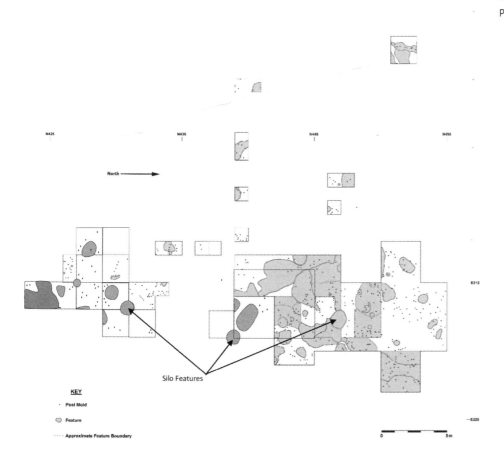

FIGURE 5.3
Plan of Barton site
(18AG3) excavations,
showing Susquehannock
community features and
post patterns

129

North ⟶

N425   N435   N445   N455

E215

Silo Features

KEY

· Post Mold

⟳ Feature

- - - - Approximate Feature Boundary

E225

0   5m

have truncated a densely occupied portion of the settlement facing the river. Again, this may reflect the linear river-edge pattern of the settlement in contrast to what is more typical of palisaded Susquehannock villages.

No Susquehannock cemetery has yet been discovered on the site, though several Mason Island and Keyser-phase burials have been exposed during the investigations on those components. The geophysical work undertaken on the site would likely have picked up signatures of even a small cemetery, but none comparable to the South Branch Valley Susquehannock

sites has been revealed. This may relate to the short period of occupation as well.

There is a large palisade trench that runs through the Susquehannock occupation at Barton, and it is much wider than the one encircling the Keyser-phase village about 50 meters to the south. This implies a small hamlet-sized occupation for the Susquehannock component, and geophysical work has not confirmed a clear village pattern demarcated by palisade lines, as with the earlier communities. To date, not enough of the palisade has been exposed by excavations to determine its orientation or size. The only other substantial palisade delineated on an early Susquehannock site in the region is the one recorded at Pancake Island, as previously described. The Pancake Island palisade appears to represent more of a linear community pattern, close to the river. The Herriott Farm site is also close to the riverbank, and what may have been a narrow palisade trench six inches deep was exposed and recorded in the 1940s (Manson and MacCord 1944:202–3). The site itself was described as semicircular and close to the river (Manson and MacCord 1941:291). This suggests the presence of a circular village pattern, but we lack details to verify this pattern, and much of the site is already severely eroded. A linear arrangement of structures close to the riverbanks would explain its rapid disappearance over just a few hundred years.

The lack of longhouses on Upper Potomac region Susquehannock sites may relate to several factors, including the brief duration of the settlements themselves and possibly the use of structures that were more typical of those in the region. The fact that Susquehannocks were newcomers to the Potomac region may have altered some of their traditional community-building practices, though their signature silo-shaped pits, material culture, and other cultural elements remained the same. The purpose of these Potomac settlements and the meaning of their diversity and function in the region are also uncertain. The Susquehannocks did use satellite camps such as small hunting-gathering-fishing stations (Jordan 2013; White 2001:39), but most of the Potomac Valley sites appear to be more substantial. The Susquehannocks are known to have raided other groups and intimidated them into cooperative agreements with regard to trading furs and so forth (White 2001:74). It is unknown if this kind of influence began with the sixteenth-century Keyser-phase peoples or residents of the nearby village at Barton or if these groups were already gone by the time the Susquehannocks arrived. The diversity of the Upper Potomac Susquehannock settlements may also have had a basis in kinship. Cultural patterns (e.g., settlement patterns, economy, wars) in Iroquoian societies were often clan based and

locally derived (White 2001:157). It has been noted that Iroquoian settlements probably included a variety of hamlets and small villages of short duration that were a consequence of factional disputes, clan-based decisions, or other reasons for community growth and decline (Snow 1991:37; White 2001:157). The same factors likely influenced the Susquehannocks as well.

Whatever the reason for establishing these Upper Potomac Susquehannock settlements, they do appear to differ substantially from the Susquehanna Valley settlements and from Iroquoian sites in general. If nothing else, the generally low density of Susquehannock occupations on sites in the Potomac Valley contrasts sharply with the densely occupied and closely packed longhouse villages of the Iroquois and Lower Susquehanna Valley Susquehannocks.

Boza Arlotti (1997), citing Braun and Plog's (1982:9) model that addresses changes in social complexity as a coping strategy, described various forms of social groupings in Susquehannock culture. Factors influencing social configurations in Susquehannock society included environmental unpredictability, trade, disease, warfare, and the introduction of new and very distinctive technologies (e.g., firearms). So the increase in social complexity, as modeled by Braun and Plog (1982), shows that cultures, in general, do respond to these factors. An example of this is the development of the new role of a tribal spokesperson for dealing with colonial traders directly, particularly with regard to the acquisition of European-manufactured trade goods. This new commercial role perhaps caused some shifts in social configurations to accommodate the new role. Relevant to the development of regionally distinct Susquehannock communities in the Upper Potomac Valley were "strategies of accommodation" (Braun and Plog 1982:11) to new social, economic, and political processes. The result was individual or clan-based entrepreneurial activities that were influenced by differential access to resources such as marketable furs. The eventual outcome, even over the short term, was the segmentation of Susquehannock societies into more complex, localized social groupings. In the

130

Upper Potomac Valley, these smaller social groups may have built smaller, more temporary village or hamlet sites without the substantial longhouses.

Longhouses of the Iroquois and Related Groups

Late Owasco cultures evolved into Susquehannock (and Iroquoian) cultures in the Upper Susquehanna region (Snow 1994:29). The smaller, subrectangular Early Owasco house types were the predecessors to the much more substantial longhouses of later centuries, so the longhouse form has a long history in the Susquehanna Valley. In the Potomac Valley, its presence is rare or absent. Primarily, oval or circular dome-shaped structures were more typical there. However, it is important to at least briefly describe the distinctions between the two house forms in this discussion.

Longhouse structures were substantial structures that housed large numbers of people compared to the much smaller dome-shaped houses found in much of the Middle Atlantic region from the Late Woodland period to the Contact period. At the Barton site, for example, a mid-fifteenth-century Keyser-phase house was oval in shape and measured approximately 7 meters by 6 meters, with a single central hearth and a single large storage pit near the south wall. In contrast, longhouses tended to have a series of internal compartments for separate families, marked by central hearths that followed a linear pattern bisecting the structures. Iroquois house patterns are usually well defined archaeologically, and houses within a village were more densely spaced over time (Snow 1994:52–53). Even early seventeenth-century Susquehannock villages in Pennsylvania were densely occupied, with houses built close together and near the palisade lines. None of these house features, or those described below, are found on Upper Potomac Valley sites (see also Wyatt, chapter 6 in this volume).

Kapches (1990) noted that as longhouse forms evolved over time, they showed greater organization of space. In general, longhouses were constructed using exterior posts for the outside walls and interior support posts (see Wyatt, chapter 6 in this volume). House interiors contained storage and refuse pits, hearths, side-wall benches, partitions, end storage pits, and cubicles. Many of these internal features were surrounded by posts of various sizes (Kapches 1990:51). Kapches (2007:178) also noted that Iroquois longhouses were typically 22–26 feet wide. Trigger (1976) describes seventeenth-century Huron houses as typically 90–100 feet long and 25–30 feet wide. Knight (1987) observed, for the Huron-affiliated Ball Site, that longhouses were recorded within 10 feet of the palisade line and that the depth of house posts was much greater than the palisade posts. There also tended to be a great deal of variation in Huron longhouses.

An example of a longhouse pattern from the Le Caron site, an early seventeenth-century Huron village, provides additional detailed information on house construction plans. One house measured 18.8 by 27 feet and consisted of 436 postholes. Rebuilding of the house is indicated by double rows of posts along the side walls near each end (Johnston and Jackson 1980:181). Palisade posts averaged 4.9 inches in diameter for an estimated 20–30 foot structure height (Johnston and Jackson 1980:193). Houses at LeCaron contained variably sized posts averaging 4–4.8 inches in diameter. At the Nodwell site, the outer wall posts were 2–3 inches in diameter, with larger interior support posts ranging from 5 to 8 inches. These figures on post sizes are all comparable to house posts in Middle Atlantic region houses, with the principal difference being the structure outlines—that is, longhouses versus circular, dome-shaped dwellings. Kapches (2007:181) remarked that structural variability, including the interior organization, relates to cultural influences. Perhaps external cultural influences, at least in part, affected the construction styles of the Upper Potomac region's early seventeenth-century structures.

Susquehannock longhouses in the Susquehanna Valley are comparable to those found in Iroquoian and Huron contexts. For example, Kinsey (1957) described a post mold pattern for a Susquehannock longhouse that was 92 feet long by 24 feet wide. Post molds averaged 2–3 inches in diameter, especially along the outer walls. Larger support posts ran lengthwise down through the center of the house and were 4–6 inches in diameter. Paired posts on both sides of the interior walls may have supported benches for sleeping.

At the Schultz site, recorded structures were 50–70 feet long by 20 feet wide with storage pits located inside houses near the walls, beneath sleeping platforms (Smith 1970:30). Other early Susquehannock sites, like the Sick Farm site (36BR50) in southern Towanda, exhibit longhouse post patterns for structures measuring 25 feet across. None of these longhouse patterns are evident on Upper Potomac Valley Susquehannock sites.

In the early Susquehannock period, sites tended to be much smaller prior to their coalescence at the Schultz site and later Susquehannock villages. Early sites in Bradford County, Pennsylvania, were small hamlets, some consisting of only a few households (Witthoft 1959:28). This would compare favorably with the Barton site and perhaps other communities in the Upper Potomac Valley. However, those communities, based on trade bead chronologies, appeared a few decades later. No Susquehannock longhouses have been identified on these late sixteenth-century northern Pennsylvania sites. Although there have been a number of sites that produced Schultz ceramics, none have produced longhouse data except for the Kennedy site (36BR43), which contained a single longhouse associated with primarily Owasco ceramics (Kent 2001:305) that most likely relate to the house builders.

Susquehannock Community Patterns

Early seventeenth-century Susquehannock communities in the Lower Susquehanna Valley tended to have densely packed structures in close proximity to many large pit features that are easily recognizable in archaeological contexts. For example, at the Schultz site (36LA7), recorded features number more than 600, including deep bell-shaped storage pits, basins, ash deposits, middens, and refuse pits that varied in size and depth. Nine obvious longhouses were exposed in Smith's excavations, along with partial sections of others (Smith 1970:30). Surrounding the densely packed community were three stockades, which bounded the community and serve as evidence of episodes of village expansion. Excavations ultimately revealed up to 27 longhouses (Kent 2001:326). Longhouses were densely concentrated in as many as six rows, and designated areas in the village were used for burials, which totaled 184 (White 2001:172). Close and parallel arrangements of wall post alignments appear to indicate wall repairs. Related to this is the linear arrangement of features, likely part of a sequence (Smith 1970; Wyatt 2012:89).

At the Washington Boro site (36LA8), pit features and houses were also densely packed across the community space, with two palisades surrounding the village (Cadzow 1936). Longhouses extended beyond the inner palisade wall, suggesting a period of village expansion necessitating the construction of a new palisade. Four cemeteries were associated with the village.

The Lemoyne site is a multicomponent community with a substantial early seventeenth-century Susquehannock component (Wyatt 2012:76, and chapter 6 in this volume), perhaps contemporaneous with the Barton site. Features include cylindrical and bell-shaped pits, basins, two palisades, and possible longhouses represented by linear features indicative of longhouse patterns. The low pit feature density noted by Wyatt (2012:90) as an indicator of the short length of occupation may perhaps be compared to the Upper Potomac sites, where lower densities of features may also imply settlements of shorter duration.

In the Upper Potomac region, using the Barton site (18AG3) as an example, there were no longhouses, and the Susquehannock community was inhabited for a much shorter period of time. This is evidenced by a lower density imprint of the Susquehannock occupation—that is, sparsely distributed silo-shaped

132

pits, basins, and middens. Scattered finds of Schultz ceramics and glass trade beads at other small sites in the Upper Potomac Valley suggest a broader and more diversified settlement pattern that included smaller villages and hamlets (long and short term), farmsteads, camps, staging areas, and other sites of varying functions. The patterning, however, appears to differ sharply from the Lower Susquehanna region.

Towns—Communities

Birch (2010:30) noted that by the late 1400s, Iroquois warfare resulted in community coalescence and the construction of defensive palisade structures. From the 1400s to 1600, Iroquois villages coalesced further, with populations reaching 1,500 to 2,000 and village sizes expanding to greater than six hectares (Birch and Williamson 2015). There is also a large body of evidence on violent conflict in the region, with tribes (e.g., Wendat) shifting away from the conflict and expressing marked territoriality over hunting territories (Birch 2015:283; Birch and Williamson 2015:143). In the late 1500s, the Iroquois attacked neighboring Iroquoian peoples as well (Birch and Williamson 2015:143). By this time (1590–1620, based on various evidence), the Iroquois Confederacy was forming (Birch 2015:291). This time of population growth and upheaval is coeval with the spread of Susquehannock peoples into the Upper Potomac region. As villages generally became larger and social complexity increased, there may have been a tendency for groups to fission, with some clan groups perhaps splitting from the main village. This could have happened prior to the village coalescence at Schultz or shortly thereafter. The attributes of Washington Boro wares present in Upper Potomac ceramics seem to suggest the latter.

The Upper Potomac region's Susquehannock sites were briefly occupied, ca. 1600–1620, a period based on the glass trade bead chronology already described. Dispersal from the Potomac Valley by the early 1620s may also relate again to a shift away from

conflicts—namely, the Second Anglo-Powhatan War in 1622 (Hatfield 2003). This may have disrupted sufficiently the important and long-term trade relationships with coastal plain sources.

Several questions can be posed regarding the origin, nature, and function of these regional settlements. In the Upper Potomac region, Susquehannock settlements could represent a sequence of diverse communities within that roughly two-decade time span rather than a sequence of durable villages, even though these sites did contain some of the elements found in villages (e.g., palisades, large storage pits). Iroquois villages were occupied for 10–12 years, and some say as long as 30 years (Abler 1970). Seneca villages were used for 15–25 years, whereas the duration of Huron villages was variable (White 2001:39).

Lower Susquehanna Valley Susquehannock villages were established and in use for a comparable length of time. Kent (2001:363) observed that Susquehannock villages contained from 15 to 100 longhouses, supporting populations between 900 and 2,900 (see also White 2001:224–25). For the Upper Potomac region, there could have been one small primary village and a number of satellite communities—possibly one primary village in the North Branch and the other in the South Branch Valley. White speculates that villages may have been moved only short distances to maintain control over a territory (2001:40). In the case of the Susquehannocks, this applied to the Lower Susquehanna Valley sequence beginning with Schultz. But the move from northern Pennsylvania in the late sixteenth century and the comparable move to the Upper Potomac region in the early seventeenth century were more dramatic and spread the population out over a large area. This is characterized by Wyatt (2012:93, and chapter 6 in this volume) as a divided risk strategy, and it contrasts with that of the Iroquois, whose settlements tended to be more focused and densely occupied. Populations also may have moved because of indigenous warfare from 1600 to 1675 (White 2001:40). Whatever the reason, the Potomac Valley may have been perceived as relatively new terrain, unfamiliar to incoming populations, necessitating the formation of much smaller, more adaptive communities.

Other notable patterns in the Upper Potomac settlements include the possible existence of paired communities comparable to the Seneca's paired towns, with a main town and a satellite on a much smaller scale. The Barton and Llewellyn sites are only a mile apart along the river, and they may have been either contemporaneous or sequentially occupied. No other sites in the Upper Potomac Valley seem to fit this pattern. Some of these separate communities may have been organized along clan lines (Brandão 1997; White 2001:41). We can speculate that if communities were paired (e.g., Barton and Llewellyn), the inhabitants of each may have belonged to separate clan groups or moieties. Partial palisades exposed at the Barton and the Pancake Island sites suggest these communities were palisaded, but were only the primary or larger communities palisaded (Abler 1970:25)? How autonomous were these communities? It is possible that the choices of areas for settlements were not necessarily centrally coordinated but may have been clan-based decisions, thereby creating even greater diversity in the Susquehannock regional settlement pattern.

Conclusions

In the late sixteenth century, the Susquehannocks made their first relocation from northern Pennsylvania (Englebrecht 2003:143). Kent (2001) described the early Susquehannock coalescence from dispersed North Branch (Susquehanna) populations into the single palisaded village at Schultz (White 2001:220). The Schultz site is recognized as the initial settlement of the Susquehannocks in southeastern Pennsylvania, where they replaced resident Shenks Ferry populations (Cadzow 1936; Humpf and Hatch 1994:68; Smith and Graybill 1977). White (2001:164) noted that most Susquehannock sites were oriented along the

river—that is, within 300 meters of the banks—and were primarily villages. Ultimately, the breakup of these kinds of villages and the subsequent movement at the beginning of the seventeenth century were due to multiple factors: population growth, trade opportunities, and the depletion of hunting/gathering resources.

It is well established that the Susquehannocks also occupied territories beyond the Juniata drainage basin and into the headwaters of the Potomac. This early seventeenth-century relocation was at least partially due to fur trade opportunities (White 2001:34). The fur trade eventually depleted game populations in some regions and changed territoriality patterns (White 2001:36). This may have something to do with the brief (two-decade-long) presence of Susquehannocks in the Upper Potomac region.

Palisaded communities in the Upper Potomac Valley—whether they contained longhouses, wigwams, pit houses, or other types of dome-shaped structures—may also have been an outgrowth of the intensification of food production, with greater reliance on maize-centered agriculture in support of larger populations. This would have encouraged the more focused and longer-term occupations that typify Keyser-phase, Late Woodland sites of the 1400–1500s. These types of communities existed in the Upper Potomac region at the very beginning of Susquehannock contact with them, ca. 1600, primarily during the Schultz and perhaps early Washington Boro phases. Unfortunately, descriptions of these settlements by the earliest European explorers do not exist. It is likely that the Late Woodland / Early Contact period communities of the Upper Potomac region were relatively diverse in their configurations.

The Susquehannocks, newcomers to the Potomac region, were adapting to new and unfamiliar landscapes, so structural forms may have been ad hoc manifestations that did not follow the patterns of traditional houses. The new early seventeenth-century Potomac Valley houses of the Susquehannocks may have displayed a variety of structural forms built for the short term, depending on the nature of the site. For example, there were likely some small hamlets large enough to accommodate several structures with associated storage pits and an enclosing palisade. These sites would have been sufficiently large to coordinate nearby clan or family-based hunting and trapping activities as well. Separate cemeteries (e.g., at Moorefield and Pancake Island) may have been established near the larger communities for the purpose of conducting mortuary activities. There may also have been an established but relatively flexible process of group fission and fusion within this new territory that bonded the entire Upper Potomac Susquehannock community together for about 20 years.

A second factor affecting the resettlement of Susquehannock peoples was warfare with the Iroquois. The Susquehannocks were fighting with the Iroquois through much of the seventeenth century (Bradley 1987; Brandão 1997; Englebrecht 2003; Sempowski 1994; Trigger 1976:97), and they were not the only ones. From 1601 to 1701, the Iroquois attacked 50 groups and were themselves attacked by 20 (Brandão 1997:31), partly to deny other groups contact with European traders (Snow 1994). Dispersal of Susquehannock populations to the Upper Potomac region may have helped reduce the frequency of Iroquois raids by putting greater distance between them and establishing dispersed and smaller settlements. It also provided the opportunity for farming the rich bottomland areas along the Potomac River. In the Potomac Valley, Susquehannock settlements are exclusively found on large floodplains. The use of floodplains is consistent with Susquehannock agricultural practices and is verified by the abundant recoveries of cultigens and wild plant foods from most of the large silo pits excavated on Potomac Valley sites.

It still remains to be seen whether the Susquehannocks expropriated resident populations (e.g., Keyser-phase, Late Woodland peoples) of the Potomac Valley or simply moved into recently unoccupied territory. The juxtaposition of the Keyser village and Susquehannock community at the Barton site suggests the latter, as there do not appear to be any Contact period materials within the Keyser village, nor are there any Keyser ceramics anywhere within the Susquehannock community. The small horticultural Susquehannock hamlets and hunting/trapping camps throughout the Upper Potomac region were likely established by ca. 1600. These small settlements may have been used for the purpose of fur trade with the recently established English settlements such as Jamestown. But the rapid changes in the seventeenth-century cultural landscape may have shortened this venture, eventually dispersing the Susquehannocks from the Potomac Valley in the 1620s, perhaps back to their Susquehanna Valley homeland.

REFERENCES

Abler, Thomas S.
1970 Longhouse and Palisade: Northeastern Iroquois Villages of the Seventeenth Century. *Ontario History* 62:17–40.

Anonymous
1889 Two Indian Cemeteries near Romney, Hampshire County, West Virginia. *The American Naturalist* 23:186.

Birch, Jennifer
2010 Coalescence and Conflict in Iroquoian Ontario. *Archaeological Review from Cambridge* 25 (1): 29–48.

2015 Current Research on the Historical Development of Northern Iroquois Societies. *Journal of Archaeological Research* 23:263–323.

Birch, Jennifer, and Ronald F. Williamson
2015 Navigating Ancestral Landscapes in the Northern Iroquoian World. *Journal of Anthropological Archaeology* 39:139–50.

Boza Arlotti, Ana Maria
1997 *Evolution of the Social Organization of the Susquehannock Society During the Contact Period in South Central Pennsylvania.* Ph.D. dissertation, Department of Anthropology, University of

Pittsburgh. University Microfilms, Ann Arbor, Michigan.

Bradley, James W.

1987   *Evolution of the Onondaga Iroquois: Accommodating Change, 1500–1655 AD.* Syracuse University Press, Syracuse, New York.

Bradley, James W., and Terry Childs

1991   Basque Earrings and Panther's Tails: The Form of Cross-Cultural Contact in Sixteenth Century Iroquoia. In *Metals in Society: Theory Beyond Analysis*, edited by Robert M. Ehrenreich, 7–17. Research Papers in Science and Archaeology. Vol. 8 (Part 2). Museum Applied Science Center for Archaeology, The University Museum of Archaeology and Anthropology, University of Pennsylvania, Philadelphia.

Brandão, José António

1997   *Your Fyre Shall Burn No More: Iroquois Policy Toward New France and Its Native Allies to 1701.* University of Nebraska Press, Lincoln.

Brashler, Janet G.

1987   A Middle 16th Century Susquehannock Village in Hampshire County, West Virginia. *West Virginia Archeologist* 39 (2): 1–30.

Braun, David P., and Stephen Plog

1982   Evolution of "Tribal" Social Networks: Theory and Prehistoric North American Evidence. *American Antiquity* 47:504–25.

Buchanan, William T.

1986   The Trigg Site: City of Radford, Virginia. Archeological Society of Virginia Special Publication 14. Archeological Society of Virginia, Richmond.

Cadzow, Donald

1936   *Archaeological Studies of the Susquehannock Indians of Pennsylvania.* Safe Harbor Report 2. Publications of the Pennsylvania Historical and Museum Commission, Harrisburg.

Englebrecht, William

2003   *Iroquoia: The Development of a Native World.* Syracuse University Press, Syracuse, New York.

Fowke, Gerard

1894   *Archeologic Investigations in the James and Potomac Valleys.* Bureau of American Ethnology Bulletin 23. Smithsonian Institution, Washington, D.C.

Fry, Joshua, and Peter Jefferson

1755   *A Map of the Most Inhabited Part of Virginia Containing the Whole Province of Maryland with Part of Pensilvania, New Jersey and North Carolina.* Thomas Jefferys, London.

Furgerson, Kathleen

2007   *Archaeobotany of the Late Woodland and Contact Periods at the Barton Site (18AG3), Allegany County, Maryland.* Unpublished M.A. thesis, School of

Archaeology and Ancient History, University of Leicester, England.

Goodwin and Associates, Inc.

1996   Artifact Inventory from Burials at 46Hy89. Prepared by R. Christopher Goodwin and Associates, Inc., Frederick, Maryland. Inventory on file at West Virginia Division of Culture and History, Charleston, West Virginia.

Hatfield, April Lee

2003   Spanish Colonization, Literature, Powhatan Geographies, and English Perceptions of Tsenacommacah/Virginia. *Journal of Southern History* 69 (2): 245–82.

Holmes, William H.

1903   *Aboriginal Pottery of the Eastern United States.* Twentieth Annual Report of the Bureau of American Ethnology, 1898–1899. Smithsonian Institution, Washington, D.C.

Horsley, Timothy, and Robert D. Wall

2010   Archaeological Evaluation of Alluvial Landscapes in Western Maryland. Report prepared for the Maryland Historical Trust, Crownsville, Maryland.

Humpf, Dorothy, and James W. Hatch

1994   Susquehannock Demography: A New Perspective on the Contact Period in Pennsylvania. In *Proceedings of the 1992 People to People Conference, Selected Papers*, edited by Charles F. Hayes III, 65–76. Research Records 23. Rochester Museum and Science Center, Rochester, New York.

Hunter, William A.

1959   The Historic Role of the Susquehannocks. In *Susquehannock Miscellany*, edited by John Witthoft and W. Fred Kinsey, 8–18. Pennsylvania Historical and Museum Commission, Harrisburg.

Johnston, Richard B., and L. J. Jackson

1980   Settlement Pattern at the Le Caron Site, a 17th Century Huron Village. *Journal of Field Archaeology* 7:173–99.

Jordan, Kurt A.

2013   Incorporation and Colonization: Postcolumbian Iroquois Satellite Communities and Processes of Indigenous Autonomy. *American Anthropologist* 115 (1): 29–43.

Kapches, Mima

1990   The Spatial Dynamics of Iroquoian Longhouses. *American Antiquity* 55 (1): 49–67.

2007   The Iroquoian Longhouse: Architecture and Cultural Identity. In *Archaeology of the Iroquois*, edited by Jordan E. Kerber, 174–87. Syracuse University Press, Syracuse, New York.

Kent, Barry C.

2001   *Susquehanna's Indians.* Revised edition. Anthropological Series 6. Pennsylvania Historical and Museum Commission, Harrisburg.

Kercheval, Samuel

1833   *History of the Valley of Virginia*. Samuel H. Davis, Winchester, Virginia.

Kinsey, W. Fred, III

1957   A Susquehannock Longhouse. *American Antiquity* 23 (2): 180–81.

1959   Historic Susquehannock Pottery. In *Susquehannock Miscellany*, edited by J. Witthoft and W. Kinsey, 61–97. Pennsylvania Historical and Museum Commission, Harrisburg.

Knight, Dean H.

1987   Settlement Patterns at the Ball Site: A 17th Century Huron Village. *Archaeology of Eastern North America* 15:177–88.

Lattanzi, Gregory

2008   Elucidating the Origin of Middle Atlantic Pre-Contact Copper Artifacts Using Laser Ablation ICP-MS. *North American Archaeologist* 29 (3–4): 297–326.

MacCord, Howard A.

1952   The Susquehannock Indians in West Virginia, 1630–77. *West Virginia History* 13 (4): 239–53.

Manson, Carl P., and MacCord, Howard A.

1941   An Historic Iroquois Site near Romney, West Virginia. *West Virginia History* 2:290–93.

1944   Additional Notes on the Herriott Farm Site. *West Virginia History* 5:201–11.

Maymon, Jeffrey H., and Thomas W. Davis

1998   A Contact Period Susquehannock Site in the Upper Potomac River Drainage: Data Recovery at Site 46Hy89, Moorefield, West Virginia. Paper presented at the 28th Annual Meeting of the Middle Atlantic Archaeological Conference, Cape May, New Jersey.

Rubino, Sara C.

2013   *A Geophysical Investigation of the Lower Leibhart site (36YO170), York County, Pennsylvania.* Unpublished M.A. thesis, Indiana University of Pennsylvania, Pennsylvania.

Sempowski, Martha L.

1994   Early Historic Exchange Between the Seneca and the Susquehannock. In *Proceedings of the 1992 People to People Conference*, edited by Charles F. Hayes III, 51–64. Research Records 23. Rochester Museum and Science Center, Rochester, New York.

Smith, Ira F., III

1970   Schultz Site Settlement Patterns and External Relations: A Preliminary Discussion and Possible Interpretation. *New York State Archaeological Association Bulletin* 50:27–34.

Smith, Ira F., III, and Jeffrey R. Graybill

1977   A Report on the Shenks Ferry and Susquehannock Components at the Funk Site, Lancaster County, Pennsylvania. *Man in the Northeast* 13:45–65.

Snow, Dean R.

1991   The Mohawk. *Bulletin of the New York State Archaeological Association* 102:34–39.

1994   *The Iroquois*. Blackwell, Oxford.

Trigger, Bruce G.

1976   *The Children of Aataentsic: A History of the Huron People to 1660.* McGill-Queen's University Press, Montreal.

Wall, Robert D.

1981   *An Archeological Study of the Western Maryland Coal Region: The Prehistoric Resources.* Maryland Geological Survey, Division of Archeology, Baltimore.

1993   Stratigraphy and Sequence in the South Branch of the Upper Potomac, Moorefield and Petersburg, West Virginia. *Journal of Middle Atlantic Archaeology* 9:49–66.

2004   The Chesapeake Hinterlands: Contact Period Archaeology in the Upper Potomac Valley. In *Indian and European Contact in Context: The Mid-Atlantic Region*, edited by D. B. Blanton and J. A. King, 74–97. University Press of Florida / Society for Historical Archaeology, Gainesville, Florida.

Wall, Robert D., and Dennis Curry

1992   Test Excavations at the Barton Complex Sites, Allegany County, Maryland. *Maryland Archeology* 28 (1): 13.

Wall, Robert D., and Heather A. Lapham

2003   Material Culture of the Contact Period in the Upper Potomac Valley. *Archaeology of Eastern North America* 31:151–77.

White, Sharon D.

2001   *To Secure a Lasting Peace: A Diachronic Analysis of Seventeenth-Century Susquehannock Political and Economic Strategies.* Ph.D. dissertation, Department of Anthropology, The Pennsylvania State University, University Park. University Microfilms, Ann Arbor, Michigan.

Witthoft, John

1959   Ancestry of the Susquehannocks, In *Susquehannock Miscellany*, edited by John Witthoft and W. Fred Kinsey III, 19–60. Pennsylvania Historical and Museum Commission, Harrisburg.

Wright, Henry T.

1963   The Herman Barton Village Site (18-Ag-3): A Stratified Late Ceramic Site in the Upper Potomac Valley. *West Virginia Archeologist* 15:9–20.

Wyatt, Andrew

2012   Reconsidering Early Seventeenth Century AD Susquehannock Settlement Patterns: Excavation and Analysis of the Lemoyne Site, Cumberland County, Pennsylvania. *Archaeology of Eastern North America* 40:71–98.

6.

Early Susquehannock Settlement in the Lower Susquehanna Valley

EVIDENCE FROM THE LEMOYNE SITE   Andrew Wyatt

ABSTRACT

The Lemoyne site is a recently discovered Susquehannock village located in the Great Valley near Harrisburg, Pennsylvania. Based on comparisons of the site's native and European-made artifacts, feature types, and feature patterning with those from the Schultz and Washington Boro sites, Wyatt (2012) proposed that the Lemoyne site was temporally intermediate between and at least partially coeval with the earlier Schultz village and the later Washington Boro village. This chapter provides a summary of the Lemoyne site's excavation and analysis, its temporal relationship with the Schultz and Washington Boro villages, and the implications of those relationships for understanding Susquehannock settlement and society in the early seventeenth century.

Introduction

The Lemoyne site (Pennsylvania Archaeological Site Survey number 36CU194), located in the Great Valley section of the Ridge and Valley Physiographic Province, occupies a relatively level upland summit overlooking the Susquehanna River in Lemoyne Borough, Cumberland County, Pennsylvania (figure 6.1). Between 2005 and 2008, excavations at the newly discovered site revealed a portion of a Contact period Susquehannock village. The Lemoyne site is located approximately 50 kilometers upriver from the better-known Susquehannock village sites in Lancaster County, Pennsylvania—the Schultz and Washington Boro sites. Prior to the Lemoyne site's discovery, Kent

(2001) proposed that these two sites were the main Susquehannock villages in the Lower Susquehanna Valley, occupied sequentially from the late sixteenth through early seventeenth centuries. Since the 1984 publication of Kent's *Susquehanna's Indians*, other archaeologists (Fitzgerald 1990; Kenyon and Fitzgerald 1986; Sempowski 1994) have suggested that Kent's dates for the Schultz and Washington Boro sites could be moved forward by 15–20 years based on their revised chronologies for the introduction of European trade items into the Northeast, particularly glass beads.

In this chapter and elsewhere (Wyatt 2012; Wyatt et al. 2011), I argue that the Susquehannock occupation of the Lemoyne site overlaps the final years of occupation at the Schultz site and the early years

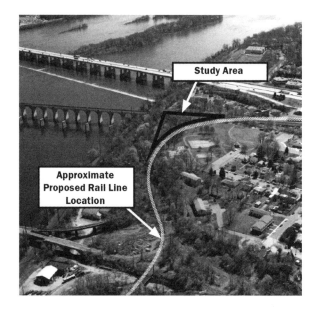

FIGURE 6.1
Location of study area

of Washington Boro based on the comparison of European trade goods and native pottery from these three sites. I also propose that the Lemoyne site was occupied between AD 1610 and 1624, accepting the glass bead chronology developed by Northeastern archaeologists beginning with Kenyon and Kenyon (1983). Because the present focus is on the Lemoyne site's chronology and relationship to the Schultz and Washington Boro sites, I begin with a brief summary of the site's excavation and results; detailed information on lithic technology and faunal and botanical remains can be found in the technical report (Wyatt et al. 2011). This summary is followed by sections on spatial patterning in the excavated portion of the site, its proposed chronology, and comparisons with the Schultz and Washington Boro sites. The Lemoyne site raises more questions than it answers in terms of its position in the Susquehannock settlement pattern of the Lower Susquehanna Valley, its relationship to Susquehannock sites in the Upper Potomac Valley, and its location far to the north of the Schultz and Washington Boro villages. I offer tentative hypotheses relevant to these issues in the final section.

Excavation History, Methods, and Results

The Lemoyne site was identified by archaeologists in 2005 during an identification-level (Phase I) archaeological survey of an unused, wooded portion of a municipal park owned by the Borough of Lemoyne.[1] Artifact counts from Phase I shovel testing were low; however, recovery of a Madison-type triangular point and a round glass "star" bead indicated a possible Contact period component at the site.[2] More intensive testing (Phase II evaluation) yielded the first clear evidence of Susquehannock occupation at the site: shell-tempered Schultz Incised and Washington Boro Incised rim sherds from a pit feature and the plow zone. The pit feature also yielded abundant, well-preserved animal bone, and a linear alignment of post molds in a nearby test trench indicated the potential for structures at the site (Wyatt et al. 2007).

Extensive (Phase III data recovery) excavations at the Lemoyne site in 2007 and 2008 were designed to assess site type, chronology, subsistence, and the site's place in Susquehannock settlement patterns. Excavations included additional test units to increase the sample of plow zone artifacts, together with machine-assisted plow zone removal to expose features. All fill from Susquehannock pit features (around 13 cubic meters) was processed by flotation and/or water-screening through one-eighth-inch mesh, and post mold fill was dry-screened through one-eighth-inch mesh. Phase III excavations exposed a portion of the site's palisade, 452 post molds within the palisade, and 41 other features that were assigned to the site's Susquehannock component. More than 215,000 artifacts were recovered from all stages of fieldwork. Phase III fieldwork alone produced more than 210,000 artifacts. Native American artifacts include 24,748 lithic artifacts, 6,734 pottery sherds and other clay-based artifacts, and 63 European-made trade items. More than 46,000 bone and shell artifacts associated with the Susquehannock occupation were recovered during the Phase III fieldwork, and more than 128,000 charred plant specimens were examined for the botanical analysis.

The Lemoyne site is located on a level upland summit or bluff on the right descending bank of the Susquehanna River, approximately 21 meters above the river. The landform slopes gently down to the east where it meets the bottom of the grade for the Lurgan Branch rail lines. The northern edge of the summit and an unknown portion of the site to the north of the study area were destroyed in the 1850s by a now inactive railroad cut (figure 6.1). Below this is an earlier nineteenth-century railroad grade. Despite these alterations, it was clear that the northern side of the Lemoyne site originally sloped steeply to the river's edge, providing a strong defensible position. To the west and south, the park has been variably graded and filled for baseball fields, tennis courts, and a walking path. Backhoe trenches excavated for the Phase II investigation indicated that the topsoil and upper subsoil has been removed from the extreme southern portion of the study area. The degree of site preservation south and west of the study area in other developed portions of the park is unknown. The soils included a modern A horizon developed on a variably thick, virtually rock-free brown silt loam plow zone. The underlying upper subsoil was a light-yellowish-brown, slightly clayey silt loam. This typical profile was buried by an eastward-thickening "wedge" of nineteenth- and twentieth-century fills and slope-wash within 20 meters of the Lurgan Branch railroad grade in the eastern portion of the study area. Artifacts were recovered from the A horizon, the plow zone, the upper 0.1 meter of subsoil, Susquehannock features, and modern fill.

The Lemoyne site is a multicomponent archaeological site, with diagnostic artifacts spanning the Archaic period and the Early to Middle Woodland subperiods, yet no features associated with these occupations were present. Nineteenth-century artifacts and features associated with the operation of the short-lived York Haven and Harrisburg Turnpike (AD 1832–50) were recovered, as were a small number

of Civil War–era military artifacts that may represent patrols from nearby Fort Couch or Fort Washington. The most extensive and significant component at the site, however, is the Contact period Susquehannock occupation. Occupation by the Susquehannocks is documented by the recovery of shell-tempered Schultz Incised and Washington Boro Incised pottery and European trade items in pit features at the site. The presence of these two pottery types and the apparent absence of Strickler Cord-Marked pottery very generally places the occupation before the mid-seventeenth-century Strickler site, based on frequency changes in pottery types first documented by Kinsey (1959) and Kent's (2001) chronology. Recovered European trade items, primarily glass beads, indicate an occupation date for the Lemoyne site in the first quarter of the seventeenth century, based on glass bead chronologies developed by Kenyon and Kenyon (1983), Kenyon and Fitzgerald (1986), and Fitzgerald (1990). The Susquehannock component consists of a portion of a palisaded village of unknown size, with interior pits and evidence of structures.

Well-preserved faunal remains from the Lemoyne site's pit features indicate a primary reliance on white-tailed deer, followed by elk and black bear, but numerous other terrestrial and avian species were represented (Weller 2011). Domestic dog, bald eagle, and turtle remains hint at possible Susquehannock ceremonial or ritual uses. Freshwater mussels, primarily eastern elliptio, were gathered in large numbers (Weller 2011). The recovery of abundant fish remains from flotation and water screening resulted in the identification of 25 fish taxa. These included year-round Susquehanna River residents (catfish and suckers) as well as catadromous (American eel) and anadromous species (American shad and striped bass; Whyte 2011). McWeeney identified abundant maize, beans, squash, gourd, and sunflower; however, examples of *Chenopodium* species, little barley, and other starchy representatives of the Eastern Agricultural Complex were not present in the analyzed portion of the botanical assemblage (McWeeney and Wyatt 2011). Lithic analysis indicated a focus on the production of small triangular arrow points from locally available cherts and quartz from pebbles and float sources (Wyatt 2011). No larger, multipurpose bifaces—also uncommon at other Susquehannock sites from the first half of the seventeenth century (Kent 2001:156–57)—were recovered, and no ground stone tools were found at the Lemoyne site.

A number of ornaments and effigies were found at the site. Four elk tooth pendants were recovered, but marine shell ornaments were much more common. The latter included one small barrel-shaped bead, three small tubular beads that fall into the size range of "Early Wampum" (Bradley 2011; Ceci 1988), and a fragment of a probable whelk shell pendant. The most common marine shell beads from the site are thin, flat, discoidal beads. A total of 84 discoidal shell beads were recovered, and 77 were sufficiently complete to allow accurate measurement. These ranged from 2.8 to 10.1 millimeters in diameter and from 0.4 to 2.9 millimeters thick. The majority (n = 60, 77.9%) ranged between 2.9 and 4.5 millimeters in diameter. In terms of total diameter range and majority range, the discoidal shell beads from the Lemoyne site most closely approximate the sample from the Seneca Dutch Hollow site (Sempowski, Saunders, and Allen 2001:263–64, figure 3–204, table 3–100), which Sempowski, Saunders, and Allen dated between 1605 and 1620 (2001:721–22). Stone ornaments were limited to a ground slate bead and a steatite/serpentine masquette, both of which were found in Susquehannock pits. One fired clay bead, one shell-tempered spoon or pipe effigy, and one shell-tempered animal effigy (most likely representing a bear) were recovered from separate features at the site.

The site's 24 metal artifacts were all recovered from Susquehannock features, but none are chronologically diagnostic. Two of these, an iron knife tang and a copper alloy kettle lug fragment are immediately recognizable as parts of finished European trade items. The remaining 22 artifacts were manufactured from copper / copper alloy sheet metal or flattened kettle fragments. The iron knife tang was flat and tapered from the butt toward the blade. The tang fragment resembles single examples from the Schultz village and Schultz-Funk Cemetery II more closely than examples from the Washington Boro site and two of its associated cemeteries. Seven copper or copper alloy beads were found in the following forms: tubular (n = 3), circular (n = 2), oval (n = 1), and flattened (n = 1). Five copper or copper alloy artifacts were classified as "bent tubes." Ten pieces of copper or copper alloys were classified as "scrap": unused waste from the manufacture of other artifacts from recycled kettles or sheet metal.

Spatial Patterning

Excavations exposed 1,200 square meters of the subsoil surface within the palisade line (figure 6.2), constituting an exposure of approximately 75% of the site within the study area. The palisade is marked by a line of large, closely spaced post molds. An interior line of smaller post molds was set in a variably preserved narrow trench. These two post mold alignments were roughly parallel and spaced 2 to 1.5 meters apart. The line of smaller posts in the trench may represent the supports for scaffolding attached to the palisade or an interior "screen" of posts. Their close spacing suggests that the two post mold lines represent an integrated defensive work rather than stages of village expansion. Plow zone stripping extended for 14.5 meters perpendicular to the palisade, which would have accommodated the maximum distance between the second and third palisades at the Schultz site (around 13.5 m; Smith 1970: figure 2) and the distance reported by Kent (2001:337) between the inner and outer palisades at Washington Boro (around 11 m). No pit features or post mold alignments were present to the east of the Lemoyne site's palisade. Together, these observations suggest that the Lemoyne site was not expanded. The preserved portion of the palisade within the study area measured 31 meters long with no appreciable curvature. Neither palisade line was preserved south of the stripped area due to deep subsoil truncation associated with the construction of Memorial Park.

Forty-one other features were assigned to the site's Susquehannock occupation based primarily on the presence of shell-tempered pottery in their fill. These were all located to the west of the palisade. They include eight cylindrical pits, two bell-shaped pits, three deep basin-shaped pits, 23 shallow basin-shaped pits, and five features that could not be easily assigned to any of these former types. Several of the cylindrical and bell-shaped pits yielded more than 16,000 Susquehannock artifacts, each exclusive of charred botanical remains. Some of the larger pits contained multiple fill layers composed of organically enriched soil, freshwater mussel shell, or ash, while others appear to have been filled with artifact-poor soil through a combination of cultural and natural processes.

Despite the presence of a palisade, storage features, artifacts indicative of a village occupation, and more than 400 post molds, no clear longhouse patterns were identified at the Lemoyne site. One possible partial longhouse pattern was identified in the western

portion of the study area and designated as House 1 (figure 6.2). It consists of two relatively straight lines of post molds oriented east to west, which might represent portions of the north and south walls of a longhouse. The distance between these post mold alignments is approximately 5.5 meters, which accords with the average width of longhouses reported for the Schultz site (Anderson 1995; Kent 2001). The full length of House 1 could not be determined due to the placement of a stone foundation along its projected north wall and subsoil truncation associated with a stone-paved road along the south wall.[3] Another longhouse may be indicated by the linear northwest to southeast–trending alignment of pit features in the central portion of the site; however, no post molds were identified that would suggest a wall parallel to this line of features. Another possible structure outline was identified in the eastern portion of the study area, designated Structure 1 (figure 6.2). It consisted of two roughly parallel rows of offset post molds aligned northwest to southeast and a line of post molds indicative of a closed-off end on the southeast side of the pattern. There were no post molds that clearly enclosed the northwest end of the pattern. The distance

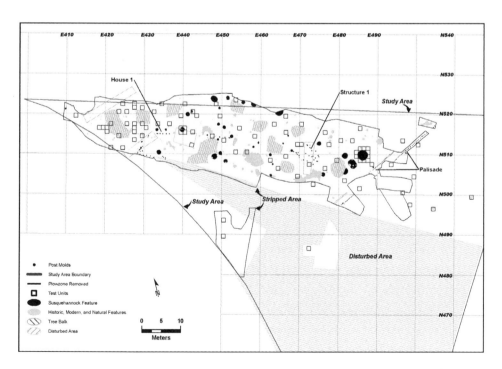

FIGURE 6.2
Excavation plan

between the two northwest to southeast–trending post mold rows was 3.8 meters, which would be much narrower than a typical Susquehannock longhouse.

In the absence of clear longhouse patterns, a preliminary model of activities in the excavated portion of the site is based on the gross horizontal patterning of pit features and their contents. Pit features within roughly 30 meters of the palisades were large and, with the exception of Features 3 and 152, held relatively low to very low numbers of artifacts from all classes. A partial possible structure pattern was located in this area (Structure 1). This portion of the site, designated as the "indeterminate use area," displayed a feature density of one feature per 31.9 square meters (total area minus tree balks). By contrast, virtually all of the pit features contained abundant artifacts beginning approximately 30 meters west of the palisade and extending to the western edge of the study area, which generally corresponded to the highest, flattest part of the site. This area is referred to as the "domestic core" of the exposed portion of the site. The density of Susquehannock features in this area was one feature per 21.6 square meters (total area minus tree balks), and it contains a possible longhouse remnant designated House 1. Another difference between the domestic core and indeterminate use area was the relative frequency of European trade goods and ornaments of native materials found in pit features. European trade items were recovered from 9 of 21 pits in the domestic core (42.9%) versus 4 of 17 (23.5%) in the indeterminate use area. Ornaments of native materials (marine shell beads, elk tooth pendants, clay and stone beads) were also discarded more frequently in domestic core pits (8 of 21; 38.1%) than in indeterminate use area pits (4 of 17; 23.5%). With a few exceptions, debitage was infrequently discarded in the indeterminate use area, while high densities of macro- and microdebitage characterized many of the features in the domestic core. Finally, evidence for pottery manufacture in the form of potter's clay fragments was common in the domestic core, occurring in 17 of the 21 pits in this area (81.0%). Only 5 of the 17 pits in the indeterminate

use area contained potter's clay (29.4%). If the assumption that features were primarily filled with soil matrix and artifacts from nearby areas is correct, the evidence for intentional filling of features with organic matrix and abundant artifacts would appear to indicate that food preparation, stone tool and pottery manufacture, and breakage or loss of ornaments occurred more frequently in the area designated as the domestic core. Although speculative, communal storage may be represented in the indeterminate use area, which contains the two largest-volume pit features exposed at the site.

Chronology

Pottery

For the analysis of the Lemoyne site's pottery, vessel lots were constructed by inspecting all decorated sherds and determining whether any mends were possible. After mends were made, sherds were grouped into vessel lots based on decorative and formal similarities. After the lots were defined, they were assigned to widely recognized Susquehannock stylistic types by reference to type descriptions, illustrations, and photographs (Heisey and Witmer 1962; Kent 2001; Kinsey 1959; Smith 1981). Two additional ad hoc types were also used: 149 shell-tempered vessel lots were constructed using 373 (48.4%) of the 752 rim or collar and collar base sherds. The distribution of the 149 shell-tempered vessel lots within types is depicted in table 6.1. The majority of vessel lots were assigned to Washington Boro Incised (n = 56; 37.6%), followed by Schultz Incised (n = 34; 22.8%); the ratio of the former type to the latter is 1.6 to 1. Two examples of probable Blue Rock Valanced (1.3%) were identified. Three vessel lots were assigned to a "Plain" category (2%), and 6 were typed as miniature vessels. Forty-six vessel lots (30.9%) were not assigned to the above types, primarily due to the small number and size of sherds assigned to these lots. These vessel lots displayed incising or punctations that occur on both Schultz Incised

TABLE 6.1 Distribution of Lemoyne site vessel lots by type

Pottery type	Vessel lots	
	Number	Percentage
Washington Boro Incised	56	37.6
Schultz Incised	34	22.8
Blue Rock Valanced?	2	1.3
Plain	3	2
Miniature	8	5.4
Untyped	46	30.9
Total	92	100

Question mark implies uncertain attribution.

and Washington Boro Incised types. No sherds in the assemblage appear to represent types indicative of Late Prehistoric or Contact period groups other than Susquehannock. Of the 149 vessel lots constructed from the Lemoyne site's shell-tempered pottery assemblage, 92 could be assigned to the Susquehannock pottery types Schultz Incised, Washington Boro Incised, or possibly Blue Rock Valanced. A preliminary indication of the Lemoyne site's chronological position relative to the Schultz and Washington Boro village sites comes from the comparison of pottery type frequencies. When the frequency of the Lemoyne site's typed vessel lots is compared to sherd-based type frequencies compiled by Kinsey (1959:95, figure 11) for Schultz village and the Eschelman midden (36LA12) within Washington Boro village, Lemoyne's pottery assemblage appears to be more similar to the Washington

Boro village than the Schultz village sample reported by Kinsey (figure 6.3). If a steady rate of stylistic change is assumed, this frequency distribution would suggest that the span of occupation at Lemoyne overlapped that of Washington Boro village rather than Schultz village. Both Washington Boro village and the Lemoyne site yielded similarly high frequencies of Washington Boro Incised in comparison to the Schultz site. The Lemoyne site may also share very low frequencies of Blue Rock Valanced and possibly Strickler Cord-Marked pottery with the Washington Boro site. At the same time, the higher frequency of Schultz Incised at the Lemoyne site (36.9%) compared to that from the Washington Boro site (27.1%) may indicate that the Lemoyne site's occupation also overlapped the final years of occupation at the Schultz site.

Other factors, however, could be responsible for the variation in type frequency distributions from these sites. First, type frequencies of Lemoyne's vessel lots may not be comparable to those based on typed sherds from the Schultz and Washington Boro village sites. Kinsey (1959:94) used sherds "large enough to determine type accurately" for his seriation. If Kinsey counted several sherds from the same vessel in his analysis, his type frequencies would not be comparable to those from the Lemoyne site. The choice to use Kinsey's (1959) pottery seriation was made because it remains the only clearly documented, quantified attempt at seriation of pottery from the Lancaster

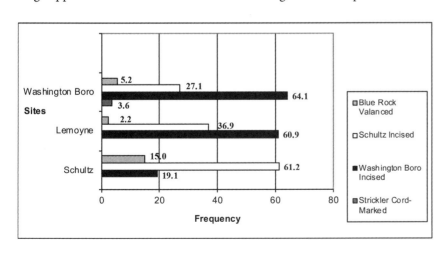

FIGURE 6.3
Frequency of pottery types at the Washington Boro, Lemoyne, and Schultz sites

145

County sites that differentiates between village and burial contexts. Second, the actual proportion of Washington Boro Incised to Schultz Incised vessels might be somewhat less than the 1.6:1 ratio indicated for the Lemoyne assemblage as a whole. In features that yielded 5 or fewer vessel lots, ratios of Washington Boro Incised to Schultz Incised pots ranged from 2.5:1 to 1.2:1 and averaged 1.6:1. However, in the two features that yielded 10 or more vessel lots, Washington Boro Incised lots outnumbered Schultz Incised lots by only 1.2:1, so it is possible that the type frequencies from the excavated sample may not represent those of the entire site. Another source of uncertainty lies in assuming that Schultz Incised pottery was replaced by Washington Boro Incised at a steady rate. Kent (2001:134), using larger pottery samples from Smith's excavations at Schultz village (Smith 1970) and two of its cemeteries (Smith and Graybill 1977), indicated that the frequency of Washington Boro Incised pottery at the Schultz site was considerably less than Kinsey's estimate. Although her analysis of Susquehannock pottery focused on its functional properties, Strauss (2000:111, figure 5–1) found that Washington Boro Incised vessel lots comprised only about 10% of the Schultz village and cemetery assemblages combined. If the population of Schultz village relocated to the Washington Boro site, as the traditional settlement model for Susquehannock sites supposes, Strauss's data may suggest that Washington Boro Incised very quickly eclipsed Schultz Incised as the dominant pottery type. Kent's (2001:134) observation in this regard, together with two- to fourfold increases in the quantity of European trade items from the Schultz to Washington Boro cemeteries, led to a "nagging curiosity about a possible missing town of some ten to 15 years duration between these two" (Kent 2001:315). Additional evidence that Washington Boro Incised did not replace Schultz Incised pottery at a steady rate comes from Susquehannock sites in the Upper Potomac Valley (see Wall, chapter 5 in this volume). Based on Wall and Lapham's (2003) assessment, the majority of incised designs on shell-tempered pottery

from these sites are more clearly linked to Schultz Incised than to Washington Boro Incised. At the same time, these authors note that glass trade bead assemblages from the same sites appear to be transitional between those found at the Schultz and Washington Boro cemeteries. The implication is that Schultz Incised pottery continued as the major pottery type on Susquehannock sites in the Upper Potomac Valley after it had been eclipsed by Washington Boro Incised in the Lower Susquehanna Valley. Despite these caveats, the Lemoyne site's pottery assemblage appears to be closer to that of Washington Boro village than to that of Schultz village.

Glass Beads

A total of 40 glass beads were recovered from the Lemoyne site: 39 from Susquehannock pit features and one from a modern fill deposit. All were assigned to specific varieties of the Kidd and Kidd (1970) classification system by the author. These assignments were cross-checked for accuracy by comparison with color photographs of glass beads in Kent (2001:216, figure 57), Fogelman (1991), Lapham (2001), and Sempowski (1994) and with glass beads in the collections of the State Museum of Pennsylvania, Section of Archaeology (SMP/SOA). The glass beads from the Lemoyne site were assigned to 19 varieties within nine larger types (table 6.2). In terms of their distribution within types, the majority are round, oval, and circular uncored monochrome beads (48.8%, $n = 20$), followed by round and circular cored beads with stripes (14.6%, $n = 6$) and round tumbled star beads (9.8%, $n = 4$). Other types, represented by only one or two beads, include monochrome tubular beads, tubular beads with stripes, cored monochrome beads, uncored monochrome beads with stripes, and faceted star beads. A date range from the late 1500s to ca. 1630 is initially indicated for the Lemoyne site by the frequency of rounded beads (Kidd classes II, IV; 87.5%; $n = 35$) to tubular beads (Kidd classes I, III; 12.5%; $n = 5$). Using glass bead assemblages from 29 sites in northeastern North America, Huey (1983:99–101) found that high percentages of rounded beads, generally greater than 80%, characterize sites with proposed median occupation dates in this range. Rounded beads from Cemetery I and II at the Schultz-Funk site comprised 100% and 83.9%, respectively (Huey 1983: figure IV).

Comparison of the small glass bead assemblage from the Lemoyne site to those from other Susquehannock sites in the Lower Susquehanna Valley with glass bead totals numbering in the thousands is potentially misleading due to the wide disparity in sample size. In addition, the Lemoyne site assemblage was recovered from village rather than burial contexts. Bead totals given in Kent (2001:218–22, table 8) for the Schultz-Funk site (36LA9) are all from burials in Cemetery I and II. Bead totals listed under the heading 36LA8 (Kent 2001: table 8) include an unspecified number from the village and from the associated cemetery sites (Keller [36LA4], Ibaugh

TABLE 6.2 Glass bead descriptions by type and variety

Type	Variety	Description	Count
Tubular	Ia5*	Small and *large*, tubular, opaque white bead	2
Tubular with stripes	Ib?	Tubular, opaque white bead, striations indicate presence of eroded/spalled stripes	1
Uncored monochrome	IIa13	Small, round, opaque white bead	1
	IIa14	Small, circular, opaque white bead	1
	IIa15	Medium, oval, opaque white bead	2
	IIa40	Medium, round, opaque, robin's egg blue bead	3
	IIa46	Medium, round, opaque, shadow-blue bead	1
	IIa55	Small and medium, round, clear bright-navy beads	5
	IIa56	Very small and small, circular, clear bright-navy beads	7
Uncored monochrome with stripes	IIb42*	Very small, circular, opaque, pale-blue bead with two redwood stripes on fragment (most similar to Kidd variety IIb42, except that variety is *medium and round*)	1
	IIb59*	*Medium*, round, translucent, bright-blue bead with three redwood stripes (Kidd variety is *large*)	1
	IIb68*	Very small, circular, clear, bright-blue bead with four white stripes (Kidd variety is *medium and round*)	1
Faceted "star"	IIIk3*	*Medium*, tubular, bright-blue with five layers (op. bright blue / op. white / op. redwood / op. white / cl. bright blue), ends ground, outer layer thin, giving appearance of blue bead with white stripes (Kidd variety is *small*)	2
Cored monochrome	IVa19	Medium, circular, bright blue with three layers (cl. bright navy / clear / cl. bright navy)	2
Cored with stripes	IVb32/35	Large, round, bright navy with two white stripes on fragment, three layers (cl. bright navy / op. white / cl. bright navy; Kidd variety unknown due to breakage)	1
	IVb31*	Small, *circular*, bright navy with six white stripes, three layers (cl. bright navy / op. white / cl. bright navy; Kidd variety is *round*)	4
Cored with compound stripes	IVbb10?	Tentative assignment based on a small fragment of a medium to large bright-navy bead with compound stripes and three layers (cl. bright navy / op. white / cl. bright navy) and stripes of opaque redwood pairs on opaque white	1
Round "star"	IVk3	Medium, round, bright navy with five layers (clear bright navy / opaque white / opaque redwood / clear bright navy / clear)	1
	IVk4*	Large, round, bright blue with *seven layers* (cl. bright blue / op. white / clear / op. redwood / clear / op. white / clear), thin outer layer giving appearance of blue bead with white stripes (Kidd variety has *five layers* and a *different color sequence*)	3

* An asterisk indicates a slight difference with the Kidd description. The differing attributes are italicized in the third column. Abbreviations are cl. (clear) and op. (opaque).

[36LA54], and possibly Reitz [36LA92]; Barry Kent, personal communication, 2008). Ira Smith's notes on the Schultz village site (36LA7) in the SMP/SOA holdings indicate that only eight glass beads were recovered from 7 of the more than 400 features excavated within the village (Smith and Graybill 1977:56). It is important to note in this regard that only four of the glass beads from Lemoyne would have been recovered using the 6.35 millimeter (0.25 in) mesh used at the Schultz site. Certainly, the larger samples of beads from these Lancaster County site complexes are more representative of the varieties selected by their inhabitants. Given the rarity of glass beads in village contexts at these early sites, it is also likely that the bead varieties recovered from the Lemoyne site also underrepresent the varieties obtained. Despite these caveats, a relatively clear pattern emerges from the comparison of glass bead assemblages from the Lemoyne site, the Schultz-Funk cemeteries, and the Washington Boro village and cemeteries. The placement of Lemoyne's bead frequencies between those of the Schultz-Funk cemeteries and the Washington Boro village and cemeteries in table 6.3 reflects the proposed intermediate temporal placement of its glass bead assemblage. The following discussion focuses on bead varieties representing 5% or more of the total glass bead assemblages from the three sites / site complexes.

The tubular white bead variety Ia5 was present in essentially equal frequencies at the Schultz-Funk cemeteries and Lemoyne but was absent at Washington Boro. Kidd variety IIa15, an oval opaque white bead, declined from 28.0% at Schultz-Funk, where it was the majority bead variety, to 5.1% at Lemoyne, to less than 1.0% at Washington Boro. Faceted, tubular "star" beads (IIIk, IIIm) were present at all three sites but were at their lowest frequency at Washington Boro. Canadian archaeologists (Fitzgerald 1990; Kenyon and Fitzgerald 1986; Kenyon and Kenyon 1983) placed sites dominated by these bead varieties, along with blue tubular and oval glass beads (Ia19, Ia57) in the Glass Bead Period (GBP) II, also known

as the "Indigo and White Horizon." These researchers dated Ontario Iroquois sites with this bead assemblage between approximately AD 1600 and 1630, reflecting the interval of intensified, historically documented French trade with the Huron, Petun, and Neutral. This range of dates was selected based on the known dates for the early French post on St. Croix Island, Maine (1604–5), and Champlain's *Habitation* at Quebec (ca. 1608–32), where the majority of excavated beads were GBP II types (Bradley 1983, cited in Kenyon and Fitzgerald 1986:15; see also Bradley 2014; Fitzgerald 1990:199–202). South of Ontario, Kenyon and Kenyon (1983:60, 62) suggested that the glass bead assemblage from the Adams site (Seneca) displays close similarity with earlier GBP I assemblages, while those from the Cameron site (Seneca) and the Schultz-Funk cemeteries bear obvious similarities to GBP II assemblages. Both of these latter sites shared high frequencies of white oval and tubular beads, variable frequencies of blue oval and tubular beads, and minor frequencies of faceted "star" beads with the Ontario sites of GBP II. Although they were present at diminished frequencies at Lemoyne, they were virtually absent at Washington Boro.

Kidd variety IIa40, a round, opaque, light-blue bead, increases in frequency from Schultz-Funk (3.6%) to Lemoyne (7.7%) to Washington Boro (34.6%), where it is the most frequent of all bead varieties. The most frequently occurring beads from Lemoyne (IIa55 and IIa56) appear anomalous with respect to the other two bead assemblages. However, if round and circular blue Kidd varieties (IIa31–48, IIa50–53, IIa55, IIa56) are combined to reduce the effects of observer error in color classification, as suggested by Kenyon and Fitzgerald (1986:17, table 2), they were present at approximately 23.7% at Schultz-Funk, 41% at Lemoyne, and 56.3% at Washington Boro. This distribution also supports an intermediate chronological position for the Lemoyne site between Schultz-Funk and Washington Boro. Increasing frequencies of round and circular blue beads on early seventeenth Susquehannock sites may have resulted from growing

TABLE 6.3 Comparison of the Lemoyne, Schultz, and Washington Boro glass bead assemblages by frequency

Kidd and Kidd variety	Schultz-Funk cemeteries (n = 2981; Kent 2001: table 8; Sempowski 1994: table 1)	Lemoyne (n = 39*)	Washington Boro village and cemeteries (n = 7351; Kent 2001: table 8)
Ia5	5.6	5.1	0
IIa11/12/13/14	< 1	5.1	4.2
IIa15	28	5.1	< 1
IIa40†	3.6	7.7	34.6
IIa46	0	2.6	0
IIa48	< 1	0	3.2
IIa52	< 1	0	5.2
IIa53	17.4	0	9.9
IIa55	< 1	12.8	< 1
IIa56	0	17.9	2.5
IIa57	8.1	0	0
IIb42*	0	2.6	0
IIb59*	< 1	2.6	0
IIb68*	0	2.6	0†
IIIk3/IIIm1	2.3	5.1	< 1
IVa11	0	0	22.9
IVa19	5.3	5.1	8.3
IVb32/35	0	2.6	0
IVb31*	0	10.2	< 1
IVbb10?	0	2.6	0
IVk3/4, IVk*	6.9	10.2	< 1

The single striped tubular bead (Ib?) is not used in this table.

† Kent (2001: table 8) assigned his varieties B14a and B15a to Kidd variety IIa53. In retrospect, Kent believed these varieties should be reassigned to Kidd variety IIa40 (Kent 2008, personal communication).

* An asterisk indicates a slight difference with the Kidd description.

trade with native societies of the Chesapeake Bay that had access to English sources of European goods. Miller, Pogue, and Smolek (1983) and Lapham (2001) have provided data indicating that round and circular blue beads dominated glass bead assemblages on both native and English sites in this region.

Rounded "star" beads (IVk3/4, IVk4*) appear to increase from 6.9% at Schultz-Funk to 10.2% at Lemoyne, but they were present at less than 1% at Washington Boro. Kidd variety IVb31 (a circular, blue, three-layer bead with six white stripes) was apparently absent at Schultz-Funk, appeared at 10% at Lemoyne, and declined to less than 1% at Washington Boro. This variety (IVa31) does, however, comprise 35.1% of the glass bead assemblage at the Herriott Farm site, an early Susquehannock burial site on the South Branch of the Potomac River in West Virginia (Wall

and Lapham 2003:163, table 2; see also Wall, chapter 5 in this volume). The single round, blue, three-layer bead with white stripes (IVb32/35) found at Lemoyne is not duplicated at Schultz-Funk or Washington Boro. Together, these bead varieties are diagnostic of Dutch Period 1 (Fitzgerald 1990:182–84), also called the "polychrome bead era" (Wray 1973) or the "Polychrome Bead Horizon" (Bradley 2007:43). During GBP II, glass bead assemblages from Iroquois and Susquehannock sites diverged from those at Huron and Neutral sites, and this divergence continued until the dispersal of the Huron around 1650. New York Iroquois sites and the Schultz site cemeteries and the Lemoyne site contained higher frequencies of polychrome bead varieties—rounded "star" beads (IVk, n); round, cored blue beads with 3 to 16 white stripes (IVb29 through IVb36); and cored white and blue beads (IVa11, 19)—than Washington Boro did. Several researchers (Bradley 2007; Fitzgerald 1990; Kenyon and Fitzgerald 1986; Kenyon and Kenyon 1983; Sempowski 1994; Sempowski, Saunders, and Allen 2001) attribute this divergence between Ontario glass bead assemblages and Iroquois and Susquehannock glass bead assemblages to the beginning of sustained Dutch trade on the Hudson and Delaware Rivers between 1609 and 1624. Their hypothesis is supported by the recovery of the same glass bead varieties found on Iroquois sites like Dutch Hollow and the Schultz site (Sempowski 1994: table 1) in archaeological deposits from Dutch glass factories that operated between 1600 and 1625 (Bradley 2007:40–46; Bradley 2014:55–58; Karklins 1974) and by significant differences with the bead varieties recovered from Fort Orange, which were deposited no earlier than 1624 (Huey 1983). Kidd variety IVa19, a circular, three-layer blue bead occurs in essentially equal frequencies at both Schultz-Funk (5.3%) and Lemoyne (5.1%), increasing to 8.3% at the Washington Boro sites. Although this variety became more common in Fitzgerald's (1990:192) Dutch Period 2 (1624–35), along with other small round and circular and cored and uncored varieties (IIa7, IIa12, IVa11/13), they were present in low frequencies at sites occupied in the second decade of the seventeenth century—that is, Schultz and James Fort (Lapham 2001).

Although wide differences in sample size exist between the three Susquehannock glass bead assemblages, the fact that all share several varieties (IIa15, IIa40, IIIk3/IIIm1, IVa19) or grouped varieties (IIa31–48, IIa50–53, IIa55, IIa56, IVk3/4) suggests close temporal relationships. The frequency of these varieties / variety groupings at the Lemoyne site either diminishes or increases with respect to those from the Schultz-Funk cemeteries and Washington Boro village and cemeteries in a regular way such that the most logical placement for the Lemoyne site's bead assemblage is intermediate between Schultz-Funk and Washington Boro. Based on the significant frequency of rounded "star" beads and the lower frequency of

striped blue beads at Schultz-Funk and their likely association with early Dutch trade, Kenyon and Fitzgerald (1986) and Sempowski (1994) have suggested that the Schultz village site was occupied into the second decade of the 1600s, which is 10 to 20 years later than the terminal date for the Schultz village site proposed by Kent. Accepting that the rounded "star" beads and other polychrome beads were introduced primarily by the Dutch, their increased frequency at the Lemoyne site indicates that it, along with Schultz village and its cemeteries, was occupied into the second decade of the seventeenth century. High frequencies of Dutch Period 1 bead types also characterized the glass bead assemblages of the Herriott Farm, Barton, and Llewellyn sites in the Upper Potomac Valley (Wall and Lapham 2003; Wall, chapter 5 in this volume). This decade corresponds with increasing Dutch presence and trade on the Hudson and Delaware Rivers.

Sporadic Dutch trading voyages in the Hudson after 1609 are suggested by Snow (1995:197), and more sustained Susquehannock access to Dutch goods might have come with the establishment of Fort Nassau (1614–17) on the Hudson River near Albany. Whether the majority of Susquehannock trade took place directly with the Dutch or indirectly through Mahican and/or Lenape intermediaries is speculative. Weslager and Dunlap recounted at least one example of direct and early Susquehannock trade with the Dutch (1961:45, 112–13, citing Brodhead 1856:13–14). Cornelis Hendricksen's 1616 report to the Dutch States General includes a passage relating his ransom of three men of the New Netherland Company, probably from Fort Nassau on the Hudson, from the Minqua (Susquehannocks) while he explored the Delaware River, "giving for them kettles, corals (beads), and merchandise" (Brodhead 1856:13–14) Some of these Dutch goods may have been introduced into the archaeological record at Schultz village, the Schultz-Funk cemeteries, and possibly at the Lemoyne site.

Intersite Comparisons

In contrast to the Lemoyne site, excavations at the Schultz village site covered a greater area, resulting in a clearer picture of site size and internal layout. Excavations at the Washington Boro village site, however, exposed an area only slightly larger than at the Lemoyne site. Nevertheless, key differences between the sites suggest a shorter occupation span at Lemoyne than those at the better-known sites. Perhaps the most striking difference between Lemoyne, Schultz village, and Washington Boro village is the configuration of their palisades. Three palisades were erected at Schultz. Smith (1970:30–32) interpreted the inner palisade as the initial defensive work surrounding the site, with the central and outer palisades representing two successive village expansions. His interpretation is supported by the layout of large circular and oval pits between the inner and central palisades and by the presence of a probable longhouse pattern between the central and outer palisades. The large circular and oval pits between the inner and central palisades resemble Feature 3 from Lemoyne, which was also located in close proximity to that site's single palisade. Excavations by Kent at Washington Boro village were successful in establishing the palisade lines at the north and south ends of the village. In one large block of plow zone removal at the southern end of the site, two distinct palisades were encountered (Kent 2001:337–38). The inner palisade was composed of four concentric, closely spaced lines of large post molds. The outer palisade was composed of a single line of large posts located approximately 10.7 meters south of the inner palisade. As noted by Kent, village enlargement is clearly indicated by the presence of pits and post molds between the two palisades. In contrast to both Schultz and Washington Boro villages, excavation on the eastern end of the Lemoyne site revealed two closely spaced rows of post molds, which probably represent an integrated defensive network.

Another contrast between the Lemoyne site and Schultz village is evidence for longhouse spacing, repair, and internal storage. In contrast to the Lemoyne site, longhouse post mold patterns at Schultz village are both closely spaced and clearly defined, the former of which is characteristic of most Iroquoian villages after AD 1500 (Snow 1994:52). The regular spacing and parallel arrangement of longhouses within the inner palisade suggests that many of the first houses at Schultz were built simultaneously and according to a plan. Longhouse "packing" at Schultz can be described as dense in comparison to Lemoyne. Schultz longhouses were built in close proximity to the inner palisade. At Lemoyne, however, there was a large area of relatively lower feature density within 30 meters of the palisade. The "indeterminate use area" contained a partial possible structural pattern (Structure 1), a few shallow basin-shaped pits, two widely spaced cylindrical pits, and a concentration of large pits that may represent communal storage. Smith (1970:30) noted that the constituent post molds of most houses at Schultz were "numerous, and the number that make up the walls suggest considerable repair and long use." Examination of the Schultz site plan clearly indicates the close, sometimes parallel arrangement of wall post molds of many of the Schultz longhouses, which, as Smith noted, is probably indicative of replacing old wall posts. By comparison, the walls of *hypothetical* House 1 at Lemoyne exhibit single lines of more widely spaced posts, which may indicate a relatively short use-life for this structure in comparison to those at Schultz village. The number of pits and arrangement of pit features within longhouses also suggests differences between Schultz village and the Lemoyne site. Schultz longhouses generally contain two parallel lines of pit features located near house walls. Many of these pits are closely spaced, which may represent sequences of use for storage, followed by filling and subsequent excavation of new pits. In contrast, the single possible longhouse pattern at Lemoyne may have contained only five pit features, which are widely spaced for the most part.

Estimates of pit feature density for the three sites partially support the hypothesis that the Lemoyne

151

site was occupied for a shorter duration than either Schultz or Washington Boro villages. Pit feature density within the palisade at Lemoyne is approximately 1 pit per 32.5 square meters. The plan of Smith's 1969 excavations at Schultz was scanned and georeferenced in the geographic information systems (GIS) program ArcView to estimate the excavated area, and the pit features were hand counted. The excavated area within the inner palisade at Schultz totals 3,539 square meters, and 363 pit features were mapped in this area. Pit feature density within the inner palisade at Schultz is estimated at 1 pit per 9.7 square meters, slightly more than three times the density at Lemoyne. Witthoft's 1949 excavations at the Eschelman midden (36LA12) within Washington Boro village totaled 599 square meters and identified 21 pit features, a density of one pit per 28.5 square meters. Based on the extant field records, approximately 536 square meters of subsoil was exposed during Kent's 1972 excavation within Washington Boro village. Twenty-two pit features were documented, resulting in a density of 1 pit per 24.4 square meters (262.6 square feet). Kent (2001), however, indicated that more than 30 pits were identified, which would result in a density of 1 pit per 17.9 square meters, although this was not confirmed by the field records. In addition, field records indicate that significant portions of the exposed areas had been deeply truncated during twentieth-century house construction. If pit features were destroyed as a result, the feature density estimate just mentioned would be too low. Finally, 473.8 square meters of subsoil were exposed and 18 pits were identified in Kent's 1975 excavations, resulting in a density of 1 pit per 26.3 square meters. The most secure estimates of pit feature density at Washington Boro village, therefore, range from approximately 1 pit per 24.4 meters to 1 pit per 28.5 square meters. Assuming that feature density is positively correlated with occupation span and/or population, the measures of pit feature density strongly suggest that the Susquehannock village at Lemoyne was of shorter duration and/or held fewer people than

at Schultz. This hypothesis is supported by evidence for village expansion, "packing" of houses, house repair, and high pit density at Schultz. Comparisons between the Lemoyne site and Washington Boro village are less clear. Pit feature density at Washington Boro is only slightly higher than at Lemoyne, but there is evidence for village expansion at Washington Boro that is not present at the Lemoyne site, which supports the hypothesis that Lemoyne was occupied for a shorter duration than Washington Boro village.

Hypotheses and Conclusions

The Lemoyne site's relative chronological position between Schultz and Washington Boro villages and the site's absolute dating have been addressed by a comparison of pottery types and glass bead frequencies. In summary, the frequencies of glass bead varieties at the Lemoyne site indicate an intermediate chronological position between the occupations at Schultz and Washington Boro village. Admittedly, the small size of the glass bead assemblage from Lemoyne precludes statistical comparisons with the abundant samples of glass beads recovered from the cemeteries associated with the two Lancaster County villages. However, the frequencies of the major Susquehannock pottery types at Lemoyne are more like those of Washington Boro village. In terms of a date range for the Lemoyne site, an occupation in the second decade of the seventeenth century (ca. 1610–24) is consistent with the dates proposed by other researchers in the Northeast for sites with significant frequencies of Dutch Period 1 beads (Bradley 2007; Fitzgerald 1990; Kenyon and Fitzgerald 1986; Kenyon and Kenyon 1983; Sempowski 1994; Sempowski, Saunders, and Allen 2001). Based on hypothesized links between suites of glass bead varieties from the Northeast and potential European sources, these authors suggested that Kent's calendar ranges for Schultz village and, by extension, Washington Boro village should be revised forward by approximately

15 to 20 years. I favor a revised chronology. Moving the terminal occupation date of Schultz village forward to ca. 1615 allows for that site's occupation during the part of the decade when increased Dutch trade in the Hudson and Lower Delaware River Valleys would have brought Dutch Period 1 bead varieties into that site's bead assemblage. The increased frequency of this glass bead set at Lemoyne, together with the low frequencies of the GBP II varieties that were dominant at Schultz village, indicates that Lemoyne was probably constructed during the last years of occupation at the Schultz site. Although not specified by Sempowski (1994), her revised chronology for the Schultz site would place Washington Boro's occupation somewhere between ca. 1615 and 1635. The two- to fourfold increase in European trade items at Washington Boro after Schultz's occupation (Kent 2001: table 19) could then be explained by greatly increased trade after the establishment of permanent Dutch settlements at New Amsterdam, Fort Orange, Fort Nassau on the Delaware River, and Claiborne's trading posts in the upper Chesapeake Bay. Partial overlap of the Lemoyne site occupation with the early years of Washington Boro village is suggested by high frequencies of monochrome blue beads and Washington Boro Incised pottery at the Lemoyne site and the virtual absence of Dutch Period 1 bead types in the Washington Boro site complex.

The possibility that more than one Susquehannock village was occupied in AD 1615 in the Lower Susquehanna Valley is clearly supported by several European sources. In that year, Champlain learned the following from the Hurons about the Susquehannocks:

> I was glad to find this opportunity for gratifying my desire to obtain a knowledge of their country. It is situated only seven days from where the Dutch go to traffic on the fortieth degree. The savages there, assisted by the Dutch, make war upon them, take them prisoners, and cruelly put them to death; and indeed they told us that the preceding

year, while making war, they captured three of the Dutch, who were assisting their enemies, as we do the Attigouautans [Huron], and while in action one of their own men was killed. Nevertheless, they did not fail to send back the three Dutch prisoners, without doing them any harm, supposing that they belonged to our party, since they had no knowledge of us but by heresay, never having seen a Christian: otherwise, they said, these three prisoners would not have gotten off so easily, and would not escape again should they surprise and take them. This nation is very warlike, as those of the nation of the Attigouautans maintains. They have only three villages, which are in the midst of more than twenty others, on which they make war without assistance from their friends; for they are obliged to pass through the thickly-settled country of the Chouontouaroun, or else they would have to make a very long circuit. (Grant 1907:286)

That Champlain was writing about the Susquehannocks is corroborated by Cornelius Hendricksen's AD 1616 report of his ransom of three Dutchmen from the Minquas (Brodhead 1856:13–14). The Dutch had referred to the Susquehannocks as Minqua since at least 1614; the symbol for a single Minqua village appears on a map of that year attributed to Adriaen Block (Brodhead 1856: facing p. 13). Unlike the 1614 map on which it is based, Hendricksen's 1616 map shows four palisaded Minqua villages on the west side of what is presumably the Susquehanna River, with Minqua territory stretching to the Delaware River (Brodhead 1856: facing p. 11). The greater detail of the 1616 map in regard to the Susquehannock villages can be interpreted as the result of the sketch maps given to Hendricksen by the ransomed Dutchmen, who were probably brought to one or more of these Susquehannock villages.

Captain John Smith also referred to the Susquehannocks as "pallisadoed in their Townes" (Barbour 1986:150) in his 1612 treatise, *A Map of*

Virginia. This textual reference, together with the five Susquehannock "King's Houses" depicted on Smith's *Map of Virginia*, is based on his 1608 encounter with the Susquehannocks at the head of Chesapeake Bay. Kent (2001:28) doubted that Smith had an interpreter in his interactions with the Susquehannocks, yet neither Smith's description of this interaction nor Powell and Todkill's version of the same event in the 1612 treatise (Barbour 1986:231) indicate whether one was present or not. Although Kent maintained that the four more northerly "Kings Houses" / villages on Smith's 1612 *Map of Virginia* are probable misinterpretations or mistranslations on Smith's part (2001:333), what Smith thought he understood about the number of Susquehannock villages is reinforced by his textual and map references. Kent also wrote that Washington Boro was the village "Sasquesahanough" indicated on this map. However, this town could now be as easily interpreted as the Schultz site if Sempowski's (1994) revised chronology is accepted. This is yet another primary source that indicates the existence of multiple contemporaneous Susquehannock villages in the first two decades of the seventeenth century.

Although the relative chronological position of the Lemoyne site with respect to the Schultz and Washington Boro villages and an estimate for the Lemoyne site's absolute date range have been suggested based on the data at hand, the origin of the people who established the Lemoyne site is less clear. Two hypotheses are offered in this regard. In the first hypothesis, the group that occupied the Lemoyne site may have fissioned from Schultz village during the last years of that village's occupation, ca. 1610–15. This scenario is supported by the increased frequency of Dutch GBP 1 bead types at the Lemoyne site and its relatively high frequency of Schultz Incised pottery compared to Washington Boro village. Under the assumption that the abandonment of the Schultz site was related to some combination of population growth and soil and firewood exhaustion, some of the Susquehannocks at Schultz may have moved to Lemoyne, while others established the village at Washington Boro only slightly

later. This hypothesis is parsimonious because it relies on data from excavated sites. The second hypothesis is more speculative but equally possible. Witthoft (1959:24) and Kent (2001:312) discuss the Smith site in the context of possible Early Schultz–stage settlement in the Great Valley. No extant collections are known from the site, although Witthoft reportedly collected Schultz Incised and Shenks Ferry pottery there. Kent placed its location approximately 4.5 kilometers north of the Lemoyne site and south of the Conodoguinet Creek / Susquehanna River confluence (2001:312). It is possible that the Smith site represents an earlier Susquehannock village, possibly coeval with Schultz, and that Lemoyne represents a village relocation from the Smith site. Although Kent (2001:312) indicates that the Smith site was destroyed by an apartment complex, testing around the margins of the saddle where it was located might produce enough pottery to shed light on its chronology. It is also possible that the Smith site was a short-term camp or hamlet used by the Lemoyne site residents or that it postdates the occupation of the Lemoyne site.

Sempowski (1994) has argued for a ca. 1610 hiatus in trade between the Seneca and the Susquehannocks. Sempowski and other researchers (Bradley 1987:89–103; Wray et al. 1987:250–51, 1991:393–94) have suggested that the majority of European trade goods and marine shell on New York Iroquois sites of the late sixteenth and early seventeenth centuries was derived from sources along the mid-Atlantic coast and that the Susquehannocks were involved in this trade. Sempowski (1994:58–60) provided data to suggest that after ca. 1610, the Susquehannocks increased their participation in an interaction sphere that linked native groups in the Ohio and Allegheny Valleys with Ontario Iroquoian groups. Increased participation in a Chesapeake Bay–Ohio Valley–Ontario Iroquois trade network may have been among the reasons that the Susquehannocks chose to settle at the Lemoyne site ca. AD 1610. The site's location adjacent to the Allegheny Path (Wallace 1998:19–20), which led to the Ohio drainage basin in the west and the Lower

Delaware River Valley in the east, may have been chosen to facilitate this trade. Other explanations for the site's location some 50 kilometers northwest of the Lancaster County villages are certainly possible. Wall and Lapham (2003:169–70; see also Wall, chapter 5 in this volume) suggested that access to additional trapping territories resulted in a possible second wave of Susquehannock expansion into the Upper Potomac River Valley, which would have placed these groups in a prime geographic position to convey native and European materials to western groups.

Settlement models proposed for the Seneca (Sempowski, Saunders, and Allen 2001; Wray et al. 1987, 1991), Onondaga (Bradley 1987), and Mohawk (Snow 1995) involve the roughly coeval relocation of paired villages in the late sixteenth and early seventeenth centuries. In each case, the paired villages were separated by a maximum distance of 6 miles (10 km), and successive village relocations were made within areas no larger than 100 square miles (259 square km) during the period of interest. While the Iroquois approach to settlement can therefore be characterized as focused or intensive, the emerging Susquehannock settlement pattern in the early seventeenth century is by contrast extensive, covering

a linear distance approaching 200 kilometers. One potential interpretation of the geographically widespread Susquehannock settlement pattern of the early seventeenth century is that it represents a divided risk strategy for dealing with intertribal conflict. Under this explanation, a dispersed settlement pattern would increase the chances that some Susquehannock groups would not be as strongly affected by raids and warfare as others. Such a strategy carries the implication that the Susquehannock communities coordinated their respective settlement choices with each other. However, I favor a different interpretation. If Susquehannock patterns of decision-making were similar to those suggested by Brandão (1997) for the individual Iroquois tribes, their extensive settlement pattern may instead reflect relatively noncoordinated decisions by autonomous Susquehannock communities to situate themselves in dispersed locations that met historically contingent needs for security and offered novel trade opportunities. The evidence from the Lemoyne site supports this interpretation and suggests that the discovery and investigation of similar sites would repay the effort in a refined understanding of Susquehannock settlement.

REFERENCES

Anderson, David A.
1995   *Susquehannock Longhouses and Culture Change During the Contact Period in Pennsylvania.* Unpublished M.A. thesis, Department of Anthropology, University of Pittsburgh, Pittsburgh.

Barbour, Philip L.
1986   *The Complete Works of Captain John Smith (1580–1631).* Vol. 1. University of North Carolina Press, Chapel Hill.

Bradley, James W.
1983   Blue Crystals and Other Trinkets: Glass Beads from Sixteenth and Early Seventeenth Century New England. In *Proceedings of the 1982 Glass Trade Bead Conference*, edited by Charles F. Hayes, 83–110. Research Records 16. Rochester Museum and Science Center, Rochester, New York.

1987   *The Evolution of the Onondaga Iroquois: 1500–1655.* Syracuse University Press, Syracuse, New York.

2007   *Before Albany: An Archaeology of Native-Dutch Relations in the Capital Region 1600–1664.* New York State Museum Bulletin 509. University of the State of New York and the State Education Department, Albany.

2011   Revisiting Wampum and Other Seventeenth-Century Shell Games. *Archaeology of Eastern North America* 39:25–51.

2014   Glass Beads from Champlain's Habitation on Saint Croix Island, Maine: 1604–1613. *Beads: Journal of the Society of Bead Researchers* 26:47–63.

Brandão, José António
1997   *Your Fyre Shall Burn No More: Iroquois Policy Toward New France and Its Native Allies.* University of Nebraska Press, Lincoln.

Brodhead, John Romeyn
1856 *Documents Relative to the Colonial History of the State of New York.* Vol. 1. Edited by E. B. O'Callaghan. Weed, Parsons and Company, Albany, New York.

Ceci, Lynn
1988 Tracing Wampum's Origins: Shell Bead Evidence from Archaeological Sites in Western and Coastal New York. In *Proceedings of the 1986 Shell Bead Conference: Selected Papers*, edited by Charles F. Hayes and Lynn Ceci, 63–80. Research Records 20. Rochester Museum and Science Center, Rochester, New York.

Fitzgerald, William R.
1990 *Chronology to Cultural Process: Lower Great Lakes Archaeology, 1500–1650.* Ph.D. dissertation, Department of Anthropology, McGill University, Montreal. University Microfilms, Ann Arbor, Michigan.

Fogelman, Gary L.
1991 *Glass Trade Beads of the Northeast.* The Pennsylvania Artifact Series, Booklet No. 70. Fogelman Publishing Company, Turbotville, Pennsylvania.

Grant, W. L. (editor)
1907 *Voyages of Samuel De Champlain: 1604–1618.* Charles Scribner's Sons, New York.

Heisey, Henry W., and J. Paul Witmer
1962 Of Historic Susquehannock Cemeteries. *Pennsylvania Archaeologist* 32 (3–4): 99–130.

Huey, Paul R.
1983 Glass Beads from Fort Orange (1624–1676), Albany, New York. In *Proceedings of the 1982 Glass Trade Bead Conference*, edited by Charles F. Hayes, 83–110. Research Records 16. Rochester Museum and Science Center, Rochester, New York.

Karklins, Karlis
1974 Seventeenth Century Dutch Beads. *Historical Archaeology* 8:64–82.

Kent, Barry C.
2001 *Susquehanna's Indians.* Revised edition. Anthropological Series 6. Pennsylvania Historical and Museum Commission, Harrisburg.

Kenyon, Ian T., and William R. Fitzgerald
1986 Dutch Glass Beads in the Northeast: An Ontario Perspective. *Man in the Northeast* 32:1–34.

Kenyon, Ian T., and Thomas Kenyon
1983 Comments on 17th-Century Glass Trade Beads from Ontario. In *Proceedings of the 1982 Glass Trade Bead Conference*, edited by Charles F. Hayes, 59–74. Research Records 16. Rochester Museum and Science Center, Rochester, New York.

Kidd, Kenneth E., and Martha A. Kidd
1970 A Classification System for Glass Beads for the Use of Field Archaeologists. Canadian Historic Sites: Occasional Papers in Archaeology and History. Vol. 1.

Parks Canada, Ottawa. (1983 Reprint in *Proceedings of the 1982 Glass Trade Bead Conference*, edited by Charles F. Hayes, 219–57. Research Records 16. Rochester Museum and Science Center, Rochester, New York.)

Kinsey, W. Fred, III
1959 Historic Susquehannock Pottery. In *Susquehannock Miscellany*, edited by J. Witthoft and W. F. Kinsey, 61–98. Pennsylvania Historical and Museum Commission, Harrisburg.

Lapham, Heather A.
2001 More Than "A Few Blew Beads": The Glass and Stone Beads of Jamestown Rediscovery's 1994–1997 Excavations. *Journal of the Jamestown Rediscovery Center.* Vol. 1, http://www.apva.org/resource/jjrc/vol1/hltoc.html.

McWeeney, Lucinda, and Andrew Wyatt
2011 Botanical Remains. In *Phase III Archaeological Data Recovery Investigations at 36CU194, Proposed Norfolk Southern Railway Company Rail Connector Project, Memorial Park, Borough of Lemoyne, Cumberland County, Pennsylvania*, 410–22. Report prepared for the Borough of Lemoyne, Lemoyne, Pennsylvania, and Norfolk Southern Railway Company, Atlanta, Georgia. McCormick Taylor, Harrisburg, Pennsylvania.

Miller, Henry M., Dennis J. Pogue, and Michael A. Smolek
1983 Beads from the Seventeenth Century Chesapeake. In *Proceedings of the 1982 Glass Trade Bead Conference*, edited by Charles F. Hayes, 127–44. Research Records 16. Rochester Museum and Science Center, Rochester, New York.

Sempowski, Martha L.
1994 Early Historic Exchange Between the Seneca and the Susquehannock. In *Proceedings of the 1992 People to People Conference, Selected Papers*, edited by Charles F. Hayes, 51–64. Research Records 23. Rochester Museum and Science Center, Rochester, New York.

Sempowski, Martha L., Lorraine P. Saunders, and Kathleen M. S. Allen
2001 *Dutch Hollow and Factory Hollow: The Advent of Dutch Trade Among the Seneca.* Charles F. Wray Series in Seneca Archaeology. Vol. 3. Research Records 24. Rochester Museum and Science Center, Rochester, New York.

Smith, Ira F., III
1970 Schultz Site Settlement Patterns and External Relations: A Preliminary Discussion and Possible Interpretation. *New York State Archaeological Association Bulletin* 50:27–34.

1981 *A Late Woodland Village Site in North Central Pennsylvania: Its Role in Susquehannock Culture History.* Manuscript on file, National Archaeological Database, Digital Archaeological Record id: 118485,

156

Pennsylvania Historical and Museum Commission, Section of Archaeology, Harrisburg, Pennsylvania.

Smith, Ira F., III, and Jeffrey R. Graybill

1977   A Report on the Shenks Ferry and Susquehannock Components at the Funk Site. *Man in the Northeast* 13:45–65.

Snow, Dean R.

1994   *The Iroquois.* Blackwell, Cambridge, Massachusetts.

1995   *Mohawk Valley Archaeology: The Sites.* Institute for Archaeological Studies, State University of New York, Albany.

Strauss, Alisa

2000   *Iroquoian Food Techniques and Technologies: An Examination of Susquehannock Vessel Form and Function.* Ph.D. dissertation, Department of Anthropology, The Pennsylvania State University, State College, Pennsylvania. University Microfilms, Ann Arbor, Michigan.

Wall, Robert, and Heather Lapham

2003   Material Culture of the Contact Period in the Upper Potomac Valley: Chronological and Cultural Implications. *Archaeology of Eastern North America* 31:151–77.

Wallace, Paul A.

1998   *Indian Paths of Pennsylvania.* Pennsylvania Historical and Museum Commission, Harrisburg.

Weller, Brenda L.

2011   Faunal Analysis. In *Phase III Archaeological Data Recovery Investigations at 36CU194, Proposed Norfolk Southern Railway Company Rail Connector Project, Memorial Park, Borough of Lemoyne, Cumberland County, Pennsylvania,* 334–403. Report prepared for the Borough of Lemoyne, Lemoyne, Pennsylvania, and Norfolk Southern Railway Company, Atlanta, Georgia. McCormick Taylor, Harrisburg, Pennsylvania.

Weslager, Carl A., and A. R. Dunlap

1961   *Dutch Explorers, Traders, and Settlers in the Delaware Valley, 1609–1664.* University of Pennsylvania Press, Philadelphia.

Whyte, Thomas R.

2011   Icthyofaunal Analysis. In *Phase III Archaeological Data Recovery Investigations at 36CU194, Proposed Norfolk Southern Railway Company Rail Connector Project, Memorial Park, Borough of Lemoyne, Cumberland County, Pennsylvania,* 403–10. Report prepared for the Borough of Lemoyne, Lemoyne, Pennsylvania, and Norfolk Southern Railway Company, Atlanta, Georgia. McCormick Taylor, Harrisburg, Pennsylvania.

Witthoft, John

1959   Ancestry of the Susquehannocks. In *Susquehannock Miscellany,* edited by J. Witthoft and W. F. Kinsey III,

19–60. Pennsylvania Historical and Museum Commission, Harrisburg.

Wray, Charles F.

1973   *Manual for Seneca Iroquois Archaeology.* Cultures Primitive, Rochester, New York.

Wray, Charles F., Martha L. Sempowski, Lorraine P. Saunders, and Gian C. Cervone

1987   The Adams and Culbertson Sites. Charles F. Wray Series in Seneca Archaeology. Vol. 1. Research Records 19. Rochester Museum and Science Center, Rochester, New York.

1991   *Tram and Cameron: Two Early Contact Period Sites.* Charles F. Wray Series in Seneca Archaeology. Vol. 2. Research Records 21. Rochester Museum and Science Center, Rochester, New York.

Wyatt, Andrew

2011   Lithic Artifacts. In *Phase III Archaeological Data Recovery Investigations at 36CU194, Proposed Norfolk Southern Railway Company Rail Connector Project, Memorial Park, Borough of Lemoyne, Cumberland County, Pennsylvania,* 278–334. Report prepared for the Borough of Lemoyne, Lemoyne, Pennsylvania, and Norfolk Southern Railway Company, Atlanta, Georgia. McCormick Taylor, Harrisburg, Pennsylvania.

2012   Reconsidering Susquehannock Settlement Patterns: Excavations at the Lemoyne Site, Cumberland County, Pennsylvania. *Archaeology of Eastern North America* 40:71–98.

Wyatt, Andrew, Brenda Carr-Weller, Charles A. Richmond, Jerry A Clouse, Robert H. Eiswert, Dane D. Snyder, and Barbara J. Shaffer

2007   *Phase I Archaeological Identification Survey and Phase II Archaeological Evaluation for 36CU194, Land and Water Conservation Fund Project Nos. 42-00640 and 42-00818, Conversion of 1.65 Acres of Section 6(f) Land to a Non-recreational Use for the Proposed Rail Connection from the Lurgan Branch to the Shippensburg Secondary, Memorial Park, Lemoyne Borough, Cumberland County, Pennsylvania.* Report prepared for the Borough of Lemoyne, Lemoyne, Pennsylvania, and Norfolk Southern Railway Company, Atlanta, Georgia. McCormick Taylor, Harrisburg, Pennsylvania.

Wyatt, Andrew, Brenda L. Weller, Jerry A. Clouse, Charles A. Richmond, Barbara J. Shaffer, Thomas R. Whyte, and Lucinda McWeeney

2011   *Phase III Archaeological Data Recovery Investigations at 36CU194, Proposed Norfolk Southern Railway Company Rail Connector Project, Memorial Park, Borough of Lemoyne, Cumberland County, Pennsylvania.* Report prepared for the Borough of Lemoyne, Lemoyne, Pennsylvania, and Norfolk Southern Railway Company, Atlanta, Georgia. McCormick Taylor, Harrisburg, Pennsylvania.

1. Archaeological investigations were conducted in response to the proposed transfer of an easement on a borough park from the Borough of Lemoyne to Norfolk Southern Railway Company for the construction of a new connector rail line. Archaeologists with McCormick Taylor, Inc., performed an initial survey in 2005 and subsequent Phase II and Phase III excavations. All phases of excavation were funded by Norfolk Southern, and the borough graciously donated all the artifacts and field records to the State Museum of Pennsylvania.

2. Evidence for a Susquehannock presence near the Susquehanna River in Lemoyne Borough was suggested by Barry Kent based on the records of William Kelker held at the Dauphin County Historical Society in Harrisburg, Pennsylvania. Kent noted that 11 Indian graves had been exposed by railroad work in 1901 near the western terminus of the Cumberland Valley Railroad bridge, although only one contained artifacts. Kent suggested that if all 11 graves were Susquehannock, "[an early Schultz phase] site of some size and importance was destroyed by railroad and other construction at this place" (2001:312). In Kent's chronology, "early Schultz times" refers to the period of the hypothesized migration of Susquehannock groups into the Lower Susquehanna River Valley between ca. 1525 and 1575. Two articles from the local *Evening Sentinel* newspaper dated August 19 and August 21, 1901, partially corroborate Kelker's observations and place the graves "on the hill" and "beyond the Vanderbilt piers." These references place the possible graves very near or perhaps within the Lemoyne site. The "Vanderbilt Piers" refers to the stone railroad bridge piers of the never-completed South Pennsylvania Railroad, also known as "Vanderbilt's Folly," which are still extant (figure 6.1). Based on the descriptions by Kelker and the *Evening Sentinel*, the "graves" were in all probability located near the railroad cut that destroyed a portion of the Lemoyne site. These sources refer to one grave with two skeletons and associated artifacts and suggest that others may have been present, although the descriptions of the graves are vague. Kelker's description clearly indicates that their openings were circular, with a depth slightly greater than the width. This could just as easily describe the two most common storage features on Susquehannocks sites prior to ca. 1645—cylindrical and bell-shaped pits. It is possible that at least some of the so-called graves were storage pits used secondarily as graves.

3. The stone-paved road is probably the York Haven to Harrisburg Turnpike (AD 1832–50), while the stone foundation may have been a tollhouse. The absence of clear Susquehannock house patterns at the Lemoyne site may reflect a combination of plow disturbance, truncation of the upper subsoil during improvements to Memorial Park, and our excavation sample.

7.

Susquehannock Stature

EVIDENCE THAT THEY WERE
A "GYANT-LIKE PEOPLE"

Marshall Joseph Becker

ABSTRACT

In 1608, John Smith described the Susquehannocks as a "gyant-like people." Confirmation of the accuracy of Smith's observation derives from two vectors: (1) the observations of Smith and several other independent witnesses and (2) the direct study of the human skeletal remains of populations that were part of the Susquehannock "Confederacy." Comparison of the calculated stature of Susquehannock skeletal samples with contemporary native populations in the nearby region reveal that Susquehannock males were significantly taller, while females were only average among these groups. The biological evidence confirms independent historical observations such as John Smith's that the Susquehannock people were unusually tall.

Introduction

By 1525, the Protohistoric Susquehannock tribe, resident in four villages along the Susquehanna River where it crosses into Pennsylvania (see Parker 1938), had begun their relocation into an area along the lower end of the Susquehanna River (Kent 1984). These Iroquoian people were spurred to make this move by several factors. The formation and growing power of the Iroquois Confederacy allowed them to take control of the pelt trade from the Great Lakes, across what is now central New York, to the Hudson River. For reasons unknown but probably due to their earlier location, the Susquehannocks were not included in the Five Nations group. By shifting their tribal territory to the area around present-day Lancaster, Pennsylvania, the Susquehannocks gained access to large numbers of pelts coming from the west. Their paired large palisaded village as well as numerous subdivisions, or outlier communities, expanded trade to the Mississippi Valley via the Ohio River route. The Susquehannocks thus had access to huge quantities of pelts that they sold to European traders.

Susquehannock trading stations or contact points along the Chesapeake may predate the Spanish mission built in that location during the 1560s. The shortest route for Susquehannock merchants who brought pelts from the west to the upper reaches of the Potomac was to take them down that river into the Chesapeake Bay. Ceramics and other features of a palisaded Native

American site (46HM73) located along the West Branch of the Potomac River, dating from the Early Contact period (ca. AD 1550), indicate that the occupants were related to the Susquehannock Confederacy of central Pennsylvania (Brashler 1987). Site 46HM73 and a nearby settlement of earlier date were early western trade outposts for the Susquehannocks (see Kent 1984), which were used to secure peltry from people to their west. It also is the source of the bones used in this study.

The Susquehannock residents at Site 46HM73, and at the even earlier village located nearby (Brashler 1987:3), could receive peltry from western suppliers covering an enormous territory. They then relayed these pelts to European buyers using routes that avoided encounters with other tribes, particularly the Five Nations. The Five Nations Iroquois, however, sought to provide "ritual" or purely sporting interactions of a lethal form that continually harassed their neighbors.

As the John Smith expedition narrative points out, Chesapeake Bay had become a major area of contact with Europeans by 1608. However, in 1622, after members of the Powhatan Confederacy attempted to exterminate the European settlers along the Chesapeake Bay, the Susquehannocks prudently shifted their trade to the Delaware River (see Myers 1912; Risingh 1653–56). While the translation of the Risingh report (Dahlgren and Norman 1988) is unreliable regarding Native Americans (Becker 1989), the original document provides valuable information concerning Lenape accommodations with the Susquehannock.

The demographic complexity of the Susquehannock Confederacy is indicated in the Risingh report of 1653–56. During that period, the Susquehannocks were coming under increasing stress from the Seneca as well as English colonists to their south. In an attempt to encourage Swedish trade and to gain Swedish military support, a delegation of "White Minquas" (Minquas being the Lenape designation for the Susquehannock) brought a petition to the Swedish Fort Trinity (now Newcastle, Delaware) in 1655. Accompanying these

delegates were "their united nations, the Tehaque, the Skonedidehoga, the Serasquacke, the true Minquas and the Lower Quarter of the Minquas" (Risingh 1653–56; also A. Johnson 1917:278; Myers 1912:140, 159–60). These five named peoples undoubtedly lived in separate villages not yet identified archaeologically (see Cadzow 1936:18).

Human skeletal remains recovered in 1985 from surface collecting at 46HM73 after a disastrous flood and from the 1986 excavations were analyzed before being returned to the property owners (Becker 1987; see also Angel 1969; Bass 1979). Through comparisons of these craniometric data (Howells 1973) and nonmetric observations (see Sjøvold 1973), it may be possible to relate this population to the other Susquehannock populations in ways similar to those employed for the Arikara (Key and Jantz 1981; see also Becker 1982, 1985, 1999a; Musgrave and Evans 1980). The focus of this review is the stature of the population from 46HM73 (Becker 1991) and comparison with other Susquehannock data and information on stature among non-Susquehannock populations. The goal is to relate these findings to the John Smith observations and to create a basis for further study of Susquehannock skeletal biology.

John Smith's first encounter with "sixtie of those gyant-like people," whom he identified as "Sasquesahanocks," took place during the summer of 1608 (1624:60). Earlier in that 1608 account, Smith (1624:29–30) described some of the "naturall Inhabitants of Virginia" as "being very great as the *Sasquesahanocks*; others very little, as the *Wighcocomocoes*: but generally tall and straight." Smith's *Map of Virginia*, compiled in 1612, was published along with Smith's observations of those Susquehannock whom he met in 1608:

[Sixty] of those Sasquesahanocks came to the discuerers with skins, Bowes, Arrowes, Targets, Beads, Swords, and Tobacco pipes for presents. Such great and well proportioned men are seldome seene, for they seemed like Giants to the English, yea and to the neighbors . . . their language it may well be-seeme their proportions, sounding from them, as it were a great voice in a vault, or caue, as an Eccho. . . . with bowes, and arrows, and clubs, sutable to their greatnesse and conditions.

These are scares knowne to Powhatan. . . . The picture of the greatest of them is signified in the Mappe. The calfe of whose leg was 3 quarters of a yard about, and all the rest of his limbes so answer-able to that proportion, that he seemed the good-liest man that euer we beheld. (Smith 1910:52–55; excerpted in Barbour 1969:342–43 and Robinson 1987:5)

Thus Smith is describing the Susquehannocks not only as tall but also as being particularly tall even when compared with their also quite tall native neigh-bors in Virginia (Smith 1624:30, 60–61). These peoples differed from the tribes on the eastern side of the bay, described as "of little stature, of another language from the rest, and very rude" (Smith 1910:54).

The human figure on Smith's *Map of Virginia* (1624: facing p. 40; Barbour 1969:342) is captioned, "The Sasques=ahanougs are a Gyant like peo=ple & thus a-tyred" (see Becker 2012, 2014a). Clearly the Susquehannocks were the standard for "tall" in Smith's eyes. In addition to the map cartoon, the Robert Vaughan engraving at the end of "Book 1" of Smith's *Historie* (1624) features several cuts clearly derived from John White's drawings. Vaughan adds two views depicting John Smith capturing the kings of Pamaunkee and Paspahegh. In both engrav-ings, Captain Smith is shown as much shorter than his prisoners, clearly violating traditional artistic conven-tions of power but strongly reinforcing Smith's desire to indicate that these Native Americans were quite tall (see Feest 1967).

As with all early recorded observations of the stat-ure of any population, the statements are always rela-tive to the observer's concept of "tall." Thus for John Smith's remarks, it would be nice to have some idea of *his* actual stature. This we do not have, leading us to

turn to proxies as proposed by historians of demogra-phy (e.g., Floud et al. 2011). As a physical anthropolo-gist, I recognize the possibility of conscription records to offer clues regarding the average stature of males in a specific population. I also recognize the failings of most of those studies that are based on cemetery data. Two adjacent cemeteries in the same town may have significantly different results from skeletal stud-ies, and both may provide results somewhat different from demographic data based on military records (Becker 2016; see also "anthropometric history of continental Europe" in Floud et al. 2011:241). In short, efforts to quantify data on stature may not be more useful than the simple observations made by some protoethnographers.

Several other comments in the early literature may be considered in regard to what they tell us regard-ing stature among two non-Susquehannock groups in the native Northeast. In Huron country in 1639, a Jesuit writing to his brother described his Indian hosts as follows: "They are robust, and all [171] are much taller than the French" (Thwaites 1898:155). This may say something about the French and/or the Jesuits. Swedish colonial Governor Johan Printz (see Becker 2006), in a letter to a colleague dated April 12, 1643, described "the inhabitants of this country," presum-ably the Lenape along the Delaware River, as being "large, strong and well built fellows" (A. Johnson 1930:150). Although Printz must have had interactions with the Susquehannock, at no place can I find them described in his records (but see Becker 2012).

In 1834, an Osage speaking to Washington Irving (1834:73) disparaged the "Delaware" [Lenape] as hav-ing short legs and being unable to run, so they had to stand and fight. Irving agreed, saying that "the Delawares are rather short-legged, while the Osage are remarkable for length of limb."

Not all Native American people were seen by European immigrants to be relatively or even unusu-ally tall, as indicated by the 1644 observation of Johannes Megapolensis on the stature of the Mohawks living in the area now central New York: "The people and Indians here in this country are like us Dutchmen in body and stature" (Megapolensis 1909:173). As we will see below, Smith was not the only observer to be impressed by the stature of the Susquehannock. However, there was a phase during the twentieth century when, without any direct supporting evidence, a group of archaeologists and historians took it on themselves to refute Smith's observations regarding the Susquehannock.

Changing "Beliefs"

There appear to be various reasons why some twentieth-century scholars took it on themselves to deny John Smith's records of the impressive stature of the Susquehannock. This effort was part of a trend to debunk various writings about "natives" of the New World (see Feest 1987:609). In addition, this new "interpretation" of Smith may derive from popular misperceptions of archaeological skeletal remains. Quite commonly, casual observers estimate the stature of skeletons seen in the ground as much greater than is indicated by calculations derived from direct measurements of an in situ skeleton or from calculations from specific bones (see the formulae of Trotter 1970; from Trotter and Gleser 1952, 1958; also Becker 1999a). Relevant to these specious reports on Indian giants, I have collected a file of 15 *New York Times* news notes, dating from 1856 to 1916, that republish accounts from all over the country regarding observations of native graves. These items, all bearing captions such as "Bones of a Giant" and "Skeletons Seven Feet Long," uniformly report individuals supposedly of extreme stature.

With the rise of physical anthropology in the early 1900s, these bizarre reports gradually faded. However, many early archaeologists were only marginally more professional in their comments to the public and were as unfamiliar with techniques of physical anthropology as any novice. This is the case with the supposed use, some 60 years ago, of "biological evidence"

to evaluate Susquehannock stature (Witthoft, Kinsey, and Holzinger 1959:101–18). After a cursory examination of 13 adult skeletons from the Ibaugh site (Washington Boro, Pennsylvania) the authors declared that Captain Smith's statements regarding Susquehannock stature were hyperbole. Their claim to have used the Hooton (1947) formulae for calculating stature has no basis in fact. No actual measurements are provided, and no Hooton reference appears in their bibliography. Witthoft (cited in Kinsey 1960:103–5) later suggested that the earlier Shenks Ferry people of central Pennsylvania were large and rugged but speculated that the Susquehannocks were short and slender. While postulating a "myth of Susquehannock giantism," these authors created a myth contradicted by all the evidence that they ignored (Witthoft, Kinsey, and Holzinger 1959:110–11). Kinsey's subsequent publication on this subject (1960) included some osteometric data, again claiming to use Hooton's (1947) methods for calculating stature. In fact, Hooton (1947:728–29) only suggested the use of Karl Pearson's (1899:169–244) formulae for reconstructing stature—methods that had long since been superseded by the work of Trotter and Gleser (1952, 1958). Sadly, Francis Jennings accepted the fantasies of Witthoft, Kinsey, and Holzinger (1959), leading him to question John Smith's basic observations as well as to construct an error-laden prehistory of the Susquehannocks (Jennings 1968:15, 17).

Materials and Methods

Excavations at a mid-sixteenth-century Susquehannock site located on Pancake Island in the South Branch of the Potomac River in Hampshire County, West Virginia (46HM73), revealed portions of a palisaded village and associated features dating from the middle of the sixteenth century. This remnant of a site, following a disastrous flood in 1986, yielded 13 relatively intact burials. Just after the flood, surface collection of skeletal material found immediately downstream of

162

the site provided long bones from at least another 18 other adults (MNI: minimum number of individuals). Calculations of the stature from 17 of the individuals represented in this sample of 31 (Becker 1987) were compared with other samples collected at earlier dates (Becker 1991).

The people from 46HM73 almost suffered a similar fate to those represented by bones discovered at other sites, most of which were entirely ignored or discarded. Thanks to the prescient actions of Jan Brashler, a recovery team was assembled that included a physical anthropologist. Reburial requirements, while speeding the analysis of this material, permitted the production of only a limited report on the skeletal remains of these people (Becker 1987). The emphasis was on data useful for comparative anthropometric studies.

At 46HM73, a total of 10 burials of adults plus a series of flood-scattered adult long bones were among the human remains selected as sufficiently intact for this review (see Becker 1987:50–53). Although the excavations resulted in the listing of 18 burials, only 12 actually were derived from excavated interments. Numbers 1 and 5–7 represented clusters of human bone later identified as bones redeposited by the flood, number 8 was a burial seen in the riverbank but left in situ, and number 11 consisted of two redeposited bits of a child. Number 18 was assigned to the entire collection of surface remains that had been washed downriver from the settlement area (Becker 1987:39, 44). Two of the 12 burials recovered (numbers 4 and 9) are young children not included in the present study.

Aside from flood damage to most of the graves, preservation of the skeletal remains was moderately good. Limitations in the time during which this material could be studied restricted the research program to basic age and sex evaluations, plus the collection of craniometric data and nonmetric cranial observations. No data concerning the stature of these people were included in the initial publication. Since these robust Susquehannock populations consumed high-protein diets (Brashler 1987), the formulae used for

calculating the stature of white Americans established by Trotter and Gleser (1952, 1958) and then Trotter (1970) were employed in generating the figures for this study.

The selection of appropriate regression formulae to calculate stature from these remains was a critical issue in this research (see Becker 1999a). Although Native Americans originally derived from Asia, according to nonnative interpretations of biological data, the connection is via a proto-Mongoloid stock who arrived as hunters and gatherers. El-Najjar and McWilliams (1978:92–93) briefly discussed this problem, noting that the Trotter and Gleser formulae for "Mongoloids" generally are inaccurate because the population from which they derive was heterogeneous (including Americans of Japanese ancestry, Indians, Filipinos, etc.). A better regional-specific New World set of formulae was generated by Genovés (1967) for Mesoamericans using a modern Mexican population. These formulae, derived from a people eating a low-protein diet, remain inappropriate for the meat-eating peoples of the Eastern Woodlands. Similarly, using the Trotter and Gleser (1958) formulae for "male mongoloids" severely distorts the statures calculated for females in such samples (e.g., Melbye 1983). Steele and McKern (1969:221) discussed this problem and agreed with Genovés (1967) that population-specific regression formulae are needed for the calculation of stature. Ideally, a set should be devised that is specific to each group in this region. The evidence here demonstrates this need, since burials 1 and 12 (table 7.1) lacked legs, and stature has been calculated using the ulna alone. The results are near the upper end of the ranges for males and females, suggesting that allometric variations in the forearms are significant.

Krogman and Iscan (1986:239, 335), recognizing that the Trotter and Gleser formulae for "Mongoloids" were not appropriate to Native American populations, modified the data from Steele and McKern. For the purposes of this chapter, where relative stature is the principal concern, the use of any standard set of formulae might be sufficient. As S. R. Saunders (1990, personal communication) points out, regardless of which regression formulae are used as standard, the calculated "stature" will show a greater metric difference than will simple comparisons of the lengths of individual long bones from which the calculations are made. Thus the formulae selected here are those calculated by Trotter and Gleser (1952) for White Americans, revised using the formulae of Trotter (1970).

The bone measurements from 46HM73 (Becker 1987: tables 4 and 5) are the basis for calculations of stature below (tables 7.1 and 7.2). No age adjustments have been factored for these statures, since our interest focuses on relative stature and not solving forensic problems involved in the identification of specific known individuals. Although age at death can be calculated for those individuals recovered from graves (table 7.1), this cannot be computed with ease for those individuals represented by scattered remains recovered from the surface. The Trotter and Gleser (1958) revised formulae for males have not been employed.

The size of the total sample from 46HM73 described here has been increased to 17 by including bones recovered from the surface. Among these remains are 26 tibia, or large fragments thereof, and 19 femurs (Becker 1987: table 5). Maximum lengths can be evaluated for 5 left and 6 right femurs (Krogman

and Iscan 1986:335, table 8.28; Steele and McKern 1969). Pairing the femurs on the basis of length as well as eight other measurements suggests that at least 7 adults are represented. Individual "D" has a difference of 7 millimeters in his femur lengths, but other measurements suggest that these were a pair. The individual "surface" bone measurements, sex evaluations, and stature calculations (based on the left femur where applicable) for 7 individuals appear in table 7.2. When combined with data from the 10 adults from grave contexts, the total sample size is 17.

Discussion of the Data from 46HM73

At least three considerations must be noted with regard to the data summarized at the bottom of table 7.2, particularly as it relates to the "statures" derived from the flood-disturbed bones (surface collected) that have been added to the figures calculated from intact burials. First, at least one of the burials noted in table 7.1 (burial 1, a female) was missing its legs, probably due to flood damage. Those "missing" leg bones may be included in the figures for table 7.2. This would mean that one of the females may be represented

TABLE 7.1 Stature calculated for each individual excavated from burials at the Susquehannock site 46HM73 (using Trotter and Gleser 1952; from Becker 1991)

Burial	Age	Sex	Long bones used	Stature (cm)
1	65+	F	L. ulna	174.32 ±4.32
2	55?	M	L. femur	174.70 ±3.27
3	60	M	L. femur and tibia	180.03 ±2.99
10	65+	F	L. humerus, femur, and tibia	160.115 ±3.51
12	60+	M?	R. ulna	179.13 ±4.32
13	70	F	L. humerus, femur, and tibia	167.737 ±3.51
14	48	M	L. humerus and femur and R. tibia	170.215 ±2.99
15	22±	F	L. humerus, femur, and tibia	159.681 ±3.51
16*	38	F??	L. humerus, femur, and tibia	167.361 ±3.51
17	65+	F	L. femur	160.063 ±3.72
Females (N = 6)	Range of statures = 159.68–174.32 cm		Average stature = 164.88 cm (5 ft 4.9 in)	
Males (N = 4)	Range of statures = 170.22–180.03 cm		Average stature = 176.02 cm (5 ft 9.3 in)	

* Burial 16, previously identified (Becker 1987) as a female, at this time is less certainly identified as to sex. This person now is noted as "F??" to indicate less certainty in the identification of sex.

TABLE 7.2 Statures in centimeters as calculated from femurs found on the surface of 46HM73* and average stature for all 17 individuals from the site (separated by sex)

Person	Bone number	Length (cm)	Bone number	Length (cm)	Sex	Stature (cm)
A	L1	439	R1	441	M	165.89 ±3.27
B	L7	444e	R4	439e	F	163.77 ±3.72
C	L2	462			M	173.37 ±3.27
D	L3	467e	R2	454	M	172.56 ±3.27
E	L6	429e	R3	434e	F	160.06 ±3.27
F	R5	399e			F	152.65 ±3.72
G	R6	395e			F	151.67 ±3.72

Females (N = 4)	Range of statures = 151.67–163.77 cm	Average stature = 157.04 cm (5 ft 1.8 in)
Males (N = 3)	Range of statures = 165.89–173.37 cm	Average stature = 170.61 cm (5 ft 7.2 in)

* Age changes are not factored. An "e" after the bone length indicates slight damage to one or more condyles. Lengths, therefore, are estimated (possible error under 2 mm).

Average stature for 17 "individuals" noted in tables 7.1. and 7.2.

Females (N = 10)	Range of statures = 151.67–174.32 cm	Average stature = 161.74 cm (5 ft 3.7 in)
Males (N = 7)	Range of statures = 165.89–180.03 cm	Average stature = 173.70 cm (5 ft 8.4 in)

twice: once as burial 1 and a second time as a set of femurs (table 7.2).

Second, the actual origins of the surface remains from 46HM73 are less well known than those from excavated burials, all of which derive from graves located inside the village palisade (Brashler 1987: figure 3). This conforms to an observation made in 1666 by George Alsop, who noted that the Susquehannocks buried their dead within the village palisade (see Cadzow 1936:96). Brashler (1987:9) recognized that the burials from 46HM73 were at variance with finds from Schultz and other Late Prehistoric Susquehannock sites, at least as claimed by Witthoft, Kinsey, and Holzinger (1959:101; Kent 1984). Stephen Warfel (personal communications, 1990) suggested that burials "found inside the Schultz palisade are usually aberrant." Some of these surface bones from 46HM73 could derive from burials from outside the palisade and might have different cultural associations.

The third consideration relates to the bimodality in the statures calculated for the surface bones as distinct from those from excavated burials. These sets may reflect burials that were inside versus outside the palisade or from graves that had been dug to shallow depths. Shallow graves were more likely to have been flood disturbed. The considerable differences in the averages in the statures of individuals recovered from excavated burials, when compared with those recovered from the surface (nearly 8 cm for females and 5.4 cm for males) may reflect different mortuary programs operative within an incipient ranked society. Within Susquehannock society, intracultural variables may be reflected in these two archaeological contexts, with higher-status individuals being buried in deeper graves. Although burial depth may relate to season of the year or to soil conditions, the individuals buried in shallow graves may reflect lower social status within the community, as is the case among the historic Lenape (see Becker 1980, 1988, 1993, 2008). Stephen Warfel (personal communication, 1990) knew of no such depth correlation from Susquehannock burials in the Lower Susquehanna Valley. If women, in general, held lower status than men at Site 46HM73, then burial depth might explain why more women than men were found "washed out" of their original loci, although women are better represented in the total population. The deeper graves, those that survived the flood, held the bones of taller individuals of both sexes, who also may have been of higher status. The figures are far too small to permit a statistical analysis at this point, but these data do form an interesting thesis for future study.

The small population from 46HM73 shows a wide range of variation in a number of characteristics not noted in the nonmetric observations (Becker 1987). For example, the gonial configuration varies considerably. Several individuals manifested everted gonial angles, while several others were turned inward. Maxillary canine length also appears to vary, with many individuals having unusually long sets. At least two dental pearls appear (burial 12). One "frequent" nonmetric trait that merits comment is the doubled anterior condylar canal, at the ventral aspect of the cranial articulation with the atlas. Some 17 examples of condylar canals were found intact in this population, of which four were double. In these few cases, the canals were not simply divided as in most populations; rather, their sizes were quite divergent, and the canals were separated by large boney pillars. The meaning of these variations remains unknown, but they must be considered as a factor in any attempt to do comparative studies.

Comparative Data: The Early Records

In a search for skeletal data to compare with the Susquehannock people from 46HM73, I turned to some earlier evidence that seemed relevant. Professor Michael Spence reported that the impressive average statures of 72 and 84 inches supposedly calculated for high-status Adena males from the Dover Mound (Webb and Snow 1959:29–32; see also Dragoo 1963:249) were not supported by any postcranial information, and these figures were later omitted (Webb and Snow 1959:41–44). Webb and Snow (1945:265, 298, table V) then calculated statures for Adena and Hopewell populations (from Manouvrier 1893). In addition, they offered averages only from the high-status individuals recovered at these excavations. Even these averages of the Adena elite fall below those

calculated for the Susquehannock people from Site 46HM73.

Comparative Data: Susquehannock Skeletal Material Inventory

All of the early excavation reports relating to Susquehannock sites (e.g., Heisey and Witmer 1962; see Kent 1984) are characterized by a general absence of osteometric information. The attention given to the human remains from these sites can be characterized by the poor treatment of the 46 individuals found at the Murry site. They became the subject of an undergraduate student report that has since gone missing (Kinsey and Graybill 1971:17).

Several excavations of cemeteries of Susquehannock populations and of related peoples were conducted during the early modern era (Dragoo 1976). Nearly 200 skeletons from Susquehannock sites in Pennsylvania were excavated between 1960 and 1990 by the Pennsylvania State Museum. These sites include 36LA52, the Conestoga Town site excavated in 1970 (Heisey and Witmer 1962:104; Kent 1984:379–91). All of the skeletons at the Pennsylvania State Museum are being curated in accordance with standards accepted by the Indian nations or have been returned to appropriate locations. Much of the Susquehannock skeletal material found in fragmentary condition during recent excavations was simply left in place, since it was determined to be too delicate for effective removal and appropriate curation (Barry C. Kent, personal communication, 1990).

Kent (1984: table 19) lists 1,100 interments identified at 10 sites. Although the tradition of collecting only intact skulls (see Morton 1839) had been superseded, not all the remains collected from these many Susquehannock burials have been given serious and respectful attention. Programs to inventory collections in the State Museum of Pennsylvania (Harrisburg) and at the North Museum (Lancaster, Pennsylvania) began by 1990 (Stephen Warfel, personal communication,

1990). In 1992, the latter museum became the North Museum of Nature and Science, an independent and nonprofit organization leasing the building from Franklin and Marshall College. Specific studies using these materials were planned. Similar considerations were discussed regarding the Monongahela skeletal material at the University of Pittsburgh and the Carnegie Museum.

The craniometric data and nonmetric observations recorded from the population at 46HM73 provide basic evidence for describing these Susquehannock in West Virginia and for comparing them with other Susquehannock and related peoples. The ideal populations for comparison include the early Susquehannock populations resident along the Susquehanna River (see Kent 1984:197–201; also the introduction to this chapter) and their immediate ancestors from areas closer to the present New York–Pennsylvania border. Programs for the study of these groups, with a focus on stature, were considered. Although the focus in this chapter is on stature, degrees of cultural affinity that will give meaning to this evidence can be determined only through craniometric or nonmetric studies and related techniques (Smith and Bettinger 1987).

Published data derived from Susquehannock skeletal material are minimal, but a brief listing of sources is useful. Some metric data may be extracted from Von Bonin and Morant (1938). Data from the 28 adults, overwhelmingly believed to be male, from the Murray Garden site, appears to have been lost as the skeletal remains were poorly curated. Parker (1938) reports elaborate stone box graves, with individuals estimated, after the fashion of the day, at over six feet tall. Cadzow's slightly earlier survey of Susquehannock archaeology included the excavation of graves at the Shenks Ferry site, where the outstanding preservation of the bones (Cadzow 1936:42, 44) is confirmed by the illustrations (Cadzow 1936:45). However, Cadzow describes the skeletons as "broken and decomposed." Craniometric data are available from burial 5 at the Shenks Ferry site (Cadzow

1936:47–48). Cadzow (1936:154–55) also provided important Susquehannock craniometric data for burials 1 and 2 at the Frey Farm burial site. While Cadzow's data are sparse, they do offer some basis for comparison and for modern verification. Although no long bone data have been published from the Ibaugh site (Witthoft, Kinsey, and Holzinger 1959), Kinsey (1960: table 2) provided metric data from some Ibaugh crania. More important here, Kinsey provided measurements from a few of the long bones from that population as well as similar information from a proximal burial that he identified as a member of the earlier Shenks Ferry population (table 7.3).

The number of sites in southwestern Pennsylvania that are identified as being of the "Monongahela" tradition has grown rapidly in the past two decades. These village-dwelling people appear to have emerged in the region around AD 1100 (see Espino 2006). While information regarding the archaeology of these people has been increasing, biological information derived from extensive skeletal collections has been wanting. Ethnohistoric evidence remains sparse (but see Pendergast 1991), since the "Monongahela" villages faded around 1630 to 1640. I believe they shifted to the east to become one of the several Susquehannock confederated tribes identified in the documents. The biological data, therefore, would be particularly valuable for understanding their relationships with the Susquehannock.

Comparative Data: Non-Susquehannock

The Iroquoian origins of the Susquehannocks are generally acknowledged (Kent 1984), and considerable archaeological evidence has been gathered to support this thesis (see Gollup and Herbstritt, chapter 2 in this volume). Osteological confirmation of the relationship, however, has not been generated despite a vast accumulation of information from the Seneca (Lane and Sublett 1972; Sublett 1965) and the other Five Nation affiliates (Forrest 2010). In her dissertation,

TABLE 7.3 Long bone data and statures from the Ibaugh site burials (using Trotter and Gleser 1952; from Becker 1991)

Susquehannock burials from Ibaugh

Burial	Sex*	Bones	Length (cm)**	Stature	
				cm	ft and in
3c	F	L. femur	423	158.58 ±3.72	5' 2.4"
		L. humerus	293		
5c	M	L. femur	463	171.60 ±3.27	5' 7.6"
7c	F	R. femur	432??	160.80 ±3.72	5' 3.3"
8c	F	R. humerus	282	152.72 ±4.45	5' 0.1"
13c	F	R. femur	445??	166.034 ±3.55	5' 5.4"
		R. tibia	368		

Females (N = 4)	Range of statures = 152.72–166.03 cm	Average stature = 159.53 cm (5 ft 2.8 in)
Male (N = 1)	"Range" of statures = 171.60 cm (5 ft 7.6 in)	

Shenks Ferry burials (Kent 1984; also Boyd and Boyd 1992)

Burial	Sex	Bones	Length (cm)	Stature	
				cm	ft and in
"Extended burial"	M	R. femur	487	168.70 ±2.99	5' 6.4"
		L. tibia	410		

* Sex determined by Becker 1991.

** Length of bones determined by Kinsey 1960.

L. P. Saunders (1986) tabulated 46 nonmetric traits from skeletons recovered at most of the early historic period sites and from several of the prehistoric Seneca sites in New York to demonstrate biological affinities among them (see also O'Connor 1987). These data provide an outstanding basis for comparison with the limited Susquehannock evidence. Recently, human skeletal data from 11 New York Iroquoian and 10 Ontario Algonquian sites have been reviewed to consider infant mortality and juvenile growth in this region (Forrest 2010). Forrest provides references to the sources for osteometric data from these 21 sites, publications that should offer data on adult femora from more than 700 adult skeletons. Her limited mention of long bone length does not separate them by sex to present average femur length (Forrest 2010: table 5.5).

Comparative data from the Lenape realm are not available, primarily due to the paucity of excavated sites and also to the poor condition of the skeletal material (Becker 1980). Similar limitations in the analysis of skeletal remains exist in New Jersey, where burials from across the state clearly are recognized as "not a biogenetic population, but a politico-geographic unit of modern times" (Clabeaux 1973:24). Clabeaux reviewed data from the 49 Native American burials then known from New Jersey, noting that little postcranial material was recovered and concluding that no estimates of stature were possible. The basic evidence from New Jersey, however, should be reviewed.

Spatially proximal to the Susquehanna Valley but temporally earlier than the Contact period Susquehannock are people represented by a skeletal population from central Delaware (table 7.4). These skeletons from the Island Field site (7K-F-17) were redated at approximately AD 700 to 1000 (Custer et al. 1990; see also Neuman and Murad 1970). The Island Field people were a nonagricultural but relatively sedentary Native American population. While temporally removed from the Susquehannock population being studied, this sample is spatially located just to the southeast of central Pennsylvania (Robbins and Rosenberg 1989). This provides important comparative information from an area that was distinct from the better-known Iroquoian-speaking peoples noted below but included a population closer in space to the Susquehannock.

Data from Canada relating to Protohistoric and historic Neutral and Huron peoples from the area around Toronto provide a useful comparison for the Susquehannock figures. These include samples from the Mackenzie site, AkGv-2 (also known as the Woodbridge site; table 7.5; S. Saunders 1986), a probable Neutral village just northwest of Toronto dated to AD 1520 ± 15 (D. Johnson 1980); the MacPherson site, a mid-sixteenth-century Neutral village just west of Hamilton (table 7.6; S. Saunders 1988); a male and a female from the Draper site, an early Protohistoric Huron village located 48 kilometers east of Toronto (table 7.7a; Williamson 1979); the Keffer site, a Huron settlement near Toronto from about AD 1500 (table

7.7b; Michael W. Spence, personal communication, 1990); and the Ball site, also a Huron settlement from about AD 1500 (table 7.7c; Knight and Melbye 1983; Melbye 1983).

Metric data from the skeletons from the MacPherson site, probably closest in date to Site 46HM73, have been recalculated from S. Saunders's (1988) report, using data that she provided. The regression formulae used by Melbye (1983) to calculate stature for both males and females from the Ball site, those that Trotter and Gleser (1958) derived for "male mongoloids," have been recalculated.

Seneca osteometric data from the Culbertson (ca. 1560–70) and Adams (ca. 1563–76) sites should be considered. Wray et al. (1987:22) provided some stature information from the three Adams site cemeteries but only as ranges. The Culbertson site information (Wray et al. 1987:179–85) is even more limited,

TABLE 7.4 Burial statures, Island Field site (7K-F-17), Delaware, AD 700–1000

Burial	Sex	Bones	Stature (cm)
1	M?	L. radius	174.266 ±4.32
7	F	L. femur	161.792 ±3.72
8A	M	R. Humerus	174.554 ±4.05
11	M	L. femur	173.984 ±3.27
12	F	L. femur	164.756 ±3.72
16	F	R. Humerus and tibia; L. femur	159.256 ±3.51
21	M	L. femur and tibia	177.17 ±2.99
37	F	L. femur*	155.617 ±3.72
44	F	L. Humerus	154.066 ±4.45
60	F	R. femur	162.533 ±3.72
68	F	R. femur	166.485 ±3.72
76	F	L. tibia	168.83 ±3.66
81	M	R. Humerus	162.85 ±4.05
82	F	R. femur	169.943 ±3.72
95	F	R. femur	166.732 ±3.72
98	M	R. femur	168.272 ±3.27
105	F	R. femur	161.792 ±3.72
107	F	R. Humerus	159.106 ±4.45
129	M	R. femur	174.936 ±3.27

Females (N = 12)	Range of statures = 154.066–169.943 cm	Average stature = 162.575 cm (5 ft 4 in)
Males (N = 7)	Range of statures = 162.85–177.17 cm	Average stature = 172.29 cm (5 ft 7.8 in)

K. Rosenberg, personal communication; excludes one person of unknown sex from Group A. These data are omitted from the problematical review in Custer et al. 1990.

* Bicondylar length used where max. L. not available

TABLE 7.5 Stature at the Mackenzie site, AkGv-2 (from S. Saunders 1986)*

Burial	Age	Sex	Bones	Stature (cm)
A.1	36	F	Femur + tibia	162.71 ±3.55
B.1	Adult	F	Radius	160.632 ±4.24
B.2	25 ±5	M	Femur + tibia	173.258 ±2.99
B.3	24 ±2	M	Radius	173.51 ±4.32
B.4	22	F	Radius	172.956 ±4.24
D.2	47(?)	M	Femur + tibia	180.368 ±2.99

Females (N = 3)	Range of statures = 162.71–172.956 cm	Average stature = 165.43 cm (5 ft 5.1 in)
Males (N = 3)	Range of statures = 173.258–180.368	Average stature = 175.712 cm (5 ft 9.2 in)

* Stature is based on the metric data provided by S. Saunders (1986:22) but computed using the Trotter and Gleser (1952) formulae for white males and females.

TABLE 7.6 Neutral stature from the Macpherson site, recalculated using the Trotter and Gleser formulae for the statures of whites (from S. Saunders; after Becker 1991)

Burial	Age	Sex	Bones	Lengths	Stature (cm)
A	20–35	M	Fibula	341	163.17 ±3.29
B	"middle-aged"	F	Femur	423	159.81 ±3.55
			Tibia	344	
C	35–39	F	Femur	393	152.14 ±3.55
			Tibia	326	
D	18–20	F	Femur	384	153.00 ±3.55
			Tibia	334	
F	44–59	F	Fibula	357	164.21 ±3.57
G	30–47	F	Fibula	360	165.09 ±3.57
H	23–39	M	Fibula	334	161.29 ±3.29
H2B2	18–19	F	Fibula	356	163.92 ±3.57
H3B1	18–20	M	Fibula	357	167.46 ±3.29
H3B2	20	M	Fibula	336	161.89 ±3.29
H4B2	40–44	F	Femur	390	150.43 ±3.72
H13B1	60+	M	Tibia	413	182.70 ±3.37
H15B1	19+	F	Femur	449	167.40 ±3.55
			Tibia	372	
H17B1	21–30	F	Radius	232	164.90 ±4.24

Females (N = 9)	Range of statures = 150.43–167.40 cm	Average stature = 160.10 cm (5 ft 3 in)
Males (N = 5)	Range of statures = 161.29–182.70 cm	Average stature = 167.30 cm (5 ft 5.9 in)

although three individuals did have one or more measurable long bones. Two Early Contact Seneca sites (Tram and Cameron, ca. 1570–85; Wray, Sempowski, and Saunders 1991) provided significant information of use in demographic and other studies of Native American biology. Sublett (1965) provided data on the Cornplanter cemetery (Seneca, ca. 1800) and information on stature for 28 adults. The absence of the long bone measurements in each case prevents standardizing this information for the present study.

The Historical Record

Early ethnographic observations of the peoples of the Americas were almost entirely limited to comments

TABLE 7.7 Huron stature from three sites (after Becker 1991)

a. Draper Site (Williamson 1979:56)

Burial	Age	Sex	Bones	Stature (cm)
2	24	F?*	L. Femur, tibia	165.59 ±3.55
6	40+	M	L. Femur, tibia	172.09 ±2.99

b. Keffer Site (M. W. Spence, personal communication, 2007)

Burial	Age	Sex	Bones	Stature (cm)
B3	45–50	M	L. Humerus, femur, tibia	169.973 ±2.99
B5	20–24	M	R. Femur, tibia	170.41 ±2.99

c. Ball Site (Knight and Melbye 1983; Melbye 1983: recalculated)

Burial	Age	Sex	Bones	Stature (cm)
2	46	M	Femur, tibia	173.53 ±2.99
4	24	F	Fibula	153.37 ±3.57
5	32	M	Femur, tibia	182.63 ±2.99

Combined data (from 2 Neutral plus 3 Huron sites)

Females (N = 14)	Average stature = 161.154 cm (5 ft 3.45 in)
Males (N = 13)	Average stature = 171.714 cm (5 ft 7.60 in)

* Williamson (1979) believed burial 2 to be male but noted that sex "was difficult to determine." Postcranial metric data suggested a very robust young woman or a young man not as robust as burial 6.

** Melbye (personal communication, 2007) considered a woman only 153 cm tall to be short "by Iroquoian standards" and suggested that the woman in burial 4 is in the bottom 1% of the sample (citing Anderson 1964:36; Melbye 1967:26) and the male of burial 5 is in the top 1% of the sample.

on dress, skin color, and stature. Comments on stature rarely offered more than a brief description relative to the observer. The account of the voyage of Giovanni Verrazano, made in July 1524, involves a failed attempt at kidnapping: "Volendo prender la giovane qual era di molta belezza, & d'alta Statura" (wanting to take the young woman who was very beautiful and very tall; Verrazano 1606:350, reverse side of page).

Andrew White made an ambiguous statement regarding the people he called Yoacomaco, who were living in the area of St. Mary's City, Maryland, and were at war with the Susquehannock. He described them as "very proper and tall men" (White 1910:42), but the text is not clear as to which group was "tall." However, only 30 years later, George Alsop (1910) specifically identified the Susquehannocks as being of "a most large and Warlike deportment, the men being for the most part seven foot high in latitude." While this is

obviously an error in estimation, Alsop's view suggests that he saw these men as taller than other groups with which he was familiar.

John Smith: First of Three Significant Observations

I introduced this chapter with John Smith's relevant remarks regarding the stature of the Susquehannock people in the early 1600s. Outside observers of these people in central Pennsylvania were few in number and perhaps relatively tall. The early Swedish and Dutch colonists on the Delaware River (Becker 1979, 1999c, 2006) as well as the Dutch on Manhattan had contact with the Susquehannock, but only Lindeström (1925:191), in the mid-1600s, recorded that the people he saw living along the Delaware River were of varying stature. What is not clear is whether he was describing only the Lenape or also the Lenopi on the east side of the river and possibly Susquehannock traders among these several groups.

During Lindeström's years in America, relentless assaults on the Susquehannocks by the Five Nations Iroquois had intensified. These culminated during the winter of 1675–76 with a devastating raid on the Susquehannock villages, which, combined with the refusal of their Maryland suppliers to provide arms, led to the dispersal of the tribe. Their history thereafter was not pleasant. Yet some of these people returned to the tribal homeland where, in 1701, they received an interesting invitation.

Queen Anne (1665–1714) was crowned Queen of England, Scotland, and Ireland on March 8, 1702. Her uncle, King Charles II, had died without legitimate heirs. He was followed on the throne by William and Mary. In 1694, Mary died without an heir, leaving William to reign as king until 1702. Anne followed William onto the throne, but her 17 pregnancies (none of which survived her) may have been a bit much. After five years, the crown was passed to George I of Hanover. In the middle of May of 1702, however, news of the death of King William first reached the very prosperous Virginia colony via a French frigate (Michel 1916:125). Over a span of several weeks, the news spread to colonists at the most distant outposts. The relative stability that had returned to England following the woes of the 1680s was widely celebrated in the colonies. On May 30, Lieutenant Governor Nicholson of Virginia announced a major event to celebrate the coronation of Queen Anne in Williamsburg on June 18–19, 1702 (Virginia Colony 1927:250, 253–55). Invitations were extended to important personages throughout the region as well as to the leaders of the many native tribes with whom the Virginia colony had enjoyed a long period of peace.

Among the guests at the June festivities was the Swiss traveler Francis Louis Michel. His account records the presence of "about forty" representatives from "four different tribes." The first tribe listed by Michel, perhaps because of their impressive stature, was the group from "pretty far up in the wilderness, a *large people*, governed by an emperor," who paid tribute in beaver and other peltry (Michel 1916:129, emphasis added). Michel further clarifies that "the permanent homes of one of the nations are at the Potomac River, several hundred miles inland or in the wilderness" (Michel 1916:130). This location plus his statement of their size clearly indicates that these people were Susquehannock from the Lower Susquehanna Valley, who, shortly before 1702, had provided a safe haven for the Piscataway and their emperor. Michel's observation of the large size of the Susquehannocks was seconded by at least one other observer attending this celebration. Regarding the other native groups in attendance, Michel observed that "they are well formed brown people, of ordinary size, but a little smaller than we" (Michel 1916:130).

Oral Tradition

A possible child of one of these Susquehannock (Conestoga) visitors to Williamsburg in 1702 was the famous John Skenandoa (ca. 1710–11 to March 1816). He, or perhaps his family before he was born, appears to have relocated from the Lower Susquehanna Valley into central New York (see Becker 2017). He was adopted into the Oneida, where he was elected as a "Pine Tree Chief." During the American Revolution, he led a force of Oneida and Tuscarora against the British. Of note here are consistent reports that his height was estimated to be 6′ 5″. Quite possibly, Skenandoa may be the person who appears in David Cusick's fabulous narrative written in 1825. Cusick included an interesting tale regarding a particular group of Oneidas whom he placed not in New York but on the Susquehanna or "river Kaunsehwatauyea" during the "reign of king Atotaro III." Cusick wrote, "There was a certain woman delivered of a male child [of] uncommon size; when he was twelve years of age he was nearly as large as [a] grown person" (Cusick 1848:24). This tall male may have been Skenandoa.

A comment from the journal of Mason and Dixon, entered in 1767, provided an observation that may well be coupled with an interesting speculation. At a station 197 miles west along their survey line, not far from the Cheat River, they noted, "On the 17th of August we were paid a visit by 13 Delawares; one of them a Nephew of Captain Black-Jacobs, who was killed by General Armstrong at the Kittony Town in 17__. This Nephew of Black-Jacobs was the tallest man I ever saw" (Mason and Dixon 1969:174).

This unnamed "nephew" was identified as a "Delaware" [Lenape], indicating his maternal affiliation and perhaps that of his uncle Black-Jacobs. This region of southwestern Pennsylvania had, after 1700, become an area claimed by Lenape, who had affiliated with the Susquehannocks and then spread west into former "Monongahela" territory. Quite possibly, this tall nephew's father was a Susquehannock (see Colonial Records of Pennsylvania 1852:19). Natives who participated in the survey and were met during that period are discussed by Strang (2012).

The belief that the Susquehannocks were a tall people also was stated by Heckewelder (1819:30), based on observations he made in about 1780. Heckewelder interacted primarily with those Lenopi originally from southern New Jersey (Becker 2008), who became one of the several groups identified as "Delaware" in the period after 1760. The people resident in that portion of western Pennsylvania and Ohio at that time included the descendants of the Susquehannocks then known as Mingoes (Becker 2017). Heckewelder recorded that "Delaware" [Lenopi] people they met in the Allegheny area were "giants" (Heckewelder 1819:30).

Discussion and Conclusions

Despite numerous archaeological excavations during the past century, the analysis of human skeletal material from Native American (and also from Colonial)

sites in the northeastern United States remains largely unstudied. Table 7.8 provides a summary of the information from seven sites, which may be compared with the data from the Susquehannock site 46HM73. Skeletal material from the Fairty site (Anderson 1964) has not yet been evaluated.

Table 7.9 provides data from Susquehannock interments in the Lancaster, Pennsylvania, region of the Susquehanna Valley recovered by representatives from the North Museum and the State Museum of Pennsylvania. The limited evidence now available suggests that Susquehannock males of the sixteenth century were taller than other Native American males in the region surrounding the Susquehanna River Valley. The higher-status males who met Captain John Smith in 1608 may have been at the taller end of their stature or perhaps even above the average of 174.7 centimeters calculated for the Susquehannock homeland (table 7.9) and a full centimeter taller on average than the 173.7 centimeters calculated here for 46HM73 (table 7.1). Smith's observations may be accepted as reliable. Comparable data on the stature of English males from the period ca. 1550–1620 is still being sought, although estimates of statures are postulated at below 160 centimeters for adult males (see Becker 2016). In 1608, these Susquehannock may have averaged 10 or more centimeters taller than Smith and

TABLE 7.8   A summary of stature data from 46HM73 (Becker 1991)

a. Susquehannock from a village in West Virginia, ca. 1550		
Females	(N = 10)	Avg. 161.74 cm
Males	(N = 7)	Avg. 173.70 cm
b. Two other Susquehannock sites		
Females	(N = 4)	Avg. 159.53 cm
Males	(N = 2)	Avg. 170.15 cm
c. Two Neutral and three Huron sites		
Females	(N = 14)	Avg. 161.15 cm
Males	(N = 13)	Avg. 171.71 cm
d. Island Field site in central Delaware		
Females	(N = 12)	Avg. 162.58 cm
Males	(N = 7)	Avg. 172.29 cm

TABLE 7.9 Long bone lengths in centimeters from Susquehanna Valley sites other than Ibaugh in the Franklin and Marshall College skeletal collection

North museum number*	Humerus		Radius		Ulna		Femur		Tibia		Fibula		Sex	Stature
	L	R	L	R	L	R	L	R	L	R	L	R		
6088	296	—	—	—	—	—	399	397	327	324	—	—	F	153.4
6089	330	330	273	273	293	288	462	465	406	404	—	—	M	176.4
6090	304	307	239	235	253	250	403	404	353	348	—	329	F	157.3
6091	341	340	272	274	297	—	483	482	420	422	—	—	M	180.9
6092	315	—	—	—	—	—	[411]	[435]	—	346	—	—	F	161.3
6093	312	309	241	241	252	262	422	427	355	355	352	—	F	161.9
6094	328	331	—	—	—	—	477	480	379	380	—	—	M	175.2
6095	309	311	351	257	272	—	443	442	372	367	367	—	F	165.5
6096	323	316	—	262	—	284	[463]	[447]	—	388	—	—	M	176.5
6097	—	—	—	—	—	264	441	434	—	366	—	—	F	164.5
6098	336	344	261	—	287	—	468	471	396	396	—	—	M	176.0
6099	317	—	244	—	264	—	457	456	371	374	364	366	M?	170.2
7126	—	342	281	282	—	—	496	498	413	—	402	399	M	181.5
7167	314	314	247	244	268	269	442	439	—	—	349	353	F	162.4
7168	309	314	—	227	251	—	423	424	347	353	—	—	F	161.1
7169	307	314	241	237	—	253	436	434	363	360	346	345	F	163.7
7170	281	—	—	205	—	226	407	402	329	330	—	320	F	155.0
7171	295	—	—	—	—	—	419	418	330	334	324	—	F	158.3
7172	—	—	—	—	—	—	487	485	—	400	—	—	M	178.5
7173	322	322	—	276	—	258	471	466	381	385	—	—	M	173.9
7174	—	272	—	—	—	—	412	411	[322]	[332]	—	—	F	155.0
7175a	—	—	—	—	—	—	475	—	—	—	—	—	M	174.5
7175b	—	—	—	—	—	—	425	—	—	—	—	—	F	159.0
7175c	—	—	—	—	—	—	474	—	—	—	—	—	M	174.4
7177a	[298]**	—	—	—	—	—	442	—	[366]**	—	—	—	F	163.2
7177b	—	—	—	—	—	—	437	—	—	—	—	—	F	162.0
7177c	296	303	227	—	—	250	431	434	341	356	—	339	F	163.0
7177d	—	—	231	—	—	—	427	429	—	365***	—	—	F	162.3
7177e	307	—	252	—	268°	—	427	436	—	—	—	—	F	161.9
7177f	—	—	—	—	—	—	482	[434, see 7177b]		—	—	—	M	176.0
7179	330	325	261	—	283	282	472	468	389	388	—	378	M	174.9
7180	345	342	—	—	—	—	477	477	413	408	—	—	M	178.9
7181a	(measurements by Becker)						—	415	(see 7182a)		—	—	F	156.5
7181b	(measurements by Becker)						459	—	—	—	—	—	M?	170.8
7182a	255	—	—	—	276°	—	414	—	—	—	—	—	F	151.0
7182b	—	—	—	—	—	—	459	—	—	—	—	—	M?	170.8
7183	—	—	255	—	—	—	—	—	—	—	—	—	M?	175.3
7185	—	—	—	—	—	—	467	467	392	—	—	—	M	175.0
7186	—	—	256	—	—	—	469	455	387	—	—	—	M	175.1
7197	300	308	240	239	—	—	418	422	357	353	347	—	F	160.9
7207	296	—	—	—	254	—	429	427	—	—	—	—	F	158.7
7208	—	—	—	—	—	—	442	439	—	365	—	—	F?	165.0
7211	—	—	—	—	—	262	—	414	—	347	—	—	F	159.0
7214	—	—	—	—	—	—	474	—	—	—	—	—	M	174.3
7217	—	—	—	—	251	—	435	—	365	—	—	—	F	164.4

North museum number[*]	Humerus		Radius		Ulna		Femur		Tibia		Fibula		Sex	Stature
	L	R	L	R	L	R	L	R	L	R	L	R		
7218a	—	—	—	—	—	[265]	418	—	—	—	—	—	F	157.2
7218b	—	—	—	—	—	—	469	—	—	—	—	—	M	172.7
7220b	—	—	—	—	—	—	460	460	—	—	—	—	M	170.8
7220c	—	—	—	—	—	—	428	—	[344]	—	—	—	F	160.5
7222a	—	—	—	—	—	246	457	—	342	—	—	—	F	164.4
7222b	—	—	—	—	—	—	—	469	380***	—	—	—	M	173.0
7225	—	—	—	—	—	—	429	—	—	—	—	—	F	160.0
7227	(Mixed and possibly deformed)						—	—	—	377	—	—	M?	173.4
7228	312	310	246	—	266	264	447	446	384	386	372	371	M?	173.8
7229	297	303	—	—	—	—	433	434	—	354	—	—	F	162.7
7235	—	322	239	235	254	—	442	—	—	—	—	—	F	164.0
7236	300	—	224	—	244	243	—	429	350	—	350	—	F	160.5
7241	—	—	—	—	—	—	—	431	—	—	—	—	F	160.5
7242	—	302	—	—	—	—	—	414	—	347	—	—	F	159.0
7244	—	—	—	—	—	263	—	—	—	—	—	—	M?	171.3
7246	—	—	—	238	—	—	—	439	—	—	—	355	F	163.5
7249	NO DATA—multiple fragments only												—	—
7262	—	—	—	—	—	—	395	403	330	330	320	—	F	155.1

Females (N = 37)	Range of statures = 151.0–165.9 cm	Average stature = 160.5 cm (5 ft 3.2 in)
Males (N = 27)	Range of statures = 170.2–181.5 cm	Average stature = 174.7 cm (5 ft 8.8 in)

The Becker transcription was reevaluated December 3, 1992, and confirmed by a 2016 reexamination; stature is from Trotter and Gleser 1952:496, 498. Measurements in brackets identify those bones not seen in 1992 but located in the 2016 study program.

* In cases where more than one person is represented by the long bones, individuals are identified by letters (a, b, c, etc.) assigned by Becker.

** The humerus "assigned" to 7177a appears too small; the left tibia could go with either of the left femurs. This is a mixed unit, and the focus will be on the left femurs only.

*** With 7177c and 7177d was a third right tibia (L = 356 cm). A third right tibia (L = 379 cm) also was with the bones of 72222a and 7222b. (These are correct figures, computed separately.)

ø The length of this bone does not appear to correlate with that of other bones. However, radius and ulna computations appear to produce generally tall readings for females.

other urban English males of the time, which certainly would merit comment in Smith's journal.

The 174.7 centimeters stature calculated for males from sites associated with the natives who met John Smith is impressive. In a modern analysis of biometric data gathered by Franz Boas (Jantz 1995a, 1995b), Stephen Langdon (1995) focused on information relating to Iroquoians. By the late 1800s, no Susquehannock population was available for study, but the tallest of the Iroquoians were the Mohawk (males averaged 174.03 cm; Langdon 1995:368, table 7), nearly 0.7 centimeters shorter than our target population of Susquehannock.

Of note regarding the ancient Susquehannock in their homeland is the finding that the females had an average stature of only 160.5 centimeters, which was shorter than the 161.74 centimeters average calculated for the females from 46HM73. Susquehannock females from both of these populations have been calculated to have had a lower average stature than two of the other comparative "populations" (see table 7.3). However, both of these archaeological Susquehannock populations are taller than the tallest females in the Boas sample (Cherokee averaged 159.72 cm; see Langdon 1995:368, table 7).

The considerable differences in the relative stature of Susquehannock males and females suggest that the diet of Susquehannock males (and possibly male food intake patterns) were quite distinct from the dietary patterns of males in other populations. While these Susquehannock males appear to have been particularly well nourished, females may not have enjoyed a parallel diet. S. Saunders (personal communication, 1990) suggested that this finding may be tested by isotopic analysis (Katzenberg and Saunders 1990; see also Sillen, Sealy, and van der Merwe 1989). Also linked to these differences in stature may be patterns of marriage among the Susquehannock, with women frequently marrying into the tribe from distant locations. Genetic studies of these populations may provide new insights into cultural patterns that may have influenced the data that have been assembled here.

Since the Susquehannocks were cultivating maize as well as hunting game and using anadromous fish in patterns similar to other horticultural peoples of the Eastern Woodlands, one might ask what combination of food-use patterns and genetics may have resulted in a notably greater stature. Webster (1983, 1984) suggested that the huge catchment area around the Susquehannock homeland, larger than that shared by the several tribes of the Iroquois Confederacy, provided vast quantities of meat (Webster 1984:41–43). He also believed that the population rose from about 1,250 in 1575 to perhaps 5,000 in 1665 (Webster 1984:56). I suggest that this reflects a concentration of population in the large defended villages rather than an actual population increase. The use of maize as a dietary staple is believed to be reflected in a number of archaeological situations that can be studied through physical anthropology. A high caries rate, high strontium value, and a low carbon 12 to carbon 13 ratio all are considered to be indicators of the use of maize as a dietary staple rather than as a simple food supplement, as was the case among the maize "gardening" Lenape (Becker 1988:80, 1991). If Susquehannock stature, at least of the males, was as distinct from neighboring populations,

as is indicated by the limited evidence now available, then the etiology of this phenomenon is well worth exploring.

The rather limited numbers of individuals from these populations that are available for study and the small differences in stature now recognized need not indicate that the Susquehannocks were significantly distinct from their neighbors in stature. That they may have been much taller than their more densely settled neighbors to the south can only be determined by further study. These findings can be tested further by subsequent studies of better-represented Susquehannock populations as well as through other allied techniques.

Acknowledgments

Thanks are due to Dr. Janet Brashler for her invitation to conduct skeletal studies at 46HM73 (Becker 1987) and to Dr. Robert Wall for his help in returning these human remains to West Virginia. Thanks are due to Alison Mallin, formerly with the North Museum, for her kind invitation to study the human skeletal remains in those collections. Martha McCartney's important aid in several aspects of this research and her continued encouragement are deeply appreciated.

Thanks are due to Dr. Mary Jackes for information from the Grimsby site (southern Ontario data), to Dr. Karen Rosenberg for Island Field site (Delaware) data, to Dr. William Johnson for data on the Campbell Farm site (Monongahela in Pennsylvania), and to Jerry Melbye for data from the Ball site. Special thanks are due Dr. S. R. Saunders for metric data from the MacPherson site (see also S. Saunders 1988) and others (Wray, Sempowski, and Saunders 1991) as well as for her careful reading of an early draft of this chapter. Thanks to Professor Michael W. Spence for data from the Keffer site and for useful comments on an earlier draft of this chapter. Stephen G. Warfel provided important information concerning materials curated at the Pennsylvania State Museum. His many important corrections and suggestions helped direct the next phase of this research. Thanks also are due to Professor K. Borre for many important suggestions and corrections. The many useful suggestions of two anonymous reviewers are deeply appreciated.

Earlier phases of this research were funded by grants from the National Endowment for the Humanities and the American Philosophical Society. Any errors of presentation or of interpretation of these data are my responsibility alone.

REFERENCES

Alsop, George
1910 A Character of the Province of Maryland. In *Narratives of Early Maryland, 1633–1684*, edited by Clayton Coleman Hall, 337–85. Barnes and Noble for the American Historical Association, New York.

Anderson, James
1964 *The People of Fairty: An Osteological Analysis of an Iroquoian Ossuary*. National Museum of Canada Bulletin 143. The Department of Resources and Development, Ottawa.

Angel, J. Lawrence
1969 The Bases of Paleodemography. *American Journal of Physical Anthropology* 30:427–37.

Ardito, G.
1977 The Epigenetic Variants in the Skulls in Some Ancient and Recent Italian Populations. *Journal of Human Evolution* 6:689–95.

Barbour, Philip L. (editor)
1969 *The Jamestown Voyages Under the First Charter, 1606–1609*. 2 vols. Hakluyt Society, Second Series, 136–37. Cambridge University Press, Cambridge, England.

Bass, William M.
1979 Developments in the Identification of Human Skeletal Material (1968–1978). *American Journal of Physical Anthropology* 51:555–62.

Becker, Marshall Joseph
1979 Ethnohistory and Archaeology in Search of the Printzhof, the 17th Century Residence of Swedish Colonial Governor Johan Printz. *Ethnohistory* 26 (1): 15–44.

1980 The Montgomery Site (36CH60): The Burial Area of a Lenape Summer Encampment During the Period ca. 1720–1733. Manuscript on file, The State Museum of Pennsylvania, Harrisburg.

1982 Human Skeletal Analysis and the Study of the Prehistory and Early History of Southern Italy: The Development of a Program of Collaborative Research Between Physical Anthropology and Archaeology. *Studi di Antichita (Lecce)* 3:133–53.

1985 Metric and Non-metric Data from a Series of Skulls from Mozia, Sicily and a Related Site. *Antropologia Contemporanea* 8 (3): 211–28.

1987 An Analysis of the Human Skeletal Remains from 46HM73: A Susquehannock Population of the Mid-Sixteenth Century. *West Virginia Archeologist* 39 (2): 37–53.

1988 A Summary of Lenape Socio-Political Organization and Settlement Pattern at European Contact: The Evidence for Collecting Bands. *Journal of Middle Atlantic Archaeology* 4:79–83.

1989 Review of *The Rise and Fall of New Sweden: Governor Johan Risingh's Journal 1654–1655 in its Historical Context*, by Stellan Dahlgren and Hans Norman (1988). *Pennsylvania Archaeologist* 59 (2): 100–101.

1991 The Stature of a Susquehannock Population of the Mid-16th Century Based on Skeletal Remains from 46HM73. *Pennsylvania Archaeologist* 61 (2): 73–88.

1993 The Lenape and Other "Delawarean" Peoples at the Time of European Contact: Population Estimates Derived from Archaeological and Historical Sources. *The Bulletin; Journal of the New York State Archaeological Association* 105:16–25.

1995 Lenape Maize Sales to the Swedish Colonists: Cultural Stability During the Early Colonial Period. In *New Sweden in America*, edited by Carol E. Hoffecker, Richard Waldron, Lorraine E. Williams, and Barbara E. Benson, 121–36. University of Delaware Press, Newark.

1999a Calculating Stature from In Situ Measurements of Skeletons and from Long Bone Lengths: An Historical Perspective Leading to a Test of Formicola's Hypothesis at 5th Century BCE Satricum, Lazio, Italy. *Rivista di Antropologia* 77:225–47.

1999b Cash Cropping by Lenape Foragers: Preliminary Notes on Native Maize Sales to Swedish Colonists and Cultural Stability During the Early Colonial Period. *Bulletin of the Archaeological Society of New Jersey* 54:45–68.

1999c Archaeology at the Printzhof (36DE3), the Only Documented Early 17th Century Swedish Site in the Delaware Valley. *Journal of Middle Atlantic Archaeology* 15:77–94.

2006 The Printzhof (36DE3), A Swedish Colonial Site That Was the First European Center of Government in Present Pennsylvania. *Bulletin of the Archaeological Society of Delaware*, n.s., 43:1–34.

2008 Lenopi, Or, What's in a Name? Interpreting the Evidence for Cultural Boundaries in the Lower Delaware Valley. *Bulletin of the Archaeological Society of New Jersey* 63:11–12.

2009 Feathered Cloaks, Foreign Affairs and War Leaders: Cross Cultural Symbolism as Represented by One Category of Matchcoats Made by Native Peoples of the Northeast Woodlands and Middle Atlantic Region. *Bulletin of the Archaeological Society of New Jersey* 64:41–55.

2010 "Late Woodland" (CA. 1000–1740 CE) Foraging Patterns of the Lenape and Their Neighbors in the Delaware Valley. *Pennsylvania Archaeologist* 80 (1): 17–31.

2012 Susquehannock Material Culture Revisited: Eight Pennsylvania Ethnographic Artifacts in the Skokloster Castle Collection in Sweden and a Possible Connection to Capt. John Smith. *Pennsylvania Archaeologist* 82 (1): 66–73.

2014a Ethnohistory of the Lower Delaware Valley: Addressing Myths in the Archaeological Interpretations of the Late Woodland and Contact Periods. *Journal of Middle Atlantic Archaeology* 30:41–54.

2014b Lenape ("Delaware") in the Early Colonial Economy: Cultural Interactions and the Slow Processes of Culture Change Before 1740. *Northeast Anthropology* 81–82:109–29.

2014c A Seed in Skokloster Castle, Sweden: Searching for the Origins of Eight Susquehannock Artifacts. *Bulletin of the Archaeological Society of Delaware*, n.s., 51:35–49.

2016 Differences in the Stature and Status of Two Populations in Medieval Cremona (Lombardy), Italy: Evidence from Human Skeletal Remains from Adjacent Urban Cemeteries. *International Journal of Anthropology* 31 (3–4): 161–84.

2017 Ethnogenesis of the Ganawese: The Piscataway Origins of the Conoy. Paper presented at the Conference on Iroquois Research, October 14, Oswego, New York, Copy on file at West Chester University of Pennsylvania.

Boyd, Donna C., and C. Clifford Boyd
1992 Late Woodland Mortuary Variability in Virginia. In *Middle and Late Woodland Research in Virginia: A Synthesis*, edited by Theodore R. Reinhart

and Mary Ellen Hodges, 225–53. Special Publication 29. Archaeological Society of Virginia, Courtland.

Brashler, Janet G.
1987 A Middle 16th Century Susquehannock Village in Hampshire County, West Virginia. *West Virginia Archaeologist* 39 (2): 1–30.

Cadzow, Donald A.
1936 *Archaeological Studies of the Susquehannock Indians of Pennsylvania*. Safe Harbor Report No. 2. Pennsylvania Historical and Museum Commission, Harrisburg.

Clabeaux, Marie Striegel
1973 The Paleopathology of the Indians of New Jersey. *Man in the Northeast* 5:7–25.

Colonial Records of Pennsylvania
1852 *Minutes of the Provincial Council of Pennsylvania.* Vol. 3. Theo. Penn & Company, Harrisburg.

Cusick, David
1848 *David Cusick's Sketches of Ancient History of the Six Nations. . . .* Turner and McCollum, Lockport, New York.

Custer, Jay F., Karen R. Rosenberg, Glenn Mellin, and Arthur Washburn
1990 A Re-examination of the Island Field Site (7K-F-17), Kent County, Delaware. *Archaeology of Eastern North America* 18:145–212.

Dahlgren, Stellan, and Hans Norman
1988 *The Rise and Fall of New Sweden: Governor Johan Risingh's Journal 1654–1655 in its Historical Context.* Almqvist and Wiksell International, Uppsala, Sweden.

Dragoo, Don W.
1963 *Mounds for the Dead: An Analysis of the Adena Culture.* Annals of the Carnegie Museum 37, Carnegie Museum, Pittsburgh.

1976 Human Skeletal Remains from the Henderson Rocks Site. In *Archaeological Investigations in the Tygart Lake Reservoir, Taylor and Barbour Counties, West Virginia*, edited by Stanley W. Lantz, 86–88. West Virginia Geological and Economic Survey, Morgantown, West Virginia.

El-Najjar, Mahmoud Y., and K. Richard McWilliams
1978 *Forensic Anthropology.* Charles C. Thomas, Springfield, Illinois.

Espino, Jason
2006 Comments on Monongahela Drew Radiocarbon Data. *Pennsylvania Archaeologist* 76 (1): 63–71.

Feest, Christian F.
1967 The Virginia Indians in Pictures, 1612–1624. *The Smithsonian Journal of History* 2 (1): 1–30.

1987 Indians and Europe? Editor's Postscript. In *Indians and Europe: An Interdisciplinary Collection of Essays*, edited by Christian F. Feest, 609–28. Rader-Verlag, Aachen.

Floud, Roderick, Robert W. Fogel, Bernard Harris, and Sok
Chul Hong.
    2011   Height, Health, and Mortality in Continental
           Europe, 1700–2100. In *The Changing Body: Health,*
           Nutrition, and Human Development in the Western
           World Since 1700, edited by Roderick Floud, Robert
           W. Fogel, Bernard Harris, and Sok Chul Hong,
           226–95. Cambridge University Press, Cambridge,
           England.

Forrest, Crystal Leigh
    2010   *Iroquoian Infant Mortality and Juvenile Growth*
           1250 to 1700 AD. Ph.D. dissertation, Department of
           Anthropology, University of Toronto, Toronto.

Genovés, S.
    1967   Proportionality of the Long Bones and Their Relation
           to Stature Among Mesoamericans. *American Journal*
           of Physical Anthropology 26:67–77.

Heckewelder, John
    1819   An Account of the History, Manners, and Customs, of
           the Indian Nations Who Once Inhabited Pennsylvania
           and the Neighboring States. *Transactions of the*
           American Philosophical Society 1:1–348.

Heisey, Henry W., and J. Paul Witmer
    1962   Of Historic Susquehannock Cemeteries. *Pennsylvania*
           Archaeologist 32 (3–4): 99–130.

Hooton, Earnest
    1947   *Up from the Ape.* Revised edition. Macmillan, New
           York.

Howells, William W.
    1973   *Cranial Variation in Man: A Study of Multivariate*
           Analysis of Patterns of Difference Among Recent
           Human Populations. Peabody Museum, Harvard
           University, Cambridge, Massachusetts.

Irving, Washington
    1834   *A Tour on the Prairies.* F. M. Lipton, New York.

Jackes, Mary
    1987   Grimsby Site Skeletal Data. Manuscript on file, The
           Royal Ontario Museum, Toronto, Canada.

Jantz, Richard L.
    1995a Special Issue on the Population Biology of Late 19th
           Century Native North American and Siberians:
           Analysis of Boas Data. *Human Biology* 67 (3): 337–516.

    1995b Franz Boas and Native American Biological
           Variability. *Human Biology* 67 (3): 345–53.

Jennings, Francis
    1968   Glory, Death, and Transfiguration: The
           Susquehannock Indians in the Seventeenth Century.
           Proceedings of the American Philosophical Society 112
           (1): 15–53.

Johnson, Amandus
    1917   The Indians and Their Culture as Described in
           Swedish and Dutch Records from 1614 to 1664.
           In *Proceedings of the Nineteenth International*

Congress of Americanists, edited by F. W. Hodge,
           277–82. United States Government Printing Office,
           Washington, D.C.

    1930   *The Instructions for Johan Printz, Governor of New*
           Sweden. The Swedish Colonial Society, Philadelphia.

Johnson, D.
    1980   The Mackenzie or Woodbridge Site (AkGv-2) and
           Its Place in the Late Ontario Iroquois Tradition.
           Archaeology of Eastern North America 8:77–87.

Katzenberg, M. A., and S. R. Saunders
    1990   Age Differences in Stable Carbon Isotope Ratios
           in Prehistoric Maize Horticulturalists. Abstract.
           American Journal of Physical Anthropology 81:247.

Kent, Barry C.
    1984   *Susquehanna's Indians.* Pennsylvania Historical and
           Museum Commission, Harrisburg.

Key, Patrick, and R. R. Jantz
    1981   A Multivariate Analysis of Temporal Change in
           Arikara Craniometrics: A Methodological Approach.
           American Journal of Physical Anthropology 55:247–59.

Kinsey, W. Fred, III
    1960   Additional Notes on the Albert Ibaugh Site.
           Pennsylvania Archaeologist 30 (3–4): 81–105.

Kinsey, W. Fred, III, and Jeffrey R. Graybill
    1971   Murry Site and Its Role in Lancaster and Funk Phases
           of Shenks Ferry Culture. *Pennsylvania Archaeologist* 41
           (4): 7–44.

Knight, Dean, and Jerry Melbye
    1983   Burial Patterns at the Ball Site. *Ontario Archaeology*
           40:37–48.

Krogman, Wilton Marion, and Mehmet Yasar Iscan
    1986   *The Human Skeleton in Forensic Medicine.* 2nd ed.
           Charles C. Thomas, Springfield, Illinois.

Lane, R. A., and A. J. Sublett
    1972   Osteology of Social Organization. *American Antiquity*
           37:186–201.

Langdon, Stephen P.
    1995   Biological Relations among the Iroquois.
           Human Biology 67 (3): 355–74.

Lindeström, Peter
    1925   *Geographia Americae.* Translated by Amandus
           Johnson. The Swedish Colonial Society, Philadelphia,
           Pennsylvania.

Manouvrier, Léonce
    1893   La determination de la taille d'après la grands os des
           membres. *Mémoires de la Société d'Anthropologie,* 2nd
           ser. 4:347–402.

Mason, Charles, and Jeremiah Dixon
    1909   A Short Account of the Mohawk Indians [1644]. In
           Narratives of New Netherland 1609–1664, edited by
           J. Franklin Jameson, 163–80. Charles Scribner's Sons,
           New York.

1969 The Journal of Charles Mason and Jeremiah Dixon. Transcribed by A. Hughlett Mason. Memoirs of the American Philosophical Society, Philadelphia, Pennsylvania.

Megapolensis, Johannes, Jr.

1909 A Short Account of the Mohawk Indians [1644]. In *Narratives of New Netherland 1609–1664*, edited by J. Franklin Jameson, 163–80. Charles Scribner's Sons, New York.

Melbye, Jerry

1967 *An Analysis of the Infracranial Material from the Orchid Site.* Unpublished M.A. thesis, Department of Anthropology, SUNY-Buffalo, Buffalo, New York.

1983 The People of the Ball Site. *Ontario Archaeology* 40:15–36.

Michel, Francis Louis

1916 Report of the Journey of Francis Louis Michel from Berne, Switzerland, to Virginia, October 2, 1701–December 1, 1702. Part 2. *Virginia Magazine of History and Biography* 24:113–41.

Morton, Samuel G.

1839 *Crania Americana; or, A Comparative View of the Skulls of Various Aboriginal Nations of North and South America, to Which Is Prefixed an Essay on the Varieties of the Human Species.* n.p., Philadelphia, Pennsylvania.

Musgrave, Jonathan, and S. P. Evans

1980 By Strangers Honor'd: A Statistical Study of Ancient Crania from Crete, Mainland Greece, Cyprus, Israel and Egypt. *Journal of Mediterranean Anthropology and Archaeology* 1:22–40.

Myers, Albert C.

1912 *Narratives of Early Pennsylvania, West New Jersey and Delaware.* Charles Scribner's Sons, New York.

Neuman, G., and T. Murad

1970 Preliminary Report on the Crania from the Island Field Site, Kent County, Delaware. *Proceedings of the Indiana Academy of Science for 1969* 79:69–74.

O'Connor, Kathleen A.

1987 A Comparative Biocultural Analysis of Human Skeletal Remains from Two New York State Sites. Paper presented at the Northeastern Anthropological Association Meeting, March 20, 1987, Amherst, Massachusetts.

Parker, Arthur C. (editor)

1938 *Report on the Susquehanna River Expedition Sponsored in 1916 by the Museum of the American Indian, Heye Foundation*, compiled and annotated by Warren King Moorehead. Andover Press, Andover, Massachusetts.

Pearson, Karl

1899 Mathematical Contributions to the Theory of Evolution, Section V: On the Reconstruction of the Stature of Prehistoric Races. *Philosophical Transactions* 192:169–244.

Pendergast, James F.

1991 The Massawomeck: Raiders and Traders into the Chesapeake Bay in the Seventeenth Century. *Transactions of the American Philosophical Society* 81, part 2, 1–95.

Risingh, Johan

1653–56 Een Kort Berattelse on Reesan till Nye Swerige, 1654–1655. Manuscript No. E433, University of Uppsala, Sweden. Microfilm copy in Becker Archives, West Chester University, West Chester, Pennsylvania.

Robbins, D. M., and K. R. Rosenberg

1989 Activity Patterns in Late Middle Woodland, Delaware [*sic*]. Abstract. *American Journal of Physical Anthropology* 78:290–91.

Robinson, W. Stitt (editor)

1987 Maryland Treaties, 1632–1775. Vol. 6, *Early American Indian Documents: Treaties and Laws, 1607–1789.* University Publications of America, Frederick, Maryland.

Saunders, Lorraine P.

1986 *Biological Affinities Among Historic Seneca Groups and Possible Precursive Populations.* Ph.D. dissertation, University of Texas at Austin. University Microfilms, Ann Arbor, Michigan.

Saunders, Shelley R.

1986 The Mackenzie Site Human Skeletal Material. *Ontario Archaeology* 45:9–26.

1988 The MacPherson Site: Human Burials. A preliminary descriptive report prepared with the assistance of Tracy Rogers. McMaster University, Hamilton, Ontario.

Sillen, Andrew, Judith C. Sealy, and Nikolaas J. van der Merwe

1989 Chemistry and Paleodietary Research: No More Easy Answers. *American Antiquity* 54:504–12.

Sjøvold, Torstein

1973 The Occurrence of Minor Non-metrical Variants in the Skeleton and Their Quantitative Treatment for Population Comparisons. *Homo* 24:204–33.

Smith, John

1624 *The Generall Historie of Virginia, New-England, and the Summer Isles.* 1966 reprint. Michael Sparkes, London. March of America Facsimile Series 18. University Microfilms, Ann Arbor, Michigan.

1910 *Travels and Works of Captain John Smith*, edited by Edward Arber. Introduction by A. G. Bradley. 2 vols. J. Grant, Edinburgh.

Smith, David Glenn, and Robert L. Bettinger

1987 Serum Proteins and North American Culture History: A Call for Samples. *Bulletin of the Society for American Archaeology* 5 (3): 7.

Steele, D. G., and T. W. McKern

1969 A Method for Assessment of Maximum Long Bone Length and Living Stature from Fragmentary Long Bones. *American Journal of Physical Anthropology* 31:215–28.

Strang, Cameron B.

2012 The Mason-Dixon and Proclamation Lines: Land Surveying and Native Americans in Pennsylvania's Borderlands. *The Pennsylvania Magazine of History and Biography* 136 (1): 5–23.

Sublett, Audrey

1965 The Cornplanter Cemetery: Skeletal Analyses. *Pennsylvania Archaeologist* 35:74–92.

Thwaites, Reuben Gold (editor)

1898 Doc. XXXI: Letter from Father François du Peron S. J. to his Brother Father Joseph-Imbert du Peron, S. J. (27 April 1639). *The Jesuit Relations and Allied Documents* 15:147–57.

Trotter, Mildred

1970 Estimation of Stature from Intact Long Limb Bones. In *Personal Identification in Mass Disasters*, edited by T. Dale Stewart, 71–83. National Museum of Natural History, Washington, D.C.

Trotter, Mildred, and Goldene C. Gleser

1952 Estimation of Stature from Long Bones of American Whites and Negroes. *American Journal of Physical Anthropology* 10:463–514.

1958 A Re-evaluation of Estimation of Stature Based on Measurements of Stature Taken During Life and of Long Bones After Death. *American Journal of Physical Anthropology* 16:79–123.

Verrazano, Giovanni

1606 Al Christianessimo Re di Francia Francesco Primo [1524]. In *Delle Navigationi et Viaggi, Volvme Terzo*, compiled by Giovanni Battista Ramusio, 350–53. Appresso I Givnti, Venetia. (Derived intact from Ramusio's [1554] *Primo volume, & seconda editione della Nauigationi et viaggi: In molti luoghi corretta, et ampliata, nelle quale si contengono la descrittione. . . .* Venetia: Nella stamperia de Giunti.)

Virginia Colony

1927 *Executive Journals of the Council of Colonial Virginia.* Vol. 2, Aug. 3, 1699, to April 27, 1705. Edited by H. R. McIlwaine. David Bottom, Richmond, Virginia.

Von Bonin, Gerhardt, and G. M. Morant

1938 Indian Races of the United States. A Survey of Previously Published Cranial Measurements. *Biometrika* 30:94–129.

Webb, William S., and Charles E. Snow

1945 *The Adena People.* 1974 reprint. University of Tennessee Press, Knoxville.

1959 *The Dover Mound.* University of Kentucky Press, Lexington.

Webster, Gary S.

1983 *Iroquois Hunting: An Optimization Approach.* Ph.D. dissertation, The Pennsylvania State University, University Park. University Microfilms, Ann Arbor, Michigan.

1984 Susquehannock Animal Economy. *North American Archaeologist* 6 (1): 41–62.

White, Andrew

1910 A Briefe Relation of the Voyage Unto Maryland [1634]. In *Narratives of Early Maryland, 1633–1684*, edited by Clayton Coleman Hall, 25–45. Barnes and Noble for the American Historical Association, New York.

Williamson, Ronald F.

1979 Non-ossuary Interments of the Draper Site. Manuscript submitted to the Social Sciences and Humanities Research Council of Canada. Museum of Indian Archaeology of the University of Western Ontario, London, Ontario.

Witthoft, John, W. Fred Kinsey III, and Charles H. Holzinger

1959 A Susquehannock Cemetery: The Ibaugh Site. In *Susquehannock Miscellany*, edited by John Witthoft and W. Fred Kinsey III, 99–119. Pennsylvania Historical and Museum Commission, Harrisburg.

Wray, Charles F., Martha L. Sempowski, and Lorraine P. Saunders

1991 *Tram and Cameron: Two Early Contact Era Seneca Sites.* Charles F. Wray Series in Seneca Archaeology. Vol. 2. Research Records 21. Rochester Museum and Science Center, Rochester, New York.

Wray, Charles F., Martha L. Sempowski, Lorraine P. Saunders, and Gian Carlo Cervone

1987 The Adams and Culbertson Sites. Charles F. Wray Series in Seneca Archaeology. Vol. 1. Research Records 19. Rochester Museum and Science Center, Rochester, New York.

CONTRIBUTORS

Marshall Joseph Becker is a professor emeritus at West Chester University and was trained at the University of Pennsylvania in all four fields of anthropology. Since 1965, he has applied archaeological and other approaches to the understanding of the human biology of people whose remains derive from archaeological contexts in the Delaware Valley as well as in Italy and throughout the Mediterranean. Dr. Becker has published more than 150 articles in scholarly journals and many book chapters. His most recent book, with Jean M. Turfa as coauthor, is *The Etruscans and the History of Dentistry: The Golden Smile Through the Ages* (2017). Dr. Becker's research has been supported by grants from the National Science Foundation, the National Endowment for the Humanities, the American Philosophical Society, and the National Geographic Society.

April M. Beisaw is a North American archaeologist who studies cultural change and resilience in the relatively recent past (AD 1300 to today). Her work focuses on challenging stereotypes, remembering forgotten events, and imagining new futures. She has recently studied the peoples and places that were sacrificed to construct the New York City water system. Since 2003, April has been conducting research on the Susquehannock Indians of central Pennsylvania. April teaches in the Vassar College anthropology department and the Native American studies (American culture) and environmental studies programs. She received her Ph.D. in anthropology from Binghamton University in 2007 and began teaching at Vassar College in 2012 after several years teaching at Heidelberg University in Ohio.

Jasmine Gollup is currently the laboratory director for TRC Environmental at the Lanham office in Maryland. She received her B.A. in history and sociology/anthropology with a concentration in archaeology from Elizabethtown College and her M.A. in archaeology from Cornell University. Her undergraduate and graduate research examined cultural change among the Susquehannock Indians during the sixteenth and seventeenth centuries.

James T. Herbstritt is a senior staff archaeologist with the Section of Archaeology at the State Museum of Pennsylvania. Currently, his multidisciplinary research is focused on the Susquehanna Valley's Middle Woodland through proto-Contact period transition of native cultures.

Lisa Marie Lauria earned her Ph.D. from the University of Virginia and taught anthropology and archaeology at UVA and the College of New Jersey before leaving academia to work for a nonprofit. In her dissertation, *Defining Susquehannock: Peoples and Ceramics in the Lower Susquehanna River Valley, AD 1575 to 1680*, she questioned the practices of equating ceramics with tribal identities and interpreting changing material culture as cultural decline or loss. She continues her interest in the complex dynamics of cultural entanglements and identity formation among both the Native American and Colonial populations of the Middle Atlantic.

Paul Raber is the series editor of Recent Research in Pennsylvania Archaeology and coeditor of three previous volumes in the series. He serves as senior archaeologist and director of archaeological

services with Heberling Associates, Inc., in Alexandria, Pennsylvania. His research interests include the evolution of technology and the archaeology of hunter-gatherers and early horticulturalists in eastern North America. He holds an M.A. and a Ph.D. in anthropology from the Pennsylvania State University and has published in *North American Archaeologist*, *Archaeology of Eastern North America*, *Pennsylvania Archaeologist*, the *Journal of Middle Atlantic Archaeology*, and the *Journal of Field Archaeology*.

Dean Snow, professor emeritus of anthropology at the Pennsylvania State University, is an archaeologist who specializes in ethnohistoric and demographic problems. In recent years, his work has led him into geographic information systems (GIS) approaches to these issues. He has conducted research in Mexico and in the northeastern region of North America, where his work on the Iroquois is particularly well known. His current research includes cyberinfrastructure and the development of large GIS databases designed to explore large-scale population movements over time and space. He is also currently researching the sexual dimorphism of human handprints and hand stencils in the Upper Paleolithic caves of France and Spain. Dr. Snow served as president of the Society for American Archaeology from 2007 to 2009 and secretary of section H (anthropology) of the American Association for the Advancement of Science from 2000 to 2006.

Robert Wall holds a B.A. in anthropology from the University of Maryland and an M.A. and Ph.D. in anthropology from Catholic

University in Washington, D.C. He teaches full time at Towson University, and he has more than 35 years of experience in Northeast, Great Lakes, and Middle Atlantic archaeology. He has developed specializations in lithic and prehistoric ceramics analysis. His work experience also includes several decades in cultural resources management. He has worked extensively on archaeological survey and excavation projects throughout the Upper Potomac region since 1980 and on the Barton site archaeological field school excavations since 1993. In 2001, he received the William B. Marye Award for contributions to Maryland archaeology, and he currently serves on the Maryland Advisory Committee on Archeology and the executive board of the Council for Maryland Archaeology.

Andrew Wyatt is a senior archaeologist at the Mechanicsburg, Pennsylvania, office of AECOM, Inc. He received his B.A. in anthropology at the State University of New York at Albany in 1988, where he had the good fortune to work on Dr. Dean Snow's Mohawk Valley Archaeological Project at the Otstungo site, learning the basics of Iroquois culture and archaeology. He worked as an archaeological reviewer at the Pennsylvania State Historic Preservation Office from 1992 to 1998 and received his M.A. in anthropology at Temple University in 2007 under the direction of Dr. Michael Stewart. His interests include Contact period Iroquoian archaeology, Iroquoian ethnogenesis, the archaeology of eastern North American foragers, and the emergence of agriculture in the region, as well as lithic and pottery analysis.

183